**SAGE** was founded in 1965 by Sara Miller McCune to support the dissemination of usable knowledge by publishing innovative and high-quality research and teaching content. Today, we publish over 900 journals, including those of more than 400 learned societies, more than 800 new books per year, and a growing range of library products including archives, data, case studies, reports, and video. SAGE remains majority-owned by our founder, and after Sara's lifetime will become owned by a charitable trust that secures our continued independence.

Los Angeles | London | New Delhi | Singapore | Washington DC | Melbourne

# We are All Revolutionaries Here

Thank you for choosing a SAGE product!
If you have any comment, observation or feedback,
I would like to personally hear from you.
*Please write to me at* **contactceo@sagepub.in**

**Vivek Mehra,** Managing Director and CEO, SAGE India.

## Bulk Sales

SAGE India offers special discounts
for purchase of books in bulk.
We also make available special imprints
and excerpts from our books on demand.

*For orders and enquiries, write to us at*

Marketing Department
SAGE Publications India Pvt Ltd
B1/I-1, Mohan Cooperative Industrial Area
Mathura Road, Post Bag 7
New Delhi 110044, India

*E-mail us at* **marketing@sagepub.in**

## Get to know more about SAGE

Be invited to SAGE events, get on our mailing list.
*Write today to* **marketing@sagepub.in**

This book is also available as an e-book.

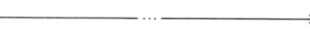

# We are All Revolutionaries Here

## Militarism, Political Islam and Gender in Pakistan

**Aneela Zeb Babar**

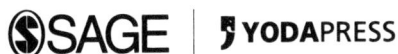

Los Angeles I London I New Delhi
Singapore I Washington DC I Melbourne

*First published in 2017 by*

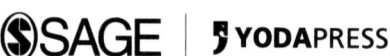

**SAGE Publications India Pvt Ltd**
B1/I-1 Mohan Cooperative Industrial Area
Mathura Road, New Delhi 110 044, India
*www.sagepub.in*

**YODA Press**
79 Gulmohar Enclave
New Delhi 110049
*www.yodapress.co.in*

**SAGE Publications Inc**
2455 Teller Road
Thousand Oaks, California 91320, USA

**SAGE Publications Ltd**
1 Oliver's Yard, 55 City Road
London EC1Y 1SP, United Kingdom

**SAGE Publications Asia-Pacific Pte Ltd**
3 Church Street
#10-04 Samsung Hub
Singapore 049483

Published by Vivek Mehra for SAGE Publications India Pvt Ltd, typeset in 10/12 pts Times New Roman by Zaza Eunice, Hosur, Tamil Nadu, India and printed at Chaman Enterprises, New Delhi.

**Library of Congress Cataloging-in-Publication Data Available**

**ISBN:** 978-93-860-6248-2 (HB)

**SAGE Yoda Team:** Sonjuhi Negi, Arpita Das, Rajesh Dey and Neha Sharma

# Contents

# List of Images

# Preface

This project is but a response to all the statements starting with 'But Why Would Pakistanis…' I have heard over the years. Let us just say that I got tired of explaining why Malala Yousafzai continues to face so much flak from certain Pakistanis (and 'good Muslims' and/or conspiracy theorists elsewhere), or why would any Pakistani woman justify the Pakistan's Council of Islamic Ideology' section to allow men to 'lightly beat their wives'. Perhaps one day I became nervous about how I felt generations of South Asians were condemned to repeat history, or that the more things changed for the region, the more our neighborhood was eager to make sure they remained the same.

Perhaps it was when I walked amongst the ruins of a Dhaka temple that was eternally condemned to live as a temple of tents and tarpaulins, marvelling how a Ramna Park once and a Ramna (suburb) again, waited out for an elusive dawn with 'Operation Searchlight' (March 1971) and 'Operation Sunrise' (July 2007) linking the love and lives of the cities of Dhaka and Islamabad forever. And there is a sun rising over Delhi and conversations about that makes it ever so important that I look inwards and share some tales. Or perhaps it will be two decades to a particular moment in Pakistan and India's history and as another generation grows in the mist of a nuclear cloud, it is important to remember how certain militaristic exercises shaped and molded our very gendered definition of peace and conflict avoidance.

I learnt a new word 'Taaq-e-Nissian', very late in my life; and now I make sure that I should never forget it. Taaq-e-Nissian can be translated as a 'niche', a shelf in the wall to consign what one has to, and to give oneself permission not to recall it for a while. I am sure there are families, families like ours in the region, whom you continue to question with a *how do you go through this?*—families who have trained themselves to place their memories, each day of December, whether it is of Dhaka or of Peshawar in a Taaq-e-Nissian of their own. My particular Taaq-e-Nissian had some essays and episodes from academic exercises in other lives, and one day Yoda Press felt it was time to share an abridged version of them with you, dear Reader.

What I should let you know, at the outset, that the following pages will not tell you the tale of all who resist the state narrative, there will be no stories of the valiant heroines and the superwomen in the everyday every person. For even as the state clamps down and conformism reigns supreme; there is the everyday Pakistani who resists and marches on to a different piper. But this project is not that forum—though there are days I am tempted to identify and acknowledge not just tales of who led and listened or who destroyed independent thought but rather who saved whom, who made sure that there continued to be spaces that resisted and inspired. Rest assured, Pakistani women continue to lead and inspire.

But for the next six chapters, I will share with you my stories of other women and other lives. But then again, this is a very subjective journey and a route map is quite disjointed. The faults that plague the text are all mine. For that I warn you now.

# Acknowledgements

Many people have supported and assisted this project in a variety of ways and many more have allowed me to forget about it and live a little.

Arpita Das and the team at Yoda Press for their tenacity and stubbornness that would rival the toughest production unit, when I, like the reluctant first-time director, sat on the film reels for quite a while claiming that there were still some final shots remaining.

Sonjuhi Negi, Nishtha Vadhera and Ishita Gupta for their fine editorial skills, an eye on the bigger picture and getting all the signatures when I was knee deep in words and jump cuts and had no idea where everything was to go. The faults that continue to plague the project are entirely my responsibility.

My mother, Mariana Babar who like an excellent critic, which she is, has already pointed out a dozen places where I missed the plot and so now none of the reviews are going to hurt.

The families and brilliant women without whom this project would have never been possible. Though they must remain anonymous, I would like to thank them for their support and assistance.

Parul Sharma and Kiran Manral for a friendship 'beyond the call of duty' and for being good spirited listeners to my endless stories. I hope they never hold the Internet against me. Sabbah Haji, Babur Majid, Raheel Khurshid for Gheebat Hellfire—I will meet you there. Lubna, Saima, Aisha, Maria for being good witches.

Archita Chanda Ray, Abanti, Devapriya Roy and Dipali Taneja for cheerleading duty. Natasha Badhwar, hail ogre well met. Tanveer Shahzad, the good soul who arranged for the copyright-mukt images at the last minute.

Ayesha, Sakeena, Raahym and Shahram for allowing me to disappear in 'script and voice' from their lives and continuing to be the pillars of strength they are. Saba Khattak for pushing me that extra mile and the dire warnings of aging film stars playing college students.

My late grandfather Habib, for our bargain the summer that he lost his eye glasses, that he would teach me my prayers and I would read him

Rushdie at night. Somehow he put everything in perspective. Mahjabina, for being my moral compass.

Gaurav, the financier for always being confident and making it all look so easy. And finally, Arhaan the trusted audience to the constant theatre of my life—though at one stage he too warned me 'It Looks Like You Are Quite Addicted To It'.

The Ideal Reader who will now finally let me go out and play.

And finally the good people of Pakistan, our million follies and foibles but twice as much fun—for assuring me ki *picture abhi baaki hai mere dost.*

# 1

# Introduction

Never before in history have so many women been empowered through 'the word', enabling them to articulate their ideas and share these with vast numbers of other women and men.... Given the explosion in technology today, vast numbers of females have at their disposal a variety of media through which they can express, analyze and above all communicate and share with each other the most radical of conceptions. —Ahmed, 2002: 27

And it was not important that all of the Faithful stood up... but it might have happened that from every one of their communities rose and left to get an understanding of the Faith and returned to the inhabitants of their area to warn them so that they did not adopt non-Islamic attitudes and refrained from [such] activities. —Surah 9 (*Al Tawbah*): 122

I have told my parents that we are a radical lot here and one day I am going to be part of Pakistan's *inqilab* (social revolution). —Interview with *madrassah* students, Khyber Pakhtunkhwa, Pakistan, November 2006

The actors in the following pages span a decade and counting of Pakistan's tryst with a difficult history. The pages they inhabit attempt to decipher the country's convoluted equation between militarism, political Islam, and gender politics, compounded by the crisis of governance and socio-economic tensions. They have all been formed by this nexus and in turn they frame the discourse of the current generation of Pakistanis. Why is it important to hear their story? Perhaps because we hope that as we retrace the journey a particular generation took, the signposts of our voyage will identify the road map a future generation should adopt to get out of the quagmire in which Pakistan finds itself.

If nothing else, the following chapters will identify the common thread that links the various incarnations of the Pakistani woman that we have witnessed over the years. On the surface these performances may seem at cross purposes. What, you may ask, might link a group of middle-class Pakistani women (some of them wives of army officers and bureaucrats), demurely sipping coffee in a living room, with the fiery young women in black *burqa*, threatening shopkeepers in Islamabad? The living room brigade is listening to an audio CD of their spiritual guru extolling the merits of their silent social revolution. Meanwhile, the other group brandishes batons, standing guard as their colleagues take to the pulpit and Pakistan's youth enter their crusade against the Pakistani government. These women and those other lives in the Pakistani diaspora they are linked to (through the new moral communities in cyber space), all aspire to have a voice in how Pakistan does religion and politics.

Three images acted together as the guiding spirit which motivated me to start writing this book. One can refer to them as the markers of the journey I referred to earlier, which Pakistani women undertook after 1947. The first of these images that sets the theme for this project was taken by photographers associated with *Life* magazine's special issue commemorating the celebrations for the brand new Pakistani state. It is of the members of the National Voluntary Guards, with the women guards themselves being a new concept for the fledgling state. The women in the photograph are fluid in their motion, parrying out and lunging with sticks as they pose for the camera amidst drills—my problems with militaristic values in the public space notwithstanding, for some this image of women might depict the hopes and aspirations of the new nation. The Pakistani nation and Jinnah, the founder patron, were aware that they had embarked on a particular experiment of political Islam—not to forget how the women's question would be articulated in the new state. As they pose for the cameras, it is clear that the young women and their well-wishers are united in the firm belief that Pakistani women will play a significant role when it comes to shaping the destiny of their new state. There was, however, the sound of rumblings on the horizon; the *mullah*s (clergy) of Pakistan had expressed their displeasure at the institution of the women guards and their presence in the celebrations of the new state. Some of the clergy had issued religious edicts against women parading with their heads uncovered and bosoms exposed, fuming that these women would be staring into the eyes of men, and be left with no shame and dignity. Perhaps their displeasure was an indication of the years ahead. Rather than writing their own destiny, the status of Pakistan's women would be the words to how the state eventually turned out.

Sixty years after these youthful images, another generation of young Pakistani women also posed for the cameras carrying sticks. However, in these images it is difficult to gauge their exuberance from the all-enveloping black cloaks that cover their bodies and faces. We know that they are equally determined as their sisters were six decades ago to play a role in Pakistan's destiny from their headbands that read 'Impose Shariah or Embrace Martyrdom'. As they posed for the foreboding images that graced Pakistan's morning newspapers, the nation knew that it stood at the brink of a social revolution that would have far-reaching consequences in the days ahead.

The third is a mental image that I carry from interviews with young students at a seminary for women. In January 2007, a young Pakistani student had looked me straight in the eye and declared, 'I have told my parents that we are a radical lot here and one day I am going to be part of Pakistan's *inqilab* (social revolution).' Remarkable sentiments these, and what was more astonishing was that this solemn declaration was being made by an eight-year-old girl studying at a seminary in Pakistan's Khyber Pakhtunkhwa. The words stayed with me till later in the month when young women studying at the Jamia Hafsa seminary (the women in black robes I refer to earlier on these pages) in Islamabad laid siege to a children's library in the city. The Jamia Hafsa (a seminary for women) and Jamia Faridia (a seminary for male students) are affiliated with Islamabad's infamous Red Mosque. The takeover of the children's library and the subsequent 'Impose Shariah or Embrace Martyrdom' conference organised by Jamia Hafsa were the first steps in their long stand-off with the Pakistan government. The students also kidnapped women whom they accused of spreading immorality, and then held hostage the policemen who had come to free them. This was followed by raiding clinics run by Chinese doctors in Islamabad and kidnapping some of them. The state did move in to crush the movement, albeit too late, and the final encounter was tragic and bloody. The repercussions of the ill-thought Operation Silence, launched in July 2007 to take over the Red Mosque, Jamia Hafsa and Jamia Faridia, still haunt Pakistani policy makers today.

At the time and even now my question remains the same: when and how will the social aspirations of an adolescent woman translate into the coming of age of a social and political revolution in urban Pakistan? Will this woman find a face, a resolution to her angst, or like Rosie the Riveter does she retreat to her cloister come daybreak? Like the Nameless Soldier, the Lal Majid student flits wraith-like through the pages of testimonies emerging after Operation Silence. She first emerges in the streets of Islamabad, an avenging force livid with the destruction of mosques in her city. With growing speed she sweeps through centres of commerce she accuses of spreading evil. However, later there are conflicting pieces of evidence: young students at the seminary claim that she is a celestial being, no mere mortal she but a tall angel who descended in the area to protect a faith in peril. The proud figure who strode the Lal Masjid compound during the Shahadat conference is later reduced to a shrouded figure in television interviews. Reciting ad nauseum the list of grievances, she gradually disappears from public space. She resurfaces only when there is talk of state torture, as one of many souls who irked a corrupt regime. I wanted her to be more than a passive, tortured woman—a stock image circulated and popularised by the reactionary press, and a mere statistic in the string of complaints against Musharraf's regime.

It is ironic that for a gender pushed to the margins in Pakistan, it is a woman who becomes the narrator for the social and political climate of a particular decade. This could be the conflicted personality of Apa Nisar Fatima. Fatima was a firebrand, a woman who had sided with General Zia as he curbed the mobility and life choices of Pakistan's women. As part of General Zia's infamous Majlis Shoora of the 1980s, Apa Nisar Fatima welcomed the spate of legislative reforms that played around with human rights and religious liberty. She would turn on women's rights groups, and had once accused them of spreading blasphemy and passing sacrilegious statements against the personality of the Holy Prophet (a crime punishable by death). It was an intriguing time in history where a Pakistani woman was asking the state to curb her personal liberties and those of fellow Pakistani women as they were vulnerable to temptation and vice. How does one reconcile to this? The 1980s also had the fleeting scandal of Naseem Fatima, a young woman who convinced her community and family to walk across the Arabian Sea (and subsequently to their death) on a pilgrimage to Iraq.

According to the sociologist Akbar Ahmed,

Naseem Fatima, 'a shy, pleasant looking-girl with an innocent expression on her face, who had a history of fits', after a series of miraculous religious experiences which were scorned by Sunni Muslims but were not inconsistent with Shia doctrine, led 38 people into the Arabian Sea at Karachi believing the waters would part and they would be transported miraculously to Shia holy sites in Karbala in Iraq. The women and children locked in five of the six trunks died. One of the trunks was shattered by the waves and its passengers survived. Those on foot also survived; they were thrown back onto the beach by the waves…. The survivors were in high spirits—there was neither regret nor remorse among them, only a divine calm, a deep ecstasy. The Karachi police in a display of bureaucratic zeal arrested the survivors. They were charged with attempting to leave the country without visas.... Rich Shias, impressed by the devotion of the survivors, paid for their journey by air for a week to and from Karbala. In Iraq, influential Shias, equally impressed, presented them with gifts, including rare copies of the Holy Quran.

For a particular moment in time Fatima transcends the limits of gender, generation and class, courtesy religion and her faith. But both she and Apa Nisar have disappeared in the archives of press clippings from their decade.

We can also neither forget nor ignore Benazir Bhutto, a paradox for many; one could tell from the tone of the requiems following her assassination how debatable her legacy and memory would continue to be in public imagination. In life she was a highly conflicted personality, straddling the liberal progressive and the deeply feudal worlds without a murmur of a conflict of interest. She challenged stereotypes of what 'good' Pakistani women of her class and generation could do and contested the public/ private space divide, but kowtowed to the constant personal theatre of the *dupatta* (veil) and the prayer beads. In death she became the elusive Salome of the seven veils in our popular imagination, with her obituaries giving tantalising hints to her real self. From a flighty young woman who consumed paperback romances and sped past us in her yellow MG searching for the closest Baskin Robbins, she turned into a thorn in the side of a military dictator, a serious foe indulging in a decade-long struggle to keep her father's name and political legacy alive. She was at times the workaholic campaigning long hours through pregnancies, a diligent politician surviving on four hours' of sleep, and then a much-maligned name with corruption and nepotism cases brought against her and her coterie. She came in at a time when the Pakistani military high command controlled women's mobility, their choices, and legal freedoms. This ranged from the repressive laws passed by their regimes to the 'instructions' given from time to time by the military elite. As the world watched the fleeting images of the first female Prime Minister of the Muslim world dying in a suicide bombing, there were a number of questions about how to understand her life and interpret her overlapping, as well as at times divergent, at times crossover, performances? Does the death of Bhutto ring the death knell of secular female political participation in Pakistan? Or was Bhutto's style at best a kind of 'liberal democracy' and not rising from a feminist consciousness at all? Is it possible that she leaves in her wake strong, politicised women involved in secular domestic politics that have yet to catch on to the democratic imagination? Or are we witnessing the coming of age of a particular generation of Pakistani women, the daughters of Apa Nisar Fatima, who are taking their first steps in political violence to usher in their own revolution. There is also the phenomenon of young, upper-middle-class women grappling with religious identity, aspiring to have a voice in Pakistani (moral) politics, who have taken to 'living room seminaries'.

Swat and 2012 gave Pakistan (and the world) a new heroine, albeit controversial: Malala Yousafzai. Like the other Pakistani Nobel Prize winner Dr Salam, Yousafzai is of Pakistan though the country looks the other way, the state shifting to a space that denies her a homecoming. Why does the figure of a young teenager divide the country so?

****

The following pages examine the various political trajectories taken by Pakistani women in the past decades and what it articulates for the days ahead for Asian women in Muslim democracies.

This project can be explained as an auto-ethnography experiment. I had set forth using a multi-methodological approach to look at my questions— this included participant observation, individual and group interviews, and when it came to the chapters dealing with Pakistani diaspora, attending the religious lectures organised by patrons of Al Huda in Islamabad (Pakistan) and Canberra (Australia). But the process was developing in not only a dialogue with the participants but also as a personal dialogue with myself, 'connect(ing) the personal to the political'. 'Auto-ethnography' emerged as one of the methods to tackle the project.

The movement toward a more 'personalised research' reflects calls to emphasise the ways in which the ethnographer interacts with the culture being researched. These texts are usually written in the first person and feature dialogue, emotion, and self-consciousness as relational and institutional stories affected by history, social structure, and culture (Ellis and Bochner, 2000). Therefore, I moved to use an approach where I could employ my own understanding of being a woman growing up Pakistani and a Muslim to investigate how others value their cultural and religious background, and employ them in their exchanges with other members of the community. I am aware of Spivak's words that one should recognise that the position of the speaking subject within theory can be 'a historically powerful position when it wants the other to be able to answer back' (Spivak in conversation with Hutnyk, McQuire, and Papastergiadis in Harasym 1990: 42). This was significant for me for instance when I spoke to Canberra Pakistani women on the issue of *hijab*. I had posed the questions with my own frame of reference towards the issue (which was very black and white!) and realised very quickly that I had to abandon my personal biases and recognise the wealth of interpretation as Canberra Pakistani women passionately articulated their choices.

A caveat: in the following chapters, when I refer to 'contesting constituencies' for Pakistanis, I refer to the constant struggle between practising ethnic South Asian customs (the 'fun cultures' of Pakistan) and a more 'official Islam'. For my Pakistani respondents in the diaspora, who in combination with all these dynamics also witness other middle-class Muslims practise being middle class and Muslim, I borrow from Werbner's definition of the 'space of fun' for diasporic Pakistanis in Manchester. Werbner studies how a majority of diaspora Pakistanis in Britain embrace two worlds: that of 'Islamic asceticism and sobriety, and the (secular) world of South Asian ('Indian') popular culture with its laughter and sensual gaiety. 'Many also partially embrace the world of Western secularism and play' (Werbner, 2002: 188).

However, with the recent rise of a more 'official Islam', that is a 'spartan Islam' after a growing Wahabi influence in South Asia, Pakistanis are seen aspiring towards a hegemonically positioned 'Muslim nation' with Arab roots. The space of fun has become a 'highly contested space' for diasporic Pakistanis, building to a situation where there might be no official cultural spaces or forums of celebration which could be deemed Islamic unless also mosque-based or religiously focussed (Werbner, 2002).

I have to disclose that on a number of occasions I was quite nervous that my interviewees would turn interrogator on me, and I constantly wondered how I would reply if the women congregating at the *dars* (religious lectures) asked me if I agreed with their particular interpretation. In an atmosphere where everyone was so conscious about their political alliances to particular community groups in Islamabad and Canberra, I believe I was very fortunate that I was never 'urged' to declare my loyalties. On most occasions I think the participants were satisfied regarding my alliances, the fact that I was sitting in on the *dars* meant to them that I tacitly agreed with the text being circulated and the discussion following. Only once while leaving an interviewee's house was I stopped by her and asked how I really felt about a particular issue I had been questioning—we had been discussing women's veiling. I was struggling with how to word my reservations, when she put her arms around me and declared that I had to meet Sister Nabeela who might convince me yet.

It was equally difficult for me when I was asked to carry back literature from an organisation in Islamabad my interviewees knew I would be visiting. I had my reservations with the text and the particular resource person's interpretations, and constantly debated with myself on how to handle these requests. However, as this was a relationship of reciprocity, I had to set aside my reservations and let my interviewees decide for themselves. Eventually, I fear I was an unwilling accomplice to the organisation's project when at my interviewees' requests I reluctantly passed on to them my personal collection of lectures on audiocassettes.

While my research at times becomes an auto-ethnographic study of the Pakistani community as I clarified earlier, I also examined the texts that were being circulated in religious gatherings conducted by the Al Huda group, by Umme Hassan and her colleagues at the Lal Masjid, and the school curriculum of the 'hybrid *madrassahs*' I will introduce in later chapters. To analyse these texts, Thanvi's *Beheshti Zevar* (Heavenly Ornaments) and Hali's *Majalis-unnisa* (Women's Society) were very useful, both books belonging to the nineteenth-century Indian advocacy of reform for Muslim women, with Hali '[p]utting into the mouths of his female characters reflections on the backward condition of the Muslim community, the stagnation of vernacular learning, and the need for girls to be educated in order better to fulfil their household and family duties' (Minault, 1986: 14).

The work is in the form of conversations among middle-class Muslim women of Delhi congregating at a female elder's house, much like the 'parallel secluded gatherings' Al Huda patrons were organising. These gatherings came about to counter the 'mixed get-togethers' organised by other Pakistanis or recreational spaces that they opposed. These 'conversations' include long narrative passages describing women's daily life, their education, and training in household management, childrearing practices, customs, and beliefs. Much of the text, situated in a particular socio-cultural and historical climate, should seem old-fashioned today until I realised how the women I was interviewing still found it relevant to their lives and concerns today. For many of them women's education is still of secondary importance. The socialisation of girls still discounts the need to be resourceful and self-sufficient, to be prepared for life on their own, to provide support to a family, to survive financially straitened circumstances, or simply to be more socially productive. The need for companionship and a harmonious relationship between spouses and in-laws, and for discipline mixed with consideration for young girls growing up in 'difficult times' are perennial social concerns.

And finally, even if events leave 'no material traces', as in not being part of history books, written texts, or other forms of media, they are indexed in the resources of memory and discourse. This theme catalogues the entanglement of people, class politics, and place for Pakistani Muslims. The reference to avenging angels in Aabpara, Islamabad, the alleged bonfire of audio and video cassettes by repentant shopkeepers in and around Islamabad, the '*milad* event' in Canberra's living rooms will all become a permanent part of public imagination of the Pakistani community. My book project thus addresses issues of how ordinary Pakistani women in their everyday life interact with Islamic rituals and cultural symbols to create their own 'negotiated truths'. The chapters revolve around particular characters, and I take the participants' stories and my interpretation to discuss these theme areas.

Chapter 2 speaks about the hybrid spaces that criss-cross Pakistan—of spatial politics and being born into being and not-being, and when the centre clashes with the margins. The chapter deals with the born-again Muslims and middle-class Pakistan which may have embraced faith but lost their soul. Through identifying the birth of the hybrid seminary in Pakistan I tackle issues of aspirational politics, political Islam and the new old-boys network. This chapter will identify the emergence of a social revolution in Pakistan with the coming of age of a particular class of young Pakistanis. It unpacks the growing popularity of a particular kind of hybrid space that is offered by the 'new' *madrassah*, and how this silent majority has given space to a problematic fringe. The chapter is based on vignettes from the field that give some understanding of the inter- and intra- Pakistani relations, and how Pakistanis articulate their national and religious identity. It identifies some of the forums they frequent in their quest for a political identity, making sense of themselves and their place in the world.

Chapter 3, 'Spatial and Ritual Politics in Canberra' covers Pakistani communities at home and in a particular diaspora community providing a snapshot of its religious and cultural performances. Like Leblanc in her *Bicycle Citizens* (1999), perched on a bicycle and negotiating the streets of Oizumi, following the 'housewife politician'[1], I negotiated the streetscapes that emerge in Canberra's Pakistan and in Pakistan's urban centres which materialised as young Pakistanis converged to form cultural spaces and networks. This has been a process of a social imaginary as they attempt to constitute a space where they can satisfy their 'Pakistani selves' and still

---

[1] By employing participant-observer methods borrowed from anthropology, Leblanc had tried to 'follow' the paths the housewife uses when she confronts the political system, so that, in the end, Leblanc too began to see the political world that the housewife saw.

be recognised as 'good Muslims'. What have been the individual, sectarian, regional and class differentiations in Pakistan that shape the discourse and politics of political Islam and led to the hybrid seminaries that dot the landscape of Pakistan? The chapter analyses the (religious lecture) sessions and other societal gatherings being organised on religious themes for and by Pakistani women, and draws from Metcalf's (1996) 'imagined maps of diaspora Muslims' and Pnina Werbner's (1996) suggestion that Muslims in diaspora connect via a 'global sacred geography'. I will catalogue the struggle of my interviewees to maintain some semblance of the richness and variety of what they see as 'traditionalism' and 'Pakistani-ness', and the constant negotiation where some religious rituals like veiling could be deemed as Islamic for the Pakistani diaspora. This chapter unpacks Al Huda's attraction for Pakistan's 'new social arrivals' and the middle class in Pakistani cities and overseas. To understand Al Huda's appeal would be to study the negotiated power struggles of a particular Pakistani generation as it gradually negotiates class and spatial politics. This particular generation has been conscious of its exclusion from certain networks dominated by the 'social elite' of Pakistan and its diaspora; their membership of Al Huda is their attempt to find their own support structures.

We come next to the ubiquitous chapter on *hijab*. The centrality of issues like control over physical appearance as well as spatial protocols of Pakistani women in the public sphere was a question that constantly came up in my debates with colleagues. It is also a popular complaint against Al Huda as the organisation is accused of exhorting Pakistani women to adopt a style of *hijab* that not only covers their bodies but also 'virtually makes them faceless' (Shamsi, 2002). When I set out to explore the multiple discursive spaces in defining Pakistani women's role in Muslim communities, the matter of *hijab* was one which most cultural groups were constantly debating and redefining as well. The decision of Pakistani women to adopt the veil or *hijab* is a very complex one. For some it is a backlash against the commentaries and descriptions in the Western media in the post-2001 world that justified the American intervention in Afghanistan with pious pontification on how and when Muslim women could be liberated from repressive 'local Muslim traditions'. Haideh Moghissi (2001) critiques such commentaries whose basic premise is how and when Muslim women can be liberated from the yoke of Muslim men. The domesticated, subjugated, unenlightened Other as contrasted to the liberated, independent and enlightened Western self was used in earlier encounters as a moral prop to legitimise colonial power relations. In earlier episodes of such encounters the subsequent 'hegemonic masculinity' in 'fundamentalist discourses' arising from cultural anxieties was complemented, as pointed out by scholars like Moallem, by an emphasised femininity thrown into relief by the symbol of the 'veiled woman':

> Discursively... the black chador carried symbolic local and global meaning. Locally, it transcended all differences of class, religion, and ethnonational origin among women; globally it created a transnational Muslim femininity... that stood in opposition to the West in complicity with the ummah. In a cultural war of representation, it was the responsibility of the woman to cover herself in a black chador. The black chador became a weapon, symbolizing belonging to the ethnoreligious community of Allah which stood in opposition to the Westernized local elite as well as to a global order. (Moallem, 1999: 332)

I hope the chapter on veiling practices serves as a space where 'our differences' can be recognised and examined. It will thus document Pakistani women as 'contextually located actors' and their relationship to veiling in the conduct of their day-to-day lives—not just in spiritual practice but as formed responses to the social and political forces governing their lives.

Chapter 5, 'Texts of War' can be read as an autobiographical chapter. It analyses Pakistan's social transformation, which we all bemoan today, where young women like me grew up dreaming of the gun and a significant section of my contemporaries justified religious violence. Pakistan's texts of war—the tale of the religio-military nexus has given birth to a discourse that firmly puts in place one's gender identity. The chapter takes up a particular moment in 1998, when both Pakistan and India conducted nuclear tests, to analyse how societal and nationalistic discourses were very much a gendered construct, with the stakeholders informed by patriarchal and gendered ideologies. When 'jingoistic' nationalism increased at the time of the nuclear tests in the public space, it affected women in particular.

Chapter 6 on 'My Lady of Lal Masjid' charts the journey of the students of the Jamia Hafsa and their benefactors as they built-up a constituency for their socio-political movement. Despite the government's crackdown over their official website and publications, or perhaps because of this censorship, their discourse has appeared in a variety of ingenious ways that might have not been earlier used. They had earlier condemned the urban Pakistani's fascination with the computer-generated world but now they emulated these practices as they created a virtual Jamia Hafsa and the Lal Masjid in cyber space. In this chapter I will identify the 'war of words' as the protagonists of the Lal Masjid uprising chronicle their version of the events of July 2007. And I pose the question whether the events of

Operation Silence and the Jamia Hafsa resistance harbour a new equation of Pakistani women and political Islam, or do they merely reinforce the traditional, static and unchanging portrayals of Muslim women?

Between these political, social and theological concepts there exists a deep inner relationship to Pakistani-ness, which I hope is reflected in the pages that will follow. Ultimately, as a Pakistani Muslim woman writing about my community, I am offering whatever insights I have been able to glean on the relationship between being Muslim, a woman and a Pakistani in recent times.

# 2

# We are All Good Muslims Here

*Hybrid Spaces, Contesting Constituencies*
*and Pakistan's Social Revolution*

Social anthropologists in recent times have frequently written about the globalised world and its interdependence, perhaps as often as security specialists deliberate upon instability in Pakistan and the consequences for global security. In November 2008, the worlds of the two overlapped as gunmen belonging to the Pakistan-based Lashkar-e-Taiba held hostage Mumbai's (India) local and expatriate population. At the end of the carnage, the lone gunman captured by the Indian security forces confessed in a televised interview:

> We were told that our big brother India is so rich and we are dying of poverty and hunger. My father sells *dahi wada* (dumplings) on a stall in Lahore and we did not even get enough food to eat from his earnings. I was promised that once they knew that I was successful in my operation, they would give Rs 150,000, to my family (Esposito 2009).

Ajmal Qasab did not study in a seminary; however, his life is representative of the cocktail of social violence, sectarianism, poverty and dispossession that pushes young Pakistanis into enrolling in problematic seminaries or adopting a life of violence.

A look at Pakistan's demography and geography clearly exhibits that there are particular regions of Pakistan that share complex ethnic and religious divisions as well as economic backwardness and lack of governance. These particular complexities need to be understood in order to examine the pressure points that exist in Pakistani society and predict how soon they will spill over into wider regional instability and volatility. As the work of Saleem Ali (2005) dealing with the *madrassahs* in Punjab, stresses, sectarian conflict in the villages and small towns of Pakistan reflect fundamental economic deprivations. The regions with the most conflicts have landlords, no prospect of land reform, are not linked to major roads that would provide the youth with easy access to urban markets and urban jobs, and they lack economic diversification. Ajmal Qasab of Mumbai fame comes from one such community. Lashkar-e-Taiba as an organisation feeds on the economic deprivation of young men like Qasab. The organisation continues to flourish in Pakistan and beyond in all its incarnations despite all attempts on the part of the Pakistani state to suppress its activities and the government's recent act of banning the organisation. The *madrassahs*' success in recruiting Pakistan's youth is an expression of the nation's underprivileged striking back at the state.

While the world is aware that any reading of Pakistan will involve a complicated lexicon of political Islam, it still struggles to understand why a significant section of (what they view) as middle- and upper-middle-class 'educated' Pakistanis will justify militancy as a vigilant action against non-Muslim forces, and how it will usher in a much-needed Islamic revolution? What makes a reading of radical Islam so attractive for certain young Pakistanis? Why is it that a particular generation of Pakistan has grown up insular, puritanical and blind to the pluralism that was South Asian Islam? The region and its Muslim community form a significant feature of global security policies. But it was important for me to write this chapter for a Pakistani audience as well. Every nation needs an understanding of how its present scripts its future, more so for Pakistan where the rise of militant Islam has erased any other reading of Islam.

# The Paradox of One: Pakistanis at Home and Abroad

We begin our journey with the allure of one.

With all the divisions of class, ethnicity, language and sectarian identity, Pakistanis have been overtly pushed to be proud of the idea of unity, of the magical power of one. They are constantly reminded through state discourse and popular media that their national idea is the supremacy of one, believing as they do in one God, the finality of the one Prophet, and guided by one ideology—the ideology of Pakistan. They are urged by the state to believe that the power of a singular 'one' will propel their lives forward rather than the multiplicity of their ethnicities and language, which will only bog them down. The landscaped hillock by the side of Islamabad Highway has the words *Faith, Unity, Discipline* set in concrete. In English as you drive into the city, Urdu as you drive out towards the airport, and the installation is whitewashed hurriedly on every state dignitary's visit. The words are from a speech the Father of the Nation Jinnah gave, where he tried to outline the guiding principles for every Pakistani. However, Jinnah's principle of 'belief in one self' was cleverly transformed to faith—a strategic use of the Urdu term *Imaan* which translates as 'believing in Islam'. When President Musharraf made moves towards a 'moderate Islam' in the early 2000s, the term *Imaan* was scrapped from the installation on the Islamabad highway to be replaced by a comparatively 'secular' *yaqeen-e-mohkim* (firm belief), which is closer to what Jinnah had envisioned when he had coined the earlier phrase. The 'change in translation' was also encouraged in print and electronic media. However, the spirit of *glasnost* was not permanent.

This particular section culled from Jinnah's speech, along with its erratic translation, has become a part of Pakistani national consciousness. The quote also forms the lines of a popular national song. As Pakistani students growing up in the 1980s we had to write essays on the theme of 'What do we believe in? We believe in one, we are one disciplined nation.' However, as I explain in the following pages, these students from 1980s' Pakistan were gradually learning through their lived experiences, at home and later as members of the Pakistani diaspora, about the anomaly of 'one'.

A significant factor contributing towards the problem of 'one nation' in Pakistan is class politics. Political scientists working on Pakistan have pointed out how class operates as a successful mobilising instrument for individual loyalties in conjunction with caste and kin loyalties in Pakistan. There are real differences in wealth, socio-economic status, and effective control of the means and surplus of production. The social strategies individuals have at their disposal are firmly embedded within a culture of groups who have grossly different access to, and control of, material and social resources in conjunction with the caste and ethnic group to which they belong. This complicates the 'myth of a unified *ummah*'. Though most Pakistanis would prefer a self-image of a monolithic nation of Islam that has remained consistent through divisions of time and space, 'reality' can be quite different as I learnt myself (and the lesson was re-emphasised during interviews). Living in their 'world of diaspora', members of the Pakistani community like reminding themselves of their 'homes of origin' and of how they differ from their host community on the issue of their religious belief. However, there are times they realise they have more in common through class and professional affiliations with their host communities than with their compatriots. There are also the competing demands of ethnicity (they might try to keep it under wraps but it does rear its head) as Pakistanis view the policy decisions of their government—for instance, being a Pathan did I view the intervention in Afghanistan in 2001 differently from a Punjabi Muslim?

## On Islamabad

My journey begins in Islamabad. On his way to interview Benazir Bhutto a decade ago, travel writer William Dalrymple had described Islamabad as:

> Islamabad—Pakistan's regimented concrete capital, home to Benazir Bhutto and ten thousand of her bureaucrats—is to Pakistan what Euro Disney is to France: it is in the country but not of it. As you drive in the early morning through its long, deserted avenues, Islamabad still looks strangely like a building site into which none has yet moved. The bureaucrats' blocks and the Saudi-financed mosques—many still shrouded in scaffolding—rise up on every side. There is little evidence of Pakistan's burgeoning population (Dalrymple, 1999: 346).

For many years, Islamabad has had an absence of the vernacular; there is little that reveals the area's cultural and ethnic roots. Spaces created as a result are not simply binary spaces of modern and traditional. In Pakistan they reflect the constant manoeuvring between the state and civil society, which is subsequently articulated as the false political of what they deem fit as Pakistani, as Islamic, and so on. Like most planners, Constantinos Doxiadis, the city planner for Islamabad, disliked the haphazard development which characterised the neighbouring Rawalpindi.[1] He quite bluntly argued that 'Rawalpindi should not have any role (in the capital). It should remain the regional center … (And) the servicing centre of the capital' (Doxiadis Associates 1960: 244). It is ironic that Rawalpindi (which houses the General Headquarters for the Pakistani Army) did just what he feared—play a significant role in the fate of Islamabad and the rest of the country.

---

[1] To assure that the vernacular did not encroach on the 'modern capital', a 'green belt' was provided between Islamabad and Rawalpindi in order to form a physical barrier between them (Doxiadis Associates 1960: 54).

I grew up in Rawalpindi, and even though our school books and the Pakistani media referred to Islamabad and Rawalpindi as 'sister cities', and for some time even as 'twin cities', the popular joke going around described Rawalpindi as the 'uglier twin' or the 'step sibling'. Even from a child's less-disillusioned eyes, driving up the Islamabad highway there were visual clues that subtly reinforced that I was driving towards something/someone which was definitely not 'my twin'. I drove from the tanks installed at Rawalpindi traffic roundabouts (as part of one city councillor's fervent 'city beautification project') to the dove and olive branch mural at Islamabad's entrance. My relatives in Islamabad would coo sympathetically, 'You know even if we are only fifteen minutes away from you, it's always two degrees cooler here.' Rawalpindi was hot, dusty and chaotic compared to Islamabad with its cool, planned and—courtesy the dove installation—diametrically opposing 'peaceful' environs. Why wasn't there any road sign welcoming us to Rawalpindi? I complained. Why weren't there any painted relief maps on the side of the roads for Rawalpindi as Islamabad had? My Islamabad friends would joke, 'But Rawalpindi is Pindi, the 'pind' (the village—a pun on the name that we had to suffer), you don't need maps for the village, do you? And welcomed to what, the markets and the military cantonments?' Later in my life when I had to travel daily to Islamabad for university, and then for work, I would notice with childish glee the encroachments on Islamabad's green belt. Eventually, most of the trees we envied were cut down as they posed a 'security threat'. Pakistan started growing onto Islamabad and the city became 15, 10, and now five minutes away from Pakistan. However, over the years, we grew to realise that actually Islamabad was Pakistan—an artificial creation that wanted to separate itself from the chaos and tenuous grip of the past. But this separation proved problematic as the Pakistani government instituted national commissions every other decade to define what Pakistani culture was and an 'official' definition at that. The rest of us outside this 'artificial' Pakistan might have had a clearer definition and sense of Muslim and Pakistani identity if left to our own personal strategies. We were expected to forget our South Asian geographical reality and our 'cultural yesterday' of a syncretic Islamic identity for one that placed our today and tomorrow in a more Arab (read Muslim) West Asia. By our school years we were well-versed in the complete separation of economic groups, of military and civilian worlds, at a relatively earlier age than our parents' generation. But in Islamabad and later as I saw reflected in Canberra, one could see the scales translating and incorporating religious parameters. 'Where are you on the religious scale?' my school teacher asked. 'Man,' she said, 'will not be judged on a social scale, the only way you can judge people is on a *taqwa* "piety" scale'. At the top rung of this ladder are the religiously pious, those who can exhibit this spirituality, and the irreligious will remain at the bottom. All eyes used to shift furtively at this stage in the lesson to the Christian students sitting in our classroom. However, Pakistan's socio-economic indicators continued to dictate this 'new improved' religious barometer. For instance, every 10-year-old sitting in the classroom knew that you must be able to afford financially the religious pilgrimage to Saudi Arabia. Every little girl in my school wanted the gold 'Allah' pendant to show that a relative had made the trip and brought back the appropriate 'religious tourist souvenir'. When a friend from my neighbourhood visited my grandmother and me with her newly acquired pendant, I was disappointed for now my pendant was not the 'status symbol' which I had been milking it for all these years in my neighbourhood. My grandmother whose pilgrimage had blessed me with the pendant was not impressed by the 'newly rich' neighbour and their equally new-found desire to acquire piety: 'Oh, but we have so many Allahs already,' she declared with a flick of her hand. I could rest easy with my newly discovered 'advantage' and all was right in my 10-year-old world.

Hull quotes from an article in the early 1970s which describes Islamabad as still a government city predominantly populated by government employees neatly divided into so many classes inherited from the colonial days:

> Today class or status (rarely distinguished with Weberian precision) is still commonly identified with government rank. In a discussion in Urdu about the social order of the city, a grade 16 government employee and long-time Islamabad resident moved fluidly among the terms *haisiyat* (status), *category,* and *scale.* In America how many statuses are there? He asked me. Following my somewhat muddled attempt to explain class in this country, he declared that, 'There should only be three categories, the low uneducated, the very high people who are very rich and well-educated, and the rest of the people in between. But here, you won't believe it, there are twenty two scales' (Hull, 2003: 97).

Many years later when I was doing research for this book, the drawing room discussions in Canberra 'of everyone knowing who you are' reminded me of the Pakistani drama serials and films that echo the everyday pantomime of the city streets. Police officer stopping a speeding car, when the man at wheel says, Don't you know who I am?', and the police officer slowly saluting the driver and saying, 'Sorry, we didn't recognise you.' Every act is thus an authenticating performance, life imitating art. Every day, we watched a slow-moving tableau on Pakistan's streets between police authority and the 'very important citizens'. For Hull, the 'Do you know who I am?' was an enunciative act, as it enunciates the idea it wants to speak out—the tacit fear or at times the indignation of a society in which your status might not be automatically known to the interlocutor and vice-versa. He writes about visitors to Islamabad asking the city residents whether they could accurately judge the status of individuals they encounter daily just from their appearance. This always provoked a lively discussion. Some claimed to be able to determine a person's exact scale and discern not only how much wealth he or she possesses, but also the legality or illegality of its source (Hull, 2003) I was reminded of how policemen in Islamabad would mournfully greet the news of a fresh parliament being sworn in in Pakistan, as it meant that every errant teenager might now be the nephew of someone new. Islamabadites, the children of bureaucrats—this being their only ethnicity, would groan that elections would bring the Sindhis and Baluchis roaming their streets looking up their relatives in the Prime Minister's Secretariat. In a country where you were frequently quizzed on your ethnicity, and your surnames were mentally checked against sectarian affiliation, the tacit question in Islamabad would concern the public service grade of the head of family. Having an ethnicity was not Islamabad, and therefore, quite un-Pakistani.

# The Eight-Year-Old Militant: Understanding Pakistan's Social Revolution

110 kilometres from Islamabad lies the small town of Khairabad, which borders the two provinces of NWFP (since renamed Khyber Pakhtunkhwa) and Punjab. It is typical of many of the little hamlets of Pakistan that clawed their way through into some kind of recognition courtesy a development not of its making but as the result of an ad hoc government decision. Khairabad might have been indistinguishable from the many other provincial check-posts in Pakistan, if it had not been for the setting up of a medical clinic for retired army personnel in the area. These were mostly the non-commissioned officers who kept guard at the bordering Cherat region notorious for small-time outlaws, and the personnel stationed on

the Punjab-Khyber Pakhtunkhwa border. At the time of my visit the clinic was facing difficulties and possibly being wrapped up due to the lack of financial and institutional support by the powers that be. The administrators had also realised that an increasing number of 'civilians' were using the facilities (though after paying a fee). The clinic had been a boon for the local populace as they would otherwise have to incur time and cost to take their sick to the closest town, Nowshera. For obvious reasons the decision to close down the establishment had the population disgruntled; it was for them further proof how the state ignored their plight by taking away even the secondary sources of infrastructure they had access to.

I was in Khairabad to visit a seminary for girls set up by the Jamat-i-Islami. I was taken there by Bibijan, a feisty old woman who worked at the clinic—it was not clear what her designation at the clinic was. She described herself as an interpreter to the doctors, a chaperone when a female patient had to be examined, a field motivator so villagers sent women to medical clinics to be treated, and an ad hoc peon for the clinic when need be. That morning her duties involved taking me to the seminary. She arrived early in the morning. Her forehead was smeared with tinsel, she had a spring in her step that has long disappeared from the area even as conservatism crept in. Earlier in the day as I took an inter-city bus to Khairabad from Rawalpindi (in Punjab) I had witnessed the change for myself. As we entered the Pakhtunkhwa province, the driver turned off the on-board TV entertainment and the stewardess drew her *dupatta* (scarf) closer to her forehead. When queried, she shrugged her shoulders and said they did not want to upset the Muttahida Majlis Amal (MMA) government that was in power in the province. Bibijan escorted me to the seminary regaling me with gossip about the people we were passing by. She stopped at the door to the establishment and grimaced as she turned away, 'I don't want to be associating with these folks; they are not for simple people like me.' Bibijan's anxiety was understandable; the growing religiosity in the region and 'controlled expression' of women's mobility did not bode well for lively personalities like her.

I entered the seminary compound hoping to interview the headmistress, but I was informed that she was out of the country—I could blame the MMA for this hiccup as well. The MMA government was at that time in power in the province and the headmistress being a protégé of the Jamat-i-Islami (an important member of the alliance) had been sponsored by the party officials to participate in the annual Hajj pilgrimage. Patronage such as this makes it clear to the students in the seminary what being a contributing member of the seminary network can do for them as they grow into adulthood. To be a part of the Hajj pilgrimage (and that too at state expense) translates as significant social capital for Pakistani Muslims. I was ushered in then to meet instead the administrator of the seminary who rattled out some facts, parrot fashion, about the seminary.

Jamia-al-Mohsinat was established at Khairabad in 1996. The building I was sitting in was inaugurated by Qazi Hussein Ahmed himself (the President of the Jamat-i-Islami from 1987 to 2009). The seminary, like other Al-Mohsinat seminaries established by the Jamat, carries out the very important task of creating and maintaining a female constituency for the Jamat-i-Islami. Jamia-al-Mohsinat gives young women from very conservative families a space to learn about the outside world but for obvious reasons their vision and impression of it is dictated by the Jamat. This particular seminary offers courses in *Aama* (equivalent to a Metric/ Grade 10) and *Khasa* (equivalent to the Year 12 Intermediate degree in Pakistani state schools). They also sit in for the Grade 8 Pakistan state school examinations that are compulsory for all students attending a seminary run by the Jamat-i-Islami. They are also coached in Mathematics and English.

The *madrassah* is exclusively for girls with students coming from Peshawar, Timargah, Swat, Bathkhela and Mansehra (towns in Khyber Pakhtunkhwa). At the time I was at the seminary, the administration was offering a concession in the school fee so that children from local villages like Akora Khattak could also join the seminary. The fee for a regular student was USD 4 per month, for concession students it was USD 1 a month, while orphan girls could study for free. I also discovered that the local children of the area and some students from other parts of the province studying at the *madrassah* could have attended an English medium school or private schools in the area but the *madrassah* administration had published and circulated pamphlets to exert pressure and 'encourage' parents to send their daughters to the *madrassah* for religious education instead.

The *madrassah* hired female teachers only; however, the year I visited the institute, they had been given funds which paid for the salary of a male teacher who was offering classes in Mathematics. For reasons of *purdah* he did not enter the main compound and took classes in a room adjacent to the *madrassah* gate.

A majority of the student population is made up of boarders from other cities, and hence, the *madrassah* has a rule of taking girls old enough to take care of themselves. There is an entry test and an interview for admission to the seminary. The teachers I spoke to disclosed that though their potential students were of a mature age, some of them did not even know the Urdu alphabet at the time of interviews. However, these students were quick to learn and caught up with their contemporaries in a short period of time. Each week there was one day when the students had to also cook for themselves. The teachers also disclosed that the parents of the students were usually not literate, and even those who had gone to school had not studied beyond Grade 10. Most of them came from families of small-time traders, shopkeepers, labourers and drivers.

My interviews were conducted in the background of certain reforms introduced by the Musharraf regime. This included the Madrassah Registration Ordinance and the curriculum review of Pakistani state textbooks—the proposed curriculum review would influence the students I was interviewing for they were to appear for the Grade 8 Middle School Exam in the coming months. However, the teachers explained that as their students are taught the translation of the Quran from the very first day, therefore, even the removal of Surah Toba (the particular verses that deal with *jihad*) from the textbooks would not make a lot of difference. Any revisions in the curriculum were ineffective as the students had already studied the translation and the commentary of the Surah as part of their *madrassah* curriculum. There were also misgivings regarding other features of the *madrassah* reforms—one pertained to the introduction of computers in seminaries. The teachers complained that there had been no thought in taking a decision regarding who would be responsible for the maintenance of the computer; if there was any problem with the functioning of the computer would the government officials help them? They introduced their students as 'simple girls' from the region of Malakand, who were interested in learning embroidery and cooking rather than new-fangled notions like computer education. The administration viewed computer education as an unnecessary complication, and were planning to introduce the subject only when their students were in Grades 9 and 10.

Parents are told at the time of admission to the seminary that it is compulsory for their wards to appear in the Grade 8 exam. However, the teachers complained that after a time the parents start protesting that they had sent their children to get only a religious education and do not want secular education (read preparing for the Middle School exam) for their girls. So they have witnessed a developing trend of parents discontinuing their wards' education once the Dars-e-Nizami or *Hifz* course is over. Parents make excuses that they want to get their daughters married off or that the mother has fallen sick and they need someone to take care of the house. But they still do have students who sit for Dars-e-Nizami and

Middle School exams and who have expressed their inclination to appear for the *Aama* and *Khasa* examinations. Some of their graduates have gone on to teach in seminaries in their own home towns or taken steps towards setting up their own seminaries.

In their interviews the young students came across as articulate young women, and expressed immense self-confidence about their hopes for a social and religious revolution within Pakistan. I was struck by their derision of the servile scraping to feet of students in 'modern schools' when a Very Important Person comes to the room, a custom that they believed should have left Pakistan with the British. They explained how their teachers and the principal have taught them to sit to attention rather than follow the 'colonial' practice of standing up when a visitor came into their room. The reason being that with the word of God (Quran) and commentaries of it in their laps, they enjoy a higher status compared to the guest. That the young women are being created in the Jamat's image was evident during my afternoons in the seminary. When asked what they understood of the upcoming educational reforms, an eight-year-old declared that their movement was against the concept of co-education and they denounced music as an academic subject. Her statement had me bewildered for a while as nothing in our exchange had brought up the issue of music. Even before this conversation took place the students had impressed me with how aware they were of what was happening in the country compared to others in their age group in Pakistan. And as I gradually learnt about their school routine I could understand where their fluency for contemporary Pakistani politics was coming from. The *madrassah* administration read out newspaper headlines to the students every day during the morning assembly. The Jamat-i-Islami finds this a necessary ritual of the early morning assembly, so that their students leave their alma mater not only grounded in contemporary politics but to be well-prepared to debate the Jamat world-view in a convincing manner. Therefore, the eight-year-olds whom I spoke to toed the Jamat-i-Islami line at a very young age—from speaking against the policies of the Musharraf government to condemning the recent inclusion of music as a subject at Punjab University.[2]

---

[2] There had been news that the Student Wing of the JI at the Punjab University (the Islami Jamiat Taliba) had agitated violently against this decision in Lahore. They viewed the inclusion of music as a subject not only as moral corruption but also a challenge to their iron-fisted control of the university campus. For years, thanks to the religio-military nexus in place in Pakistan, they had enjoyed a great amount of influence in the running of the university. Under their 'regime', university faculty had little control over the curriculum and the student examination; the IJT had a say in what was taught, and challenged faculty

The students I interviewed were mostly from Swat and other small towns in the Malakand region, while some were from areas neighbouring Khairabad which housed the seminary. Cities like Swat in Malakand are areas that have experienced extreme Talibanisation and in those days were witnessing the rise of illegal FM radio channels that broadcast sermons of radical firebrand clerics. These changes in their world-view had brought about less tolerance for Muslims of sects other than theirs, and also the erasure of their Buddhist and pacifist past. Some of the students shared with me in their interviews their plans of setting up their own *madrassahs* in their home towns in Swat and elsewhere. They explained that not all of the girls in their villages could leave their homes to take admission in the *madrassahs* of Peshawar and elsewhere, so they planned on taking the message of Jamia Mohsinat back to their young friends. They also viewed becoming a *madrassah* teacher a more useful means of employment than taking up any other profession, expressing a clear disdain for the other professional choices I discussed with them, their reasoning being that they would truly feel 'accomplished' if they had participated in Pakistan's revivalist movement. This was reiterated as they expressed their contempt for 'secular' education, the only purpose of which was producing 'American agents' and 'cultural stooges' in Pakistan for the West.

Khawar Mumtaz has explored the phenomenon of seminary education for women and how it evolved over the years. Mumtaz writes that the religiously defined parties of Pakistan took a long-term view of instilling their Islamist ideology amongst a wider section of women in the country. The *madrassahs* for women are one attempt to instil not only their particular version of Islam amongst women students but also to prepare them for jobs in segregated settings as teachers of Arabic and Religion in government primary and girls' high schools across Pakistan. In the words of the *madrassah* Faisal-ul-Banat, (a seminary Mumtaz investigated) their mission is to rectify the neglect of women's spiritual education 'and (to) counter Westernisation that has effected women, who under the pretext of emancipation and liberation are in reality spreading obscenity and

---

decisions. They also controlled the lives of the students and frowned upon male and female students fraternising with each other. They vehemently protested the setting up of the Music Department and declared that parents sent their children to get an education in something decent and did not want their wards to be misled by faculty and 'indulging in debauchery'. Their protests came from a subterranean fear that there were changes afoot, and if they did not challenge this, the days of their holding sway over the university would soon end. I had been following the turf wars in Lahore through the print media but little did I know that I would meet their ideological comrade-in-arms in a small seminary on the border of NWFP.

immorality' (Mumtaz, 1994: 231). Mumtaz explains that the impact of the time spent in each of these seminaries can be well imagined given the nature and content of the education imparted combined with the formative ages of the students. Consider the hundreds of girls and young women as they lead isolated lives in an over-protected environment, following rigid routines, living away from reality, and only receiving a narrow and often bigoted view of the world through selected Islamic texts. They can only imbibe a particular kind of ideology. The implications are indeed far-reaching and have certainly contributed towards generating retrogressive thinking and reinforcing patriarchal structures (Mumtaz, 1994: 239).

My day in Khairabad corroborated Mumtaz's hypothesis and I could see for myself that the students of Jamia-al-Mohsinat were leaving with the warped and narrow world-vision of their teachers. It was clear to me that the only skill they were trained in would be to regurgitate their curriculum with none of the analysis. There is increasing talk of nepotism and class hatred that a secular education brings about which does not bode well for any project that aspires to have a non-sectarian and non-violent political reading of Islam and national identity in Pakistan. These young women were also ready to participate in the insurgency against the Pakistani state; however, at this stage they were not clear how. What was evident to all observers was that these young women had become agents of the changed social demography and the growing Talibanisation in the Malakand valley. As later ethnographic studies in the region showed, these young women were eager to support the firebrand clerics and their challenge to the Pakistani state in later days. As news started trickling in over the coming months of the women of Swat contributing their golden bangles to Mullah Fazalullah and chastising their husbands if they shaved their beards or supported the Pakistani state, I wondered to myself how many of them had been present on that particular afternoon in Khairabad.

While I was in the area I heard the news of the bombing of a seminary in Bajaur (in Pakistan's FATA region) by drone planes hunting for militants.[3] The government claimed that they had received reports that there were dangerous Al Qaeda operatives and ammunitions in the building while the seminary faculty screamed hoarse that there were only students. The sight of shrouded bodies (including that of little boys) had many in tears as they viewed the media images. The Bajaur incident followed me as I travelled across the country speaking to seminary students. There were

---

[3] I refer here to the events of October 2006. Bajaur would continue to be in the news for drone attacks conducted by the US and suicide bombings by 'their own' in the coming years.

many who would confront me and ask me why 'we' (as in secular Pakistan) hated them; they would question why my contemporaries could attend their educational institutions, no questions asked, while they were killed for attending theirs. As a young student in the city of Quetta asked me, 'Why do all of you hate us so?' Quetta is now in the news for hosting the infamous Quetta Shura that acts as a state within state, challenging the edict of the Pakistani government and responsible for terrorist activities across the region.

Many viewed the initial pictures of the carnage as 'our ground zero'— drawing parallels with New Yorkers, if their grief was legitimate for the world, then why not Bajaur's? Just as a decade later the hashtag of Je Suis Paris, Beirut, Charlie Hebdo and Aylan Kurdi would compete with each other in social media. Perhaps those who were in charge of the Bajaur site then wanted to invest in connections with other pilgrimages of grief in keeping alive the memories of the day. The inter-relationships between pilgrimage, grief and memory are never power-free and the vision of the building in ruins and a site contested was successful in evoking powerful emotions—an outcome that the *madrassah* administration and their affili- ates were looking forward to utilising for their own purposes.

As I read news reports that narrated the visits of ordinary Pakistani citizens to the site I could witness for myself the power of ritual, pilgrim- age, and politics produced by the Bajaur site. One report recounted the actions of 'a clean shaven man in ultra-white', and how he was 'witnessed collecting sand from the site of the *madrassah* and graves of the victims at some distance from there, and rubbing them with his neat and clean clothes. When asked why he was doing so, the Urdu-speaking man replied that he had come from Rawalpindi and wanted to go back with the gift of the sand of the graves of 'martyrs' for his family. The media took care in pointing out his ethnicity (Urdu-speaking) in order to comment upon the pan-Pakistan support to Bajaur—bear in mind that Bajaur is in Khyber Pakhtunkhwa and so the bombing of the seminary is shown as an affair that concerned and had in rage groups from regions other than the Pashtun heartland alone.

I believe the Bajaur actors had been very shrewd in investing in these rituals and encouraging discourses dealing with these themes—with all narratives concluding with an emphasis on the injustice the community faces from state and external actors, and suggestions for a possible road map for their future. There was a clear understanding that any strategic action for securing their political future could only happen by allowing visitors to the site and by ensuring that they went through the rites of grief. Assisting pilgrimages to the site, having the ritual of 'viewing', and keeping a memory of their community's grief alive in the personal day-to-day life of the Pakistani citizen proved useful. However, in less than six months the Lal Masjid movement and the subsequent Operation Silence against it created a situation much more disturbing than the one in Bajaur. There were now images of Jamia Hafsa, a seminary under siege in Islamabad that graced the front pages of Pakistani newspapers.

But the discourse of these ill-fated seminaries may continue, at times adopted by forums previously never imagined. A far cry from the modest establishment in Khairabad and the gloomy environs of the Jamia Hafsa, a new generation and class of Pakistani students buckle down for their morning studies in cosmopolitan Karachi and the prosperous suburbs of Islamabad. They are students of the new face of the Pakistani seminary. In spaces I label as 'hybrid' they offer a world class education and training in the Quran and Hadith. In present-day Pakistan, the Pakistanis have witnessed the mushrooming of billboards that publicise these institutions with their credentials superimposed on a set of scales that has the Quran on one side of the scales and a globe on the other—very clichéd but basically emphasizing the institutions' promise of offering the best of both worlds.

It is essential to study these institutions as they signify the changed mindset of civil society in Pakistan, and in addition, they challenge the statistics that the Pakistan government offers regarding enrolments in seminaries. The former Pakistani President Musharraf's statement on the issue of seminaries 'that only two percent of Pakistani children go to seminaries' can be challenged—for government statistics fail to acknowledge these particular seminaries as they are not perceived as 'conventional' *madrassahs*. They confound definitions of both conventional schools and *madrassahs* in Pakistan. The emergence of such spaces have escaped any earlier research on seminary education in Pakistan as these have concentrated on traditional religious seminaries, the allegations of terrorism, or at most, profiles of urbanised members of the Jamat ud Dawa.

## Enter the Hybrid Seminary

The evolution of the hybrid seminary has been a gradual process. It started with a decree of 'equivalence' for *madrassah* degrees and academic degrees awarded by Pakistan's Ministry of Education. The process was instituted 1979 onwards in response to pressure from religious seminaries, when President Zia agreed to extend to *madrassah* graduates the same level of respect that applied to other Pakistani graduates. However, the ad hoc nature of a Dars-e-Nizami degree issued by the seminaries and other issues related with a seminary education were causing conflicts when it came to the accreditation of a *madrassah* degree in other educational and job sectors in Pakistan. Therefore, over time there have been reforms and structural changes within the seminaries towards a relatively more formalised structure of awarding degrees. The following two tables list the educational qualifications recognised by the Ministry of Education in Pakistan, the degrees offered by the *madrassahs*, and their equivalents in the 'mainstream' government educational system. Table 2.1 lists the various degrees conferred by the various Pakistan Education Boards. Table 2.2 lists the various degrees conferred by the *madrassahs* and their equivalent in the Pakistan Education Board system. At the high school level, this meant that graduates from *madrassahs* at the *Aama* level were recognised as having the same qualifications as matriculation or 'O level' students. The employment implications of this are obvious: *madrassah* graduates have increasingly since 1979 had general access to employment in government departments, and study in professional, tertiary colleges. Of course, the *madrassah* graduates who receive equivalence need also to have completed at the matriculation level a minimum of three additional electives beyond the *Aama* curriculum—for example, English is one of those options (see below for details). This 'compromise' was reached as a result of intensive *madrassah*-government negotiations. Similarly, the *Khasa* curriculum is recognised as the equivalent of the Intermediate

**Table 2.1**

*Pakistan Education Degrees*

| Level | Grade | Age Group of Students |
|---|---|---|
| Pre-school | Kindergarten and Montessori | 3–5 years |
| Primary | Grades 1–5 | 5–9 years |
| Secondary | Middle School (Grades 6–8) | 10–12 years |
| High School | Metric, Grades 9–10 | 13–16 years |
| Higher Secondary | Intermediate, Grades 11–12 | 15–16 years |
| Higher Education | Bachelors (2 years degree pre-2002, 4 years degree since 2002) | 17 years and over |
| Higher Education | Masters, 2 years | |
| Higher Education | PhD, 3–4 years | |

*Source*: Author.

**Table 2.2**

*Degrees Offered by* Madrassahs

| Grade | Level | Class | Duration | Equivalence with Mainstream System |
|---|---|---|---|---|
| Ibtidai | Nazera (Primary) | 1–5 | 5 years | Primary |
| Mutawassit | Hifz (Middle) | 6–8 | 3 years | Middle |
| Sania Aama | Tajvidh Qirat (Secondary) | 9–10 | 2 years | Matriculation |
| Sania Khasa | Tehtani (Higher Secondary) | 11–12 | 2 years | Intermediate |
| Aalia | Mouquf-Alaih (College) | 13–14 | 2 years | Bachelors |
| Alamia | Dora-e-Hadith (University) | 15–16 | 2 years | Masters |

*Source*: Author.

Certificate or the A Levels, depending on the student also having completed the subjects required by the Ministry of Education of Pakistan.

Over the years we have seen a silent revolution where Pakistani families who as a rule might have sent their children to private and English medium schools now have an incentive to send their children to these new 'hybrid' institutions. They are doing so, so that their children can learn to memorise the Quran to boost their chances of gaining admission in medical and engineering colleges on reserved seats for Hafiz Quran (someone who has memorised the Quran) and for the extra marks in college transcripts.[4] Parents are now inclined to tell their children to consider memorising the Quran in order to get into the academic programme of their choice; they are not saying memorise the Quran in order to become a better Muslim! This is a paradoxical result, because from the viewpoint of a religious purist such attitudes could be seen as undermining the very purpose of a 'religious' education. Yet, despite this fine point the pressure to implement

---

[4] Since the 1980s, a new 20-point incentive system has been introduced into Pakistan to encourage students to memorise the Quran (*Hifz*). Those who have committed the Quran to memory receive an extra 20 points at the time of their entrance into professional colleges in Pakistan. The debate over equal citizenship as guaranteed by the Pakistani constitution aside, what is more important to acknowledge is what memorising the Quran now means for Pakistani families and an average school student. What should be a task pursued mainly for gaining religious merit becomes a means of getting ahead in life as it is a conduit to enter professional and bureaucratic organisations in Pakistan. It is these changes that the Mutahida Majlis Amal (a major Islamic coalition that formed two of Pakistan's provincial governments and a significant influence in the National Assembly post the 2002 election) and the General Zia administration before have introduced to Pakistani society. And a cadre of seminaries today cater to meeting the need of Pakistani students to gain this worldly 'merit'.

the system of 20 additional marks is increasing, especially because right-wing political parties such as the MMA are monitoring the system to ensure that it is observed. Moreover, being a Hafiz Quran or going to a particular seminary has real clout in Pakistan these days as members of the Jamat-i-Islami and other right-wing religious political parties are on the selection board of the Federal Public Services Commission, the engineering and medical universities and other institutions.

Thus, over the past decade one has observed institutions such as Reflections, Iqra Educational Foundation and the Yaqeen Model School becoming popular choices of alma mater for young people in Pakistan. These institutions have also risen from the needs of a certain class of Pakistani Muslims (living at home and in the diaspora) who want to emphasise how their family's life choices (whether it is what they speak, how they dress or live) do not follow the hotchpotch of Western culture and Pakistani traditions. Instead, they hope they can advocate a way of life for their family, friends, and colleagues 'that is complete unto itself.'

Khalid Bashir, who established the Reflections Model School, describes in an interview the institution he set up as the culmination of a 'personal journey'. He describes himself growing up as an agnostic. Though he says he was educated at the prestigious (and secular) Karachi Grammar School and attended colleges in Canada, he did begin to wonder whether 'it was wise to live my life as if there is no God (Siddiqui and Sherazi, 2009: 84–87).' He mentions his self-awakening leading to a new phase in his life which coincides with one being adopted by his larger family: 'My family was embarking on its own religious journey. My mother already prayed regularly. My sisters were attending a course in Quran' (ibid.). The course that his sisters were attending was one organised by Al Huda—a trans-national religious network instituted by Dr Farhat Hashmi. The organisation started out in the cities of Karachi and Islamabad in Pakistan and now has affiliates in North America, United Arab Emirates, United Kingdom and Australia. Two years ago Dr Hashmi migrated to Canada and now runs Al Huda from there. Bashir's sister suggested that they set up a short lecture-based summer course named 'Islamic Fundamentals' in collaboration with Al Huda so in 2001 he decided to set up a summer camp for teenage boys. The two hired a group of *maulvi* (clergy) to impart *tajvid* (religious commentary) to the students. Upon the insistence of their students they extended the summer school as a weekly programme run for three hours in the evening. The boys are taken for 'Islamic' field trips to the beach so they can offer prayers there and set up in their own words a 'thriving Islamic environment'. One of the field trips included taking a group of 20 boys on a 10-day trip to Pakistan's Northern Areas. They were accompanied by an Islamic scholar who was given the task of offering sermons to the young men during the day. Bashir believes that the trip taught the campers not only to travel on their own and be self-sufficient, but was also useful in imparting to them good Islamic morals. Therefore, parents like Rukhsana Azeem, whose son studies at Reflections, are happy that their children have the opportunity to 'study in an English medium school but one that also emphasised (sic) on Islamic teachings and moral values.'

Iqra schools (short for the Iqra Roza Itfal Trust) have also become extremely popular with the middle classes precisely because they offer *hifz* classes (memorisation of the Quran) in an environment which is perceived by these families as being sophisticated learning institutes that are also committed to modern educational methods and curricula. The Iqra Roza Itfal Trust was founded on 4 April 1984 in Karachi, Pakistan and a brochure for the institute explains the aims and objectives of the institute as to bring the memorisation of Quran to all Muslim households, to reform character and behaviour, along with establishing good quality modern and religious educational institutions for girls and boys who have memorised the Quran. (The translation of the Iqra brochure from Urdu is mine).[5]

The Iqra schools I visited were non-residential and guided by modern parenting practices that prohibit corporal punishment. In short, they are ideal for Pakistan's middle classes wishing to avoid the authoritarianism, rote learning, and stifling environment of what they regard as the conventional *madrassah*.

It is important to stress that the appeal of the Iqra Roza Itfal Trust is so extensive that many imitations have emerged; there are many competing Iqra schools that seek to benefit from the original Iqra reputation but do not belong to the Iqra Trust *madrassah* system. Indeed, a newspaper report in Peshawar (December 2006) carried a photograph and story about a young boy whose swollen face was attributed to discipline imposed by an Iqra teacher. The Iqra Roza Itfal Trust sprang to its defence, pointing out that this was the work of another Iqra that did not belong to its system. What this also reveals is the competition between *madrassahs* for students—in

---

[5] The Iqra Roza Itfal Foundation was founded by Maulana Jamil, the founding patron and motivating force behind the formation of the Jaish-e-Mohammad. The first schools were set up on land donated by his father. Maulana Jamil also belonged to the Almi Majlis Khatam Nabuwat. He gave particular attention to establish Iqra schools in Pakistan Northern Areas to counter the influence of the Agha Khan Rural Support projects and the alleged 'Ismaili' missionary activities. Maulana Jamil was gunned down in Karachi by unknown assailants.

this case, not merely on the basis of sectarian identity but simply for reasons of commercial success. Despite these developments, the Iqra Roza Itfal Trust refuses to copyright its name believing that 'imitation is the best form of flattery'.

Iqra expanded its educational system to give importance to pre-school training based on the Montessori principles and playgroup. This programme admits under five-year-olds into a *roza* programme where they are taught the Urdu and English alphabet, basic conversation and numeric skills. This is in strong contrast to conventional *madrassahs*, the majority of which are residential, where a young person can only be taken in if 'they can look after themselves'. A three-year-old, for example, would not be studying at a *madrassah*, but Iqra recruits three-year-olds believing that the sooner they begin their education, the better. In the past, ambitious parents would have sent their young children to a Montessori school; now they can send their children to an Islamic 'Montessori'. This pre-school system allows Iqra students to undertake an accelerated programme of Islamic and Pakistani school curriculum at all subsequent levels. Students more than five years old are placed in *Qaeda* where they are introduced to the *Noorani Qaeda* (Arabic primer) and a special Iqra primer. At this stage children go through *nazera* (reading of the Quran) classes. On completion of *nazera*, children go through *Hifz*, classes (memorisation of the Quran) that should at least take them four years. As Iqra teachers explained, a five-year-old student is an ideal age as Iqra wants students to finish the *hifz* by their tenth birthday. Therefore, a six-year-old will be taken only as a special case. After completion of *hifz*, students are prepared to appear for Grade 10 examinations under an accelerated six-year programme. Though they follow the curriculum set by the particular Pakistan Board of Education that an Iqra branch is affiliated with, students can take extra classes in Arabic, commentary of the Quran (the Quran commentary has been written by Iqra) and *fiqh* (Islamic jurisprudence). The students, if they wish, can also prepare for and appear in examinations conducted by the federation of *madrassahs*, and teachers at Iqra will guide them. For example, if a student later discovers a passion for religious learning and wishes to transfer into a conventional *madrassah*, Iqra offers to facilitate this by preparing the student for the requisite entrance exams.

The Iqra school heads and teachers interviewed by me were very disparaging about other English medium private schools and even Pakistani government English medium schools. They were seen as providing an unsuitable environment for young children. My interviewees asked me why such institutions took pride in providing 'unnecessary' education to students. 'Unnecessary education', in their view, involves parroting English nursery rhymes that they felt had little relevance to a Muslim child's life, of the school administration emulating Christians, and/or employing Christian teaching staff.

Iqra addresses the question of women's education by being a co-educational school that has mixed gender classes on some campuses (depending on the needs of a locality). Relative to this, very few conventional *madrassahs* provide for women memorising the Quran or getting any educational qualification in religious or any other kind of education. My interviews with other seminaries had also brought up the question of *hifz* (memorisation of Quran) for women. While some of the faculty associated with *madrassahs* other than Iqra declared that they do make provisions for women to memorise the Quran, in the same breath they did clarify that they do this with serious misgivings because 'women had weak memories and could not retain complex information after graduation'. This happened, in their view, because Pakistani women get involved with housework and forget what they have learnt. Men had better memories because they did no housework!

The Iqra teachers interviewed were very proud that their institution was accommodating young Pakistani women desirous of acquiring a religious education, as none of the *madrassahs* had allowed women to memorise the Quran or obtain any educational qualifications in religious subjects. Iqra regards itself as a pioneer of female religious education in Pakistan. Of course, this also means that Iqra will have a growing influence on the lives of young women, and ultimately the family. In providing religious education that tolerates mixed genders, Iqra is also building a powerful advocacy group in higher levels of education, in the job market and ultimately in society. Recently one Iqra female graduate attracted publicity because she was awarded a government merit scholarship to study at an engineering college in Karachi. Such successes appeal to the Pakistani middle classes.

The principal of one of the Iqra Roza Itfal schools in Karachi explained to me that it is not necessary that all his students (and Pakistani students in general) go on to take up life as a religious scholar or become clerics.[6] He does see them as majoring in medicine, liberal arts, and engineering. However, he feels that all Pakistani students should have a rigorous training in religious and moral education, which only institutions like Iqra can provide. Once Iqra graduates step into professional life they will have

---

[6] Personal interview, Karachi, December 2006.

shared religious values and a network of contacts. It is very significant to acknowledge the importance of this network of contacts, as particular *madrassah* alumni are emerging as parallel 'old boys clubs' in Pakistan. The Iqra administrators interviewed explained for me in great detail the tumultuous circumstances which they feel have brought the Muslim community to a crossroads much akin to a personal crisis in life. At this point of the interview they juxtaposed the post-9/11 environment with the aftermath of the War of Independence in 1857—in both cases Muslim communities were torn between being either with them (Westerners) or against them. The administrators feel that the present resembles an earlier situation where Muslims had to choose between an alliance with personalities like Sir Syed Ahmed Khan (the pioneer of Aligarh Muslim University, and an advocate of learning English and 'modern' sciences) or a refusal to assimilate (the *madrassah* Darul-uloom Hind of the past). The Iqra Roza Itfal administration saw the Aligarh model as too westernised and the *madrassah* Darul-uloom Hind as too divorced from life. The Iqra way is viewed as the 'middle path', their own brand of 'enlightened moderation'.

Table 2.3 offers a translation of the Iqra brochures that list the accomplishments of Iqra Roza Itfal schools for consumption by Pakistani families. This repeats information noted above, but it is important to catalogue how Iqra self-consciously promotes itself to the Pakistani public.

The last two points in Table 2.3 demonstrate how the Iqra administration does not want us to forget how their students are 'well-prepared' even when it comes to state examinations. Student exams results were advertised in Iqra brochures as they provided an added incentive for parents to enrol their children in this particular hybrid *madrassah* as it caters for both religious and non-religious education, thus proving a convenient alternative to the current practice of sending their wards to different schools at different points in their student life so that they can obtain both a religious and secular education.

The general impression conveyed by Iqra is that this is an educational institution that emphasises egalitarian values and a vision of Pakistan as a classless society. For instance, there is no canteen/tuck shop on the school premises; at lunchtime a *dastarkhwan* (a table cloth) is placed on the ground and the students share the food that they have brought from home. This communal meal is a new development, again being imitated by other schools.

Nevertheless, problematic features remain in the Iqra system. Sectarianism has not been overcome. Iqra is a Deobandi institution and some Barelvi families began to complain that the teachers were 'converting'

**Table 2.3**

*Specific Characteristics of Iqra (Translated from Urdu Brochures and Publicity Material)*

- First pre-primary education institution in Pakistan based on Islamic principles
- Hifz (memorisation) of Quran, followed by Metric (Grade 10) and higher academic levels
- Special provision of character-building and good social conduct under the guidance of learned teachers
- Learning in an atmosphere free of beating and scolding
- Education and training provided by computers and other modern apparatus
- Smart and graceful uniform
- Beautiful and roomy school buildings
- Transportation to school
- Appealing atmosphere and courteous staff
- Grading by report cards and observation
- Sponsorships by religious elders and intellectuals
- Network of school with branches from Karachi to Gilgit
- 129 branches
- 45,401 students currently enrolled (25,809 boys and 19,592 girls)
- 3,273 teachers (1,722 male and 1,591 female)
- 12,494 students who have memorised the Quran to date (6,874 boys and 5,620 girls)
- Iqra Hafiz Secondary Schools' Metric (Grade 10) Results to date: 733 students have given exams (319 boys and 414 girls)
- 316 boys and 410 girls have cleared examinations giving us a pass rate of 99%. 238 students got A+ grades (32.78%), 258 students got A grade (35.63%), 155 students got B grade (21.34%), 70 students got C grade (9.64%), 5 students got D grade (0.68%)

*Source*: Author's Translation of Iqra brochures.

their children. For example, at prayer time all the students prayed together with the result that the Deobandi prayer mode was followed even by Barelvi students. Teachers have responded to this criticism saying that they always encourage non-Deobandi students to follow their own customs. Of course, this may be difficult to implement in practice, as all young people tend to conform to the behaviour of the majority of their peers.

The administrators are not as accommodating on matters of ethnicity and local languages. I observed a gradual weeding out of local ethnic aspirations amongst students and moves towards a pan-Pakistan Urdu-speaking environment. The Urdu language that is encouraged as the *lingua franca* of the Iqra schools reflects the ethnic affiliation of the Karachi-based Iqra pioneers. At the same time, local languages such as Sindhi or Punjabi or Pashtu are regarded as pre-Islamic languages and in their very essence would introduce images and concepts that cannot conform to the Islamic environment that Iqra seeks to develop. In particular, such regional languages would remind the students, teachers and parents of the cross-border cultural affiliations that Pakistan shares with 'enemy' countries such as India and Afghanistan. Such regional discourses are both natural and indeed popular in Pakistan, but it is something that the pan-Islamic Iqra schools seek to eradicate.

All the resource persons associated with the hybrid seminaries I surveyed emphasised the British as colonising Muslim minds in the past, and the Americans today being very intelligent in using education as an inducement to encourage the Muslims to belittle their own culture and particular mode of education. Their task is to challenge this new coloniser as it sets forth to 'ruin the current Pakistani generation'. There is an attempt towards modernisation in these new seminaries—but only to the extent to master the technology and languages of teaching. One cannot find anything in the curriculum and the mindset to celebrate as a harbinger of a non-violent reading of Islam, and their agenda remains to build new networks to usher in their particular social revolution.

## Conclusion: Understanding the Social Revolutionaries amidst Us

The meteoric rise in the rate of success of certain right-wing groups in building a base among the professional, urban, and upper-middle-class Pakistani groups has confused the traditional as well as the modernist/ secular groups in the Pakistani community. One can borrow from Göle in analysing the 'ambiguity of signs' posed by the mass appeal of this particular social movement (Göle, 2002: 173–90). Göle has studied the surprising crossovers between 'Muslim' and 'modernity', and between secular and religious practices taking place in Turkey, which have unsettled the fixity of positions and oppositional categories. Göle's work catalogues the new social imaginaries being shaped by these circulatory, transcultured, and crossover performances. As her study of Islamists in Turkey shows, though these groups are in an oppositional political struggle with the modern secularists, they often mirror them and search for public representatives who speak foreign languages and belong to the professional and intellectual elite. This was reflected by a similar move in Pakistan to recruit youth icons that belonged to similar elite backgrounds—Pakistan's cricket team and their recent wave of evangelism is a case in point.

Junaid Jamshed, the popular singer-turned-devotional speaker, is a case study of this particular social revolution. Jamshed, the son of a former Air Marshal is credited for ushering in Pakistan's popular music revolution in the 1990s. While studying at Lahore's University of Engineering and Technology he was initially pursued by the Jamat-i-Islami and various other missionary groups. These groups persevered and a decade to the day when Jamshed first ruled Pakistan's air waves he became the poster child of Pakistan's new social revolution. Though Jamshed declares that since his change in life choices he has not only lost a number of friends and well-wishers but also suffered significant financial losses, a look at his personal business (of luxury Islamic goods) and paid public speaking declares otherwise. In August 2009, Jamshed participated in a televised panel discussion. I refer to the incident as it illustrates how Pakistan's new social revolutionaries give religious licence to turning a blind eye to the problems that irk Pakistan. The panel was discussing the death of a group of women as crowds stampeded for free rations. Jamshed came up with an interesting theory of the religious merits of not challenging your social location chiding the deceased for lining up for handouts in the first place. In the words of the social scientist Tazeen Javed who has offered a brilliant social commentary of Jamshed's tirade:

> According to Maulana Junaid Jamshed, it is ok if rich Muslims do not follow the religion, but if poor Muslims let go of the sacred religious teachings, the whole society would collapse. He repeatedly made references to '*Ghareeb ka Imaan*' (poor people's faith) and '*Ameer ka Imaan*' (rich people's faith) as if your class is responsible for your levels of faith and piety. He further went on and said that when poor people embrace the true values of Islam, they are endowed with the gift of self-respect, restraint and integrity. His theory was that even if people are poor and hungry, their self-respect—endowed only through strict adherence to Islam—will not allow them to go beg for food…. Junaid Jamshed further said that if poor people just practice restraint and stay hungry for three days, Allah will provide food for them for one whole year (Javed, 2009).

Javed's words struck a raw chord with some of her readers as they reprimanded her for criticising Junaid Jamshed[7] and his views regarding exercising restraint in the face of adversity—all evidence of the growing religiosity and intolerance towards dissent in today's Pakistan.

---

[7] While the book was in press, Junaid Jamshed passed away in a plane crash on 7 December 2016.

Pakistan's young go through generational angst like anyone else and feel that they lack any support networks. The new age Islamic schools I refer to, Reflections, its inspiration Al Huda, Iqra and the other hybrid *madrassahs*, the new social revolutionaries that masquerade as enlightened Islamic scholars, all deprive their students of the will to change or challenge all that is flawed in the Pakistani society. What they do, as Riffat Hassan (2002) criticises in her analysis of Al Huda's *dars* (scripture reading) culture, is to maintain the status quo and make certain age-old interpretations more palatable and acceptable to young people. However there is no attempt to bring in any revolutionary change and challenge Pakistan's flawed distribution of resources. So young people enrol in these schools, willingly participate in the meetings and excursions organised, and along with their parents feel good as they think they have performed their religious duty and pleased God. These schools teach them that only their Muslim identity should become dominant in their day-to-day practices, as this alone will give them some understanding of the world. For a group that needs some kind of mandate to continue with their established behaviour of indifference towards those lesser than them, what can be better if it is coming with a religious licence? Any angst at the growing realisation of the inequality of distribution of resources in Pakistani society, the skewed class structure of the Pakistani community and lack of governance and accountability in society is suppressed. Somewhere along this process is their absolution of the militant fringe for they feel that these radical groups are fulfilling their own mandate of taking on the evil West.

There is none of the *ijtihad* or revolutionary spirit Pakistani society badly needs as it takes on an enemy claiming to challenge the Pakistani state and kill thousands of innocents in the name of Islam. What is ironic is that both groups—those that turn a blind eye to Pakistan's challenges and those that spread terror claim that they are ushering in the supremacy of Quran and Sunnah, and that they want to impose good Muslim practices. However, they do so in a manner that is dangerous to the Pakistani nation. The latter has a problematic reading of political Islam and God's instructions of a 'just war' and the former feels Islam condones their apathy towards Pakistan's problems with governance and class differences and their religious duty lies in subcontracting the 'just war' to the militant fringe.

Today if one were to walk down the narrow lanes of Karachi's Sadar Bazaar, an area bustling with frenzied crowds jostling to get a closer look at the electronic goods, mobile phones and accessories on display, one cannot help but be distracted as I was by a colourful announcement for innovative 'Islamic' products. I share here an image of one of the products that I witnessed which is but one in a long line of consumer items influenced by the Islamisation of public culture in Pakistan (Image 2.1). The lines from the poster read:

> *Khush Khabri! Khush Khabri!* (Good News! Good News!)
> *Ovaiz Raza Qadri Ki Maqbool Naatey* (Ovaiz Raza Qadri's Popular Odes to the Prophet)
> *Musical Horn Aur Ghenti ka Neymul Badal* (In lieu of Musical Horns and Bells)
> *Ghar, Office, School aur Madrassah Ko Musical Ghenti Sey Bachaye* (Save Your Home, Your Office, School and *Madrassahs* from Musical Bells)

**Image 2.1**

*A poster of Ovaiz Raza Qadri's hymn-playing horns and doorbells*

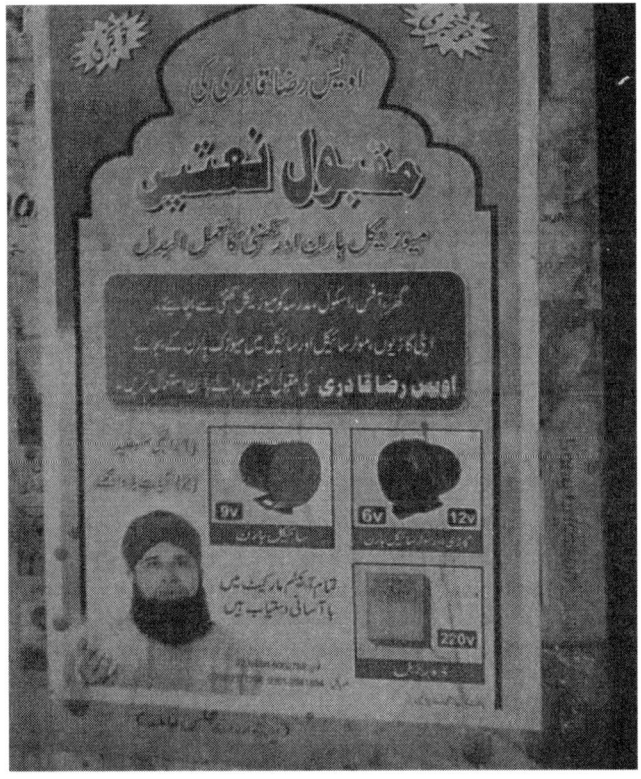

*Source*: Author.

*Apnee Ghariyo, Motor Cycle, Aur Cycle May Music Horn Key Bajaye Ovaiz Raza Qadri Ki Maqbool Naato Waley Horn Istimaal Karey* (In your cars, motor cycle and cycle use the Horn offered by Ovaiz Raza Qadri that plays his popular hymns to the Prophet instead of music.)

The Naát (hymns to the Prophet are):

1) *Nabi Muhammadiya*
2) *Aaya Hai Bulawa Mujhey*

*Tamam Item Bazaar May Ba Asani Dastiyab Hain*
The poster ends with the reminder that all items are easily available in the market.

The text under the images for the '9V Cycle Horn', '6 and 12 V' motorcycle and car horn and the '220 V' doorbell elaborate on their use. The gentleman in the poster is the famous Ovaiz Raza Qadri referred to in the announcement, and we are provided with the telephone and mobile contacts for the retail firm. This is just one sample of the cultural change that the technicians (with Islamic mindsets as the principal of Iqra promises) who graduate from these hybrid *madrassah*s have ushered in Pakistan.

The relationship of Pakistani Muslims with consumer items distinctly Islamic is not new. But I wonder where Pakistani society will end up as they set fervently on this quest. For history is witness to the fact that the Pakistani community's experiments with identity politics have always managed to have disastrous results. It is obvious that the move towards cultural nationalism has ushered in a process of 'othering' but what scares observers is the xenophobia being unleashed as it is obvious by this poster. Is the average Pakistani now scared of being tempted towards the path of evil by the chime of a doorbell or the ring of a bicycle bell? Are the new social revolutionaries hell bent on driving away any melody from the average Pakistani life?

With the paucity of debate and the Pakistani state brutally repressing dissent—it is ironic that it has been primarily the problematic religious lobby which has managed to mount a credible challenge to the Pakistani state regarding its crisis of legitimacy. Abdul Rashid Ghazi, the former patron of the problematic Red Mosque, had declared in the midst of his confrontation with the Pakistani state, 'We are only a student protest. We do not want to overthrow Musharraf as such. We want to overthrow the entire Pakistani system, which serves only one percent of the population.' These groups have provided a forum to critique the government's political policies and challenge global forces perceived by these groups as out to get Pakistan. *Madrassah* groups and their benefactors declare their agenda of ushering in social justice and reform in Pakistan. 'We want our rulers to be honest people'—they claim in interviews, perhaps a thought shared by many silent spectators in Pakistan who now lean towards the far-right and militant groups.

# 3

# Cultural Underpinnings

*Pakistani Muslim Women's Conceptions of Hijab in Islam*

## Voices

Naz, the female protagonist in Maniza Naqvi's *On Air*, fills in as a late night radio talk show host in Karachi, Pakistan. Earlier in the evening an irate male caller has chastised her: 'A woman's voice, going into stranger's houses at this time of the night, into strange bedrooms ... is very bad. It is simply indecent ... obscene' (Naqvi, 2000: 9).

The tirade is followed by another phone call, this time a young woman supporting her for hosting the show. Naz thinks to herself:

Here is a woman as indignant and bewildered as I am ... I gave the producer a double thumbs-up sign.

The caller, though, goes on to say, 'I think he is wrong because after all being on the radio is like wearing a hijab [literally, veil or curtain], isn't it? After all,' the caller continued, 'women in hijab can go anywhere, their movement is unrestricted, their motives are unquestionable. The point is that no one should see them and they should not be able to incite men to immorality. The radio is like a hijab'.

And you think that's what women do, incite men?

Well, it has to be, you see, because men are men and so women should be more responsible ... do you wear the hijab? You sound as though you did ... to me you sound confident. Like the way I sound when I'm in the hijab on a bus, or at college talking to professors or fellow students. I feel they're all in awe of me, a bit scared of my grandeur.

Grandeur?, I asked.

Yes, in the hijab I feel as though I represent all the great ladies of our Islamic history, I'm a symbol of Islam and our morality.

Maybe I sound as though I'm wearing a hijab because you've become used to being just a voice…behind a hijab, without a face, without an identity, and that is what I am for you right now. My voice is with you but you cannot see me.

Maybe. But I think you are being very unfair by saying that the hijab leaves me without an identity. My eyes are my identity and so are my ideas. You don't have to see my face for my identity. The reason I'm wearing it is to assert my real identity! (Naqvi, 2000: 37–40).

# Introduction

The above passage reflects the struggle I have often gone through when I try to tackle the issue of the veil. As a teenager I giggled reading a passage in Rushdie's novel *Shame* when the family's matriarch approves of her daughter-in-law keeping her *dupatta* (scarf) on: 'So Bilquis was forced, one evening … to recount her nudity in the Delhi streets. "Never mind," Bariamma pronounced approvingly, when Bilquis was shaking with the shame of her revelations, "at least you managed to keep your dupatta on"' (Rushdie, 1984: 76).

For me, Rushdie summed up (what I felt at the time) the pretence of my school teachers who were only concerned that we carried our scarf to school as a symbol of the faithful, paying no attention to whether we were growing up virtuous or not. Growing up in Pakistan in the 1980s meant hearing persistent threats of placing women in '*chadar* and *chardevari*' (*chadar*: shawl draped around the body; *chardevari*: four walls), and seeing women burning their *dupattas* (scarves) in the street in protest. For me, women who chose to cover themselves up were passive victims who had been co-opted by the state. It took some time before I could see them as they see themselves, as active participants seeking mobility and changes in their respective societies.

I hope this chapter serves as a space where 'our differences' will be recognised and examined, and a way whereby I can relate across these differences. It will also serve to analyse the conflicts faced by Pakistani women everywhere because of social, structural, cultural, and global influences and differences.

But at the outset I have to clarify that Muslim women's dress codes are often misleadingly referred to generically as veiling or the *hijab*. This obscures both historical changes in modes of dress and cultural contexts—and thus the fact that people may be talking of quite different modes of dressing when they refer to increased veiling or women's *hijab*. In the case of Pakistanis, whether in Pakistan or in the diaspora, there are wide variations in the physical and behavioural details of *purdah* (literally, veil) observance. These relate to differences in class, income, place of residence, level of education, occupation, religious or sectarian affiliation, and individual life circumstances. These range from the different styles of *burqa* (concealing cloak), the *chadar* (the shawl) and the *dupatta* (the scarf draped across the breasts, around the neck or over the head), and now the *hijab* (the head scarf).

It is this last, the *hijab* adopted by the urban upper-middle-class women, that has created a stir in the Pakistani community both at home and in the diaspora. For social groups and a media in Pakistan that has grown over the years to place actors under rigid definitions, this 'ambiguity of signs' may have confused them initially for they see these women as belonging to urban, upper-middle-class groups and now looking for 'liberation within Islam'. Even though these women are ill-at-ease with being called Islamic fundamentalists, they may tend to take stands similar to these groups on certain issues like women's right to work, sexuality, a woman's testimony and so on.

A spate of commentaries in the Pakistani media has described these groups thus:

> Considered to be a manifestation of a mullah mentality, hijabis (those taking the headscarf) are snidely labeled 'fundos' with the association of female oppression, another correlation borrowed from the West. Traditionally, though, a so-called fundo would have been likely to be clad in some bizarre variant of the burqa (a full coat and head covering). And she would most likely have been compelled to do so. But the headscarf is a recent Arab adoption and more often donned as a choice rather than a compulsion. It is also just one aspect of a drift towards understanding Islam. Many hijabis are women with college degrees, some working, others not, and the particular brand of Islam they have adopted springs from reason and research (Shamsi, 2002: 142).

Göle (2002) observes the surprising crossovers between 'Muslim' and 'modernity', and between secular and religious practices taking place in Turkey which unsettle the fixity of positions and oppositional categories.

Her work catalogues the new social imaginaries being shaped by these circulatory, 'transcultured', and crossover performances. As her study in Turkey shows, though these groups are in an oppositional political struggle with the modern secularists, they often mirror them and search for public representatives who speak foreign languages and belong to the professional and intellectual elite:

> In Turkey, one of the arguments widely used against the headscarf is that it has been appropriated as a political symbol, so the desire to wear it is not a disinterested one. Many will say they are not against their 'grand-mother's headscarf', that on the contrary they remember it with affection and respect. This is certainly true to the extent that 'grandmothers' either sat in their corners at home and didn't step into the sites of modernity or took off their headscarves as they walked out from indoors but today the play has changed and so have the actors. The Islamic headscarf is deliberately appropriated, not passively carried and handed down from generation to generation (Göle, 2002: 181).

# Voices Within: Dialogues with Women on Hijab

When I started speaking to young Pakistani women in Canberra I may have started observing them as 'contextually located actors in the conduct of their day-to-day lives'—their lived realities, not just their spiritual and religious practices but also how they responded to the community, spatial, social, and political dynamics governing their lives. Would Pakistani Muslim women in the diaspora adhere to the rigid fundamentalist positions? Would they find support and sustenance by 'upholding the faith'? Or would they look for 'liberation' by reinterpreting certain codes? Would they reinterpret portions of Islamic discourse that they are ill at ease with? The intention was to select women from a similar background and then see the range of belief, interpretation and attitude within the group on this issue.

Canberra, like other communities hosting the Pakistani diaspora, was a regular host to visiting Pakistani government delegations and there was a subtle emphasis in the community there on being seen as maintaining Pakistani norms. However, by their choices of which community centre they would choose to socialise in, and the mosques which they would worship in, the members of the Pakistani community were engaged in placing themselves in several different diasporas—South Asian, Muslim, nationalist Pakistani, Punjabi/Pathan. As Werbner writes of the Pakistani community in Manchester, each of these communities is a hybrid diaspora, each with its own aesthetics and ethics. Being Pakistani, far from referring to a reified identity, encompasses a historically produced multiplicity, created in response to diasporic and subcontinental movements—of Islamisation, Empire, modernism and nationalism—further embedded in quite different regional and linguistic traditions (Werbner, 2002).

The Pakistani community in Canberra was also being shaped by the 'spiritual leaders' who visit diasporic communities to provide blessings and advice. These continued relations between 'home' and 'host-country' institutions transform religious practice, discourses, and relations in both 'home' and 'host' contexts. For instance, as stated before, the *hijab* is seen in Pakistan as a 'recent adaptation' and an 'Arab import' introduced by these globalised socio-religious networks.

When analysing any debate on the issue on veiling, one has to discriminate between two distinct dimensions: what people actually do—the decisions they make, secretly entertain or display—and the discourses they develop for themselves. One is about reality and how people adapt to rapid change in time; the other is about self-presentation and identity-building (Mernissi, 1991). The need for the Pakistani Muslim diaspora to claim so vehemently in interviews that they are traditional, and that their women have miraculously evaded social change, has to be understood in terms of the imperatives of self-representation and must be classified not just as a statement about daily behavioural practices, but rather as a psychological need to maintain a minimal sense of identity in a confusing and shifting reality. Finally, women's and men's positions relative to religious-rights discourses on women's dress codes or female modesty can be likewise diverse.

In Canberra the degrees of veil observance among the Pakistani community varied. The operation of the institution of *purdah* amounts to secluding women's and men's living spaces at home or setting aside separate spaces in public on social occasions. As previously studied by the anthropologist Hanna Papanek, the allocation of space provides physical and visual isolation between women and men and is intended to prevent accidental contact. Men entering the spaces set aside for women must signal their intention, and women must withdraw if necessary (Papanek, 1982). Where it operated, this arrangement was a visible sign on the part of families not only about their attitudes of conformity to a particular ethnic group, but also of their ideological bent within Islam (ibid.: 211) However, it could also be applied flexibly in some families for 'close family friends', or as in my case, where the fact that I was seen as visiting and doing research in Canberra allowed me to 'overstep' my gender on social occasions in '*purdah* households'. I would frequently be invited to sit instead with the male invitees during community dinners and participate in their discussions.

Another element of the *purdah* was expressed in the choice of paid work taken up by the women in the community. The allocation of work is the analogue of the allocation of living space—women working with other women or young children in and around the home was a preferred choice. Most Pakistani women in Canberra were busy running day care centres for children or food catering services in their own homes or working incrèches outside. These forms of *purdah* provide, as Papanek explains, 'symbolic shelter' for the women in the community. They permitted Pakistani women to be defined simultaneously as important to the Pakistani family unit and very vulnerable when they move into the world outside the home (Papanek, 1982).

The final aspect was the form of dress code the women chose enabling them to move out of segregated living spaces while still observing *purdah*. The *burqa* (cloak with veil) has been viewed by many, like Papanek who researched veiling practices in Pakistan, as operating as 'portable seclusion' (ibid.: 195) and a liberating invention for some as it enabled women to move out of segregated living spaces while still observing the basic moral requirements of separating and protecting women from unrelated men. As Papanek writes:

> Women's proper behaviour, as sheltered persons, becomes an important measure of the status of their male protectors, and the achievement of symbolic shelter is valued by the men of the family as a measure of control over their environment. In a culture where male pride is a significant and also a fragile element of identity and status, the seclusion of women is an important aspect of male control (ibid.: 193).

However, in some households this consideration worked in reverse. Some of my interviewees who wore the *chadar* in Pakistan were asked by their husbands to choose some other less distinctive form of covering up in Canberra as they wanted to be seen as fitting in with Anglo-Australian society. This led to a lot of guilt and heartache for some women. Hashmi's (and other religious speakers visiting Canberra) lecture sessions usually feature a question from the audience regarding whether they could defy their husband's dictates and still be considered good Muslim wives. In some cases they had complied with their husband's requests and tried to compensate for such visible regression on their part by other forms of piety so they could still be considered 'good Pakistani women.' For instance, one interviewee had convinced her husband to insist that her children watch only Pakistani programmes on cable television and that the family not speak in English at home.

In the broadest sense, the *purdah* system is related to 'status, the division of labour, inter-personal dependency, social distance and the maintenance of moral standards as specified by the community' (Papanek, 1982). The problem arises as most Muslim societies in general have mainly followed a view that women are mentally and morally deficient creatures on whom 'virtue' has to be externally imposed. At the heart, so to speak, of Muslim religious right groups is their concern with women:

> Where logically one might expect a focus on the (gender neutral) five pillars of Islam—the profession of belief in Allah and the prophet, the five daily prayers, the annual month-long fast, the giving of a tenth of one's goods for charity each year, and the pilgrimage to Mecca—there is instead a preoccupation with women. It is women's dress and behaviour that is frequently made a symbol of new 'Islamic' orders (Imam, 1997: 15).

In Pakistan, Abul Ala Mawdudi (the founder of the Jamat-i-Islami) considered the preservation of women's chastity through *purdah* (in the broad sense of seclusion from men) to be one of the basic principles of human rights in the Islamic world. He instructed that women should wrap themselves well in their *chadars* and should draw and let down a part of the sheet in front of the face. Another Islamic jurist in Pakistan, Justice Aftab Husain argued that *purdah* keeps both sexes chaste and prevents them from gazing at one another (Chaudhry, 1991: 107–8).

The elaborate detail with which Ashraf Ali Thanvi's book *Behishti Zevar* outlines the ideal Muslim woman has remained an agenda for perfection, impossible for most Pakistani Muslim women to attain. It is distributed as 'a classic manual of Islamic Sacred Law' to young women in Pakistan, particularly at the time of marriage and looked upon almost as required reading for women in the Pakistani diaspora who belong to Islamic reform movements in the West. In it women are ordered to cover their bodies from head to toe, and not to expose their bodies to *ghair mehram* (all those with whom marriage is permissible):

> It is permissible for an old woman to expose her face, palms and feet below the ankles but not to expose the rest of her body. At times the head covering (of young women) drops slightly and she goes in the presence

of *ghair mehram* in this way. This is not allowed. Not a single strand of hair should be exposed in the presence of *ghair mehram*. In fact, the hair that falls off her head while combing her hair and the nails which she has clipped should be left in such a place where *ghair mehram* will not be able to see them. If a woman is not cautious in this regard, she will be sinful ... it is compulsory to make *hijab* with the 'disbelieving women' who come into one's home. This also applies to maids and domestic servants who are not Muslims (Thanvi, 2002: 297–98).

On the rare occasion when the women did go out of the confines of their four walls, they were expected to don the *burqa*—that portable statement of *purdah* or physical seclusion and the cultural marker of the status of whole families as well as individual men (Jalal, 2002). As it was in the times when Thanvi wrote *Behishti Zevar*, the *ulema* (religious elite) today in Pakistan are determined to strictly confine Pakistani women to the sacred geography of the Muslim household. Even today, women in the *ashraf* (respectable class) conception remain 'ornaments of their homes' and it is preferred that they remain confined to the *zenana* (women's quarters).

The coloniser's 'impure and tainted' ideology then, and fear of modernity now should not be seen as reaching the home, where women protect and preserve cultural traditions to shield the beleaguered self. The whole process symbolised protection of Islamic identity, communal dignity, and social and cultural continuity, and it draws the boundaries between 'Muslim culture' and the non-Muslim other. The 'zenana' was the 'essential space of Indian femininity' (Suleri, 1992: 92) Instances when the 'zenana' was violated in colonial times and the veil removed were therefore akin to the impregnation of the woman and had strong sexual connotations: '[O]nly after such a sanctum had been penetrated that the Anglo-Indian can claim to "know" the Indian' (Suleri, 1992: 93).

This is also reflected today in South Asia in popular literature and electronic media where the veil bestows a certain kind of mystique to the woman. The accent is always on the physical beauty of the protagonist and therefore on the veil that hides that beauty. The veil thus hides what all men desperately want to see (Kazmi, 1994). Pakistani wedding songs, for instance, conjure up an eroticised picture of the 'woman hiding behind the veil' as an object of desire.

The variant of Pakistani nationalism in the period immediately after independence was that of liberal modernism, an approach which advocated emulation of some Western practices while preserving what are constructed as traditional cultural practices in other areas (Gardezi, 1997).

This normally entailed the granting of political, economic, and social rights which could bring some changes to the lives of women of the upper classes, but a continued or intensified emphasis on women's primary role in the family. In state discourses, the ideal woman continued to be a middle-class/lower-middle-class urban housewife whose function was to be the *chiragh-e-ghar* (the light of the house) rather than the *shama-e-mehfil* (the bright light of public occasions), not too different from the 'angel of the hearth' in Victorian spheres.

Islamisation was a strategy of General Zia's martial law regime in the 1980s, a period which forms the formative years for my interviewees. Even before this, Bhutto in the 1970s had responded to the crisis of the creation of Bangladesh brought about by the secession of East Pakistan in 1971 by turning to pan-Islamism and a resurrection of the 'Muslim world' in the Pakistani imagination (Toor, 1997). This later enabled General Zia-ul-Haq to play the Islamisation card. As Gardezi explains, the most profound changes undertaken in the course of Islamisation were directed towards women:

> A vow to maintain the sanctity of the *chadar* and *chardivari* (the veil and the four walls of the home) figured prominently in General Zia's initial speeches to the nation …. The government issued directives requiring women to wear *chadar*s in government offices, on television and in public schools (areas over which the government could exert some direct control) …. General Zia made a common practice of presenting *chadar*s as gifts to women he met in his official function as head of state (Gardezi, 1997: 90–91).

The existing feudal elites found the patriarchal, anti-minority stance of the Islamists and the state useful for furthering their own economic and political interests. Therefore, even though Islamisation was a strategy of a martial law regime, it nevertheless enjoyed a significant level of popular consent. Thus, not all women viewed General Zia's laws for compulsory veiling and rendering women's testimony secondary as repressive. Toor points out that the fact that these laws differentially impacted the most vulnerable sections of the population may also explain why middle- and upper-class women did not react in line with their 'gender interests' (Toor, 1997). Ayesha Jalal makes an argument for the 'convenience of subservience': given that a particular group of women operated in a privileged social context, most of these women chose the path of least resistance. Their decision was thus in favour of their class and gender interests (Jalal, 1992). Whether one buys Jalal's argument completely, it certainly illustrates the complexity of analysing the relationship between Pakistani women and the state. A significant group of my interviewees were of a generation that had grown up under these conditions prior to moving to Australia, and one shouldn't overlook how certain cultural traditions are transmitted and internalised through the socialisation process, thus continuing to frequently work as an important control mechanism in the case of the Pakistani diaspora.

During the initial phases of the Islamisation process in Pakistan, efforts were made by conservative Muslim men, who were threatened by women's presence in 'public space', to put them in the '*chadar* and *chardevari*' (the veil and within four walls). Not satisfied with 'the outer garment' prescribed by the Quran for Muslim women in a specific cultural context, some conservative Muslims also sought the help of *Hadith* (traditions ascribed to the Holy Prophet), whose authenticity is dubious, to compel women to cover themselves from head to foot, leaving only the face and hands uncovered. Due to various reasons these efforts were not immediately successful, especially amongst urban elite women. In the 1980s, female students scoffed at the *chadar* directives. The Pakistani religious right wing in the 1990s decided to take a longer-term view of imparting their ideology among a wider section of Pakistani women. As a measure to actively mobilise women belonging to an emerging middle class, there was a mushrooming of religious seminaries in the major cities and towns of Pakistan. These institutions imparted a selective reading of Islamic texts and discourses and prepared women for jobs in segregated settings as teachers of Arabic and religious studies in state-run schools. Mumtaz notes that the stated reason for establishing one such institution, Madrassah Faisal-al-Banat in Lahore, was to rectify the neglect of women's spiritual education—as considered essential in the *madrassah* (religious seminary) brochures, which publicised their services as countering the Westernisation that had affected women, who under the pretext of emancipation and liberation were in reality spreading obscenity and immorality (Mumtaz, 1994: 231).

But later, personalities like Farhat Hashmi (Image 3.1), who started running religious seminaries for women, have been far more successful in their Islamisation campaign since her followers seem to have voluntarily adopted a style of *hijab* that not only covers their bodies but also virtually makes them faceless. Farhat Hashmi is also the pioneer of the *dars* (religious lectures) visits to Pakistani communities in the diaspora and she visits Australia regularly. Hashmi has been questioned why she advocated a particular style of *hijab*, which is more of an Arab cultural

**Image 3.1**

*Dr Farhat Hashmi*

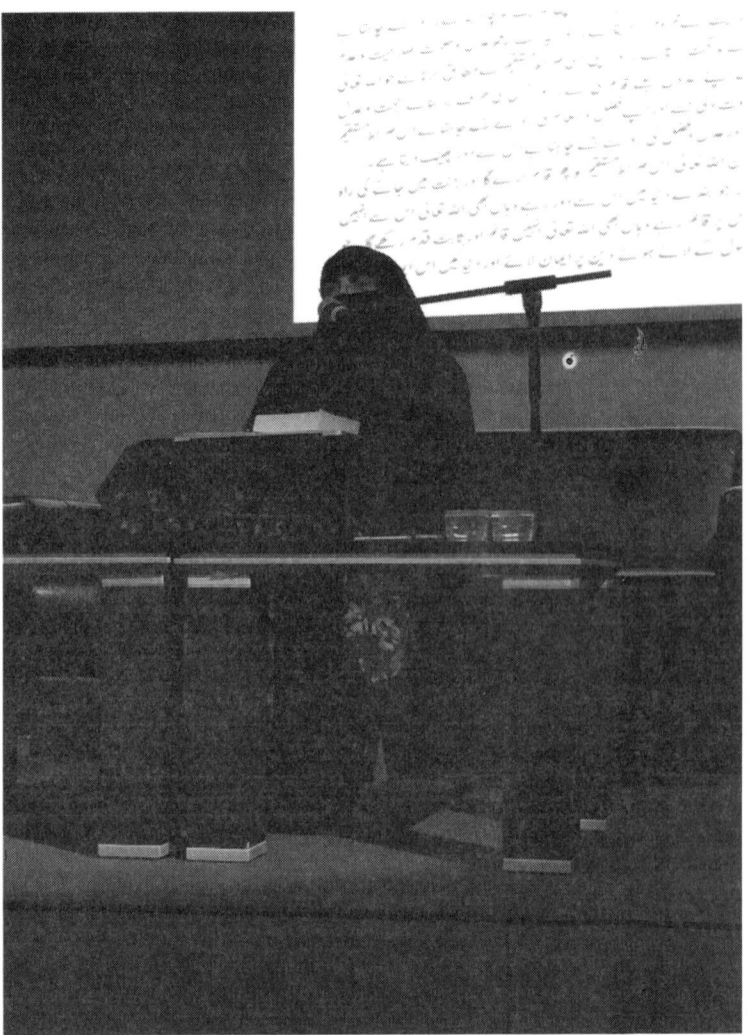

*Source*: Al Huda Publications.

custom, rather than the code of dress considered as modest for Pakistani women. In an interview with Samina Ibrahim, Hashmi shared her view:

> I am not prescribing the design of what a woman should wear. It is up to the woman to adapt whatever form of covering that is convenient for her. I don't think that one is following the Arab way of dress, but when one is translating [the] Arabic [of the religious texts] there will be some influence of that language. The Islamic code of dress is to hide your beauty, however you choose to do it. It is, however, clearly stated that there should be a head covering that also covers the upper part of one's body. It can be a scarf, a *chadar* [or a] *burqa*. According to religious research, a woman's hair is part of her beauty. Just look at all the beauty parlours in Pakistan; their main work is to beautify hair! (*Newsline*, February 2001)

Farhat Hashmi and her group, however, prefer to interpret the *hijab* in a very restrictive way. In a poster campaign they compared the woman in *hijab* as a 'hidden pearl' (Image 3.2) and pointed out that whenever the women of *Jannat* (Heaven) are mentioned in the Quran:

> [T]heir quality of being hidden and preserved is also mentioned which further enhances their beauty. They have been called *Azwajun Mutahharatun* (purified wives) and *Lulu-el-Maknoon* (pearls kept hidden). Allah says, 'And beside them will be *Qasirat-at-Tarf* (ones with lowered, restrained eyes) with wide and beautiful eyes, (Delicate and pure) as if they were (hidden) eggs (well) preserved.' (As-Saffat: 48–49) If we desire to be amongst these women in the gardens of Paradise, we will have to develop these qualities within ourselves from this world onwards to become one of the HIDDEN PEARLS (*The Hidden Pearls*, 2004).

A constant refrain repeated during my interviews with women who had attended these seminars or the visiting lecturers' sessions in Canberra was their belief that it is best to keep men and women segregated, because the intrusion of women into the public space defined as the 'men's area of control' is seen as leading to the disruption, if not the destruction, of the fundamental order of things. This is so because she appears to be in violation of what traditional societies consider being a necessary barrier between 'private space' (i.e., the home) to which women belong and 'public space' (i.e., the rest of the world) which belongs to men. They explained that this 'invisible barrier' between these two unequal spaces is called *hijab*, that the *hijab* is not just a piece of material worn by women but literally translates as a 'curtain' between the men and 'unrelated' women. The interviewees quoted a popular *hadith* of the Prophet that whenever

**Image 3.2**

*'The Hidden Pearls' Poster/Sticker*

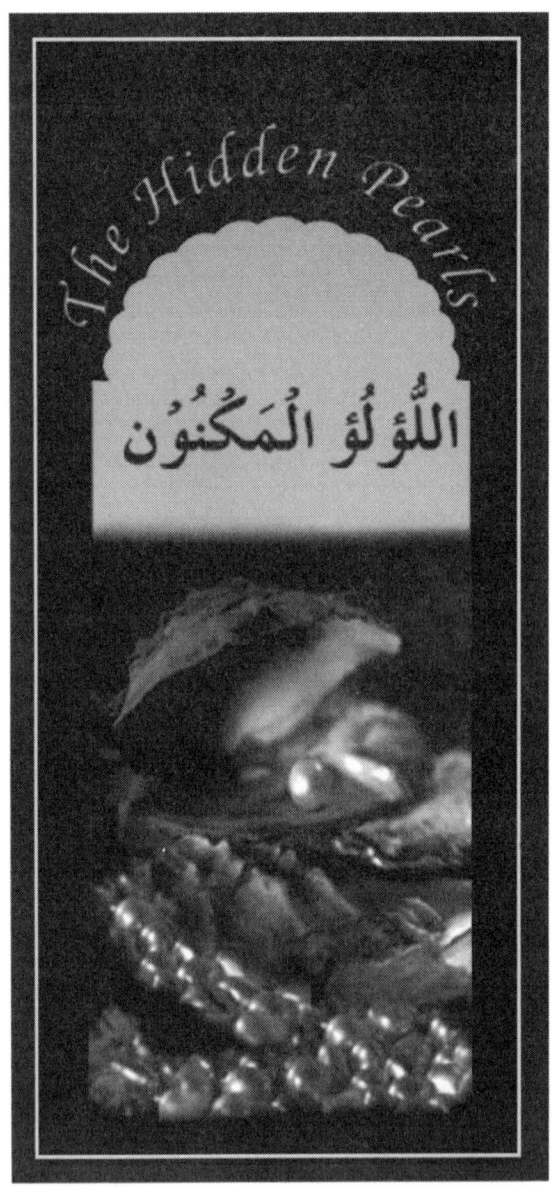

*Source*: Al Huda Publications.

a man and woman are alone, Satan is bound to be there, referring also to the sections of the Al Huda syllabus that unpacks this issue:

> The *hijab* is not a hindrance but rather a blessing for the Muslim woman. If an entire nation can go around wearing masks to save themselves from catching the SARS disease, why can't Muslim women do so to save themselves from other kinds of social ills? If a surgeon can perform the most delicate of tasks covered from head to toe, wearing a mask, why must a Muslim woman's sight, hearing or breathing be obstructed by a cloth? *Hijab* is not a means of blackening the faces of women and reducing them to mere objects! Rather, it is the culture of obscenity that is making women mere objects of attraction and a feast for the eyes (*The Hidden Pearls*, 2004).

What was also emphasised was that women could only obtain an elevated social status and respectable image in the public space as long as they stayed within the boundaries of a notion of modesty. More importantly, within these boundaries women were not expected to compete with men on an individual basis, rather, they had to be seen as willingly supporting them in public life without undermining the moral fabric of Islam. They were also assigned the responsibility to coax those who were seen to have overstepped boundaries which were divinely sanctioned. For a community which finds itself displaced as an immigrant community in a foreign nation, it tries to overcome its subordination by positioning its own religious and cultural heritage as the purest private space which it has to safeguard against corrosive outside influences.

The mythical unity of ethnic 'imagined communities', which divides the world between 'us' and 'them' in the diaspora, is culturally maintained and ideologically reproduced by a whole system of diacritical emblems, which Armstrong (1982) called symbolic 'border guards'. These 'border guards' can identify people as members or non-members of a specific collectivity. They are closely linked to specific cultural codes, styles of dress and public conduct, as well as to more elaborate bodies of customs, literary and artistic modes of creativity, and of course, language. Symbols of gender play a particularly significant role in this articulation of difference. Women's distinctive ways of dressing and behaving very often, especially in minority situations, come to symbolise the group's cultural identity and its boundaries. In Canberra women who had decided that they did not want to cover their heads disclosed that on social occasions a particular group of women constantly urged them to do so: 'There is one group which considers itself the "right" group, and they always raise the issue of *hijab*; by some excuse or other they take my class [lecture me incessantly] because I don't wear one, and they find some way to scold me.'

So women will place themselves in charge of surveillance, supervision, and management of other women in the community, thus acting as agents of patriarchal control. There is constant interrogation about their dress code, absence from religious lectures, choice of work and so on. I inquired of one of them indirectly about her views regarding convincing women to veil:

> One has to set a standard ... when I was younger there was none of this *purdah*, like *purdah* was there in the villages but not amongst us in the city. When we went to the village, we had to pull the *chadar* over our head. You see our family were the *Qazis* [the religious and social elite group in her community] and if we didn't cover up everyone would remark, 'see, the high-and-mighties' women don't cover up'; we were setting a standard. I remember if the scarf slipped from our head the women on the streets would taunt us '*dheedupattakaj*' [daughter, cover your head now] ... Our women make these excuses that they will get into trouble because of the *hijab*. Now you can't argue against the *hijab*, I keep on telling these girls to find another way, in what other way can you wear it? Can't you tie a scarf? Use caps or hats instead. Basically, you have to cover your hair. See I cover my head with a scarf if I am stepping out; it doesn't take long, does it? When I came here initially I was among the first women to wear *shalwar kamiz* [the traditional Pakistani shirt and loose trousers], cover my head. No one took a second look. We should cover our head and ask others to. God will keep count of this.

In the following pages I analyse Pakistani women's relationship with the veil based on the recognition of the various intersecting social relations of belief systems, age, ethnicity, class, gender, and sexuality and the positioning of self. This is reflected by the instrument of veiling which they have chosen (among other life choices). Werbner declares the process of positioning of the self as sited social 'boundaries', that is, the identity markers of inclusion or exclusion highlighted situationally (Werbner, 2002). The Pakistani community in diaspora is significantly also a social field, not a 'closed', bounded group. Its actors, men, women and youth are positioned differentially in terms of their access to symbolic, cultural, and financial 'capital'. This was reflected in my interviews when the respondents specified *when* they veiled and *from whom* they veiled themselves.

# Social Performances

Naseem Ali made a conscious decision to reconstruct her life according to what she considers to be the fundamental dictates of Islam. Coming from an urban, middle-class family, she had a fairly traditional but not a rigidly religious upbringing, and despite having to conform to certain traditions she was not prevented from pursuing her interest in getting a degree in psychology. For a while after getting married, she also taught as an assistant professor in Karachi. Her husband gained a scholarship to study in Canberra and she moved there with him and their two sons. The initial years with her husband as a student were very difficult, so she helped out by taking up odd jobs as a checkout clerk. She had her third son while in Canberra and with time she was more confident that their personal circumstances were improving. In her initial years in Australia she had always believed that once their sons grow up she would start 'working' (as in regular work in her 'field of specialisation') or maybe take up a further degree at university. However, once they were in her own words 'settled', she quickly realised that now her 'changed thought process is coming in the way' of following up on these dream projects. She now believed that women should not step out of the house 'just for amusement or to please themselves', and if husbands can support the family there remains no need for women to step out for paid work or these self-growth projects—the only reason to do so would be to appease their own spirit, which may not be the moral thing to do.

How necessary it is to work rather than working outside the home as a life choice, and considering this the parameters under which women would choose to take up paid work (and Naseem's distinction between choices when the family was financially struggling and when they were settled) accomplishes two things: first, it validates women's primary role as homemakers and privileges 'the family' as a natural and/or inevitable social unit. Second, it ultimately suggests disapproval should a woman choose not to marry and exercise the option to work instead, or decide to continue to work for personal satisfaction when married (Rouse, 1997). Thus, the Pakistani community seemed sympathetic to women who stepped out of the house to support the family, but community members were quick to point out that women work only because they must. Women who stepped out from the household to work for personal satisfaction (and therefore violating the instrument of *purdah* and the domestic space) were seen as 'out of the ordinary' and therefore could not speak on issues relevant to most (other) Pakistani women. A flawed logic of this kind ultimately reproduces notions of normalcy of women's position within the household as nurturers and caretakers. It continues to operate within the broader framing of the issue of gender which denies agency to women, except insofar as they strive to 'better' the family. It also potentially provides the basis for reaction against all women who work outside the home. 'Necessity' and the need for 'respectability' further inhibit women's ability to choose what kind of work to take up; for instance, most families were more comfortable seeing women working with children or running a home-based enterprise. Such insistence and justification serve as the basis of self-identification for 'good Pakistani' women and constitute the marker of separation from those 'other', non-respectable women—the professionals dubbed as 'westernised'—and also working class women who are cast as the objects of pity and/or contempt (ibid.).

As Naseem described her current situation, she had ample leisure time now with her children away in school, so she had decided to keep herself busy in something spiritually satisfying. She started participating in the *dars* lectures organised by some former students of Dr Farhat Hashmi. They usually used to play an audiocassette of Dr Hashmi's lectures, while everyone listened and there used to be a discussion following it.

After attending these classes she decided to be a bit more serious where matters of *hijab* and *purdah* (seclusion from male company) were concerned. She also made a conscious decision to avoid 'gents' and 'mixing unnecessarily with them' from then on. What one notes here is a resort to the veil as a signifier of *shurfa* (the genteel). Therefore, the act of taking the *hijab* and opting for a conscious division of space are not socially neutral concepts; indeed, they are situated in and produced by social relations of domination and exclusion.

For some women, as Papanek explains, *purdah* observance can be related to recent migration, the perceived dangers of an unfamiliar environment, and the sense of isolation felt by these families far away from the supportive environment of the home communities (Papanek, 1982: 199). For example, among the community where Naseem comes from in Pakistan it is often reported that women do not wear the *burqa* in their local streets but only put it on when going to other areas in the city. So as Naseem explains:

> Ever since I started wearing the *hijab* I have become secure. Earlier I always wanted someone to accompany me, used to feel insecure when I used to go out shopping. I used to ask my sons, who are so small, to accompany me! Now that I am covered I feel no one will harm me.

Though I did have doubts about how wearing the veil would give her security and pointed out incidents when even women who had worn the *burqa* or *hijab* had been molested in Pakistan or elsewhere, or had incidents of violence committed against them, even instances of someone grabbing the *hijab* off a woman's head, I had to respect Naseem's reply that wearing the veil did 'make her feel better' as it gave her the privacy she wanted.

Yes, these incidents of violence against women happen but I still think *hijab* is security. I feel that with me even gents who knew me don't talk so much with me now, no unnecessary conversations. They respect me now, none of the jokes that men pass, you know when couples hang around they make these jokes. All that has stopped and I feel good about it; it really makes me feel better.

For Naseem the style of dress she has adopted, in general, but particularly secluding herself to her home is 'privacy's metaphor' as Guindi (1999) describes it. For Guindi the concept of sanctuary that connects sacred places, like mosques and pilgrimage centres, also applies to women, women's quarters, and family—a connection that brings out the significance of the idea of the sanctity in these contexts. The veil, veiling patterns and veiling behaviour are therefore, according to Guindi's analysis of Muslim culture, about sacred privacy, sanctity and the rhythmic interweaving of patterns of worldly and sacred life, linking women as the guardians of family sanctuaries and the realm of the sacred in this world. Guindi argues for the centrality of the cultural notion of privacy, as one that embodies the qualities of reserve, respect and restraint as these are played out in a fluid transformational space (Guindi, 1999).

Later on in the week while she is driving down to a *dars* meeting, Naseem is comfortable with only her headscarf on. However, at the meeting she hides behind the door every time her friend's husband passes by, and her friends have to caution their male relatives not to enter the room as Naseem is in *purdah*. I ask her later about the contradiction in her actions, considering she is a 'victim' of the male gaze while driving her car as well. Why do different rules apply? Her reply is interesting, as she clarifies that there are distinctions in place as she clearly draws boundaries of whom she veils from: 'But why hide from them? They are not one of us.'

By 'them' Naseem would mean the 'others', the average (Caucasian) Australian on the street and not members of the Pakistani community in Australia. It is an interesting twist to the inside/outside debate. Inside, the private space is the domain of 'Muslim culture' where she has to exhibit her 'piety', while the street/public space is for the 'non- Muslim' other. Secluding herself and covering her face in front of the men of her community could be interpreted as an opportunity for her to show how committed she was to being 'moral' and that she has a 'sense of honour tied to her family'—the boundaries of place then are flexible in relation to space and ethnicity. When I took up the issue with her again in a later discussion, Naseem also clarified that in her car she did feel secluded and secure from the male gaze. Could the car for her then be a literal translation of Papanek's 'portable seclusion', just like the *burqa* was for Pakistani women in the home country? This is similar to what young Pakistani women go through at home and in the diaspora regarding what family members will 'allow them' to wear. So outfits that are seen as too Western would be allowed to be worn to a girlfriend's party if they were being driven there, for as a mother explained, they would 'only be stepping out of their house into a car and then the friend's house, not on the streets'.

Naseem's decision to go into *purdah* coincides with the decision of her sister in Pakistan to do so as well:

> I heard my middle sister has also changed her lifestyle, she wears gloves and socks now when she goes out (in addition to the head covering and overcoat), she used to teach boys before, but has stopped doing that now, has taken off all the paintings in the house ... well, she had a dream one night, you know God shows you the path if He wants to guide you. God just wanted to give her *hidayat* [guidance].

Writer V.S. Naipaul described this life change and outward forms of piety as an opportunity to 'give quite simple people [the] possibility of constant personal theatre' (Naipaul, 1998: 323) when he visited Mansoura, a city that Pakistan's Jamat-i-Islami has built for themselves outside Lahore, Pakistan. (Mansoura is a literal inside/outside divide of a city—inside are the devout Muslims living their lives according to the true faith, while outside are those who are not one of them and have not found the truth.)

In Mansoura, Naipaul meets a family where the daughter has gone into *purdah*, her head and face covered with a loosely wrapped, light-coloured cotton cloth. The girl could not absolutely say why she had gone into *purdah*. She had just felt one day she should go into *purdah*. And she felt that she was much calmer now. Naipaul imagines how it would have been an endless topic of conversation to people there:

> It was possible to imagine the drama of this sister of Saleem's going into *purdah*, 'Have you heard? Saleem's sister is thinking of going into

*purdah.'*—'She is going into *purdah.'*—'She's gone into *purdah.'*—'It's a question everybody asks me. I just thought one day I should go into *purdah*. I feel much calmer now' (Naipaul, 1998: 323).

Our Naseem, other than feeling calm also believes that taking the *hijab* has led to a new-found respect and status for her in the Pakistani community and in her immediate social circle. She believes that she has found 'my voice now':

> I believe once I have taken the *hijab* I have become very confident. Earlier
> I always kept quiet in a corner, now I speak out about what I feel strongly,
> I express my views. Before I used to listen to everything said to me, now
> I can argue.

For at times the signifiers of Islamic values, such as the veil or seclusion for women and a particular cut of the beard and style of dress for men, are more than an indication of a psychological need with regard to cultural identity. These signifiers and the lifestyle that they emblematise are the site of their struggle for power in the immediate community. Considering Naseem's husband was one of the challengers of the current governing council of the Pakistan Australian Friendship Association, an organisation the couple felt did not reflect 'true Pakistani culture and values', there was a lot more to Naseem's decision to take up the *hijab* than it being the moral thing to do.

## Identity Politics

Tayyaba was confronted, as she saw it, by the banality of the expatriate woman's world, which consisted of 'clothes, cooking, children and the like' and a society, which in her perception was 'amoral'. It was at this stage that she found herself grappling with questions regarding her own life and her identity:

> I feel when we were growing up we had a normal religious background, we
> were culturally Muslims, but I don't think we took it seriously. We were not
> a rigid, religious family. I have really started thinking about religion since
> we came here. I started thinking about these issues, started learning about
> our religion as we are going through an identity crisis. How can people
> here tell from looking at us whether we are Muslims or not, if I don't cover
> up? Do I really justify being called a Muslim? I think covering our head is

a symbol that it's our identity, it's not security as such as some would tell you. Otherwise some people think you are Indian, I don't like that either.

We were conducting this interview at her workplace. She pointed to the business suit she was wearing and said:

> These are my work clothes and if I am not wearing *shalwar kamiz* I don't cover my head or anything. Yes when I go the Fyshwick markets, these crowded fresh food markets, I cover my head as then men respect you and would not brush against you or anything … you just feel a bit secure. If there is a congested place, and my head is covered I feel safe. See, in Pakistan, you feel the need. Over here too you get respect, they talk properly if your head is covered.

When Tayyaba veils, whom she veils from echoes the class issues and concerns which are very much part of Pakistani society. There is also this discomfort of not being confused for being Indian or Bangladeshi, in a situation where the question of what forms a Pakistani identity has yet to be resolved. At the moment I am only addressing the issue that Tayyaba introduces here—that of veiling and stratification.

For instance, Guindi's research of Assyrian Law revealed a connection between women who *must* and those who *could not* veil (Guindi, 1999). Exploring a number of relevant laws, Guindi could discern the following differentiations: 'ladies by birth' (noble women) versus 'concubines and servants'; respectable, married women versus 'those of loose character' and; free women versus slaves. Women of nobility *had* to veil. Servants, according to the laws had to veil too, but *only* when accompanying noble women (Guindi, 1999: 14–15). (Words to remember when I was doing field research in Mansoura, Pakistan with a male colleague, and we were ushered into the house by a young female servant not in *purdah*; I made my way to where the 'women of the house' lived segregated from their male in-laws and any male visitors.)

Meanwhile, coming back to Canberra and Tayyaba—Tayyaba described herself as coming from a comfortable background from Pakistan and thrown into the anonymity of Canberra society. She attempted to explain the everyday struggle of finding herself in Australian society missing the cordial respect, which was accorded to her in Pakistan. For her the performance of covering her head and getting respect from the men in the shops is associated with family honour and the higher respectability and morality of the more privileged classes. In Pakistan, particularly in the rural areas, *purdah* is a way of demonstrating the affluence of a family, since only wealthy families can do without woman's agricultural labour.

In the cities, *purdah* becomes an important component of middle-class practice. As Mumtaz and Shaheed clarify:

> This cultural pattern continues in the cities where the lower middle class is most anxious to maintain *purdah* since it is often the only visible sign that differentiates them from the working class. And in case seclusion within the four walls of the home is not possible, an external symbol of 'respectability', i.e., a *burqa* or *chadar*, is available at a cheaper price (Mumtaz and Shaheed, 1987: 30).

So veiling and its style, the colour and material employed will signify belonging to a particular ethnic or sectarian community in Pakistan. Even the material used for the *hijab* or *chadar* itself varies considerably, signalling clear differences in class and wealth. The notion that the *hijab* fights consumerism and erases class distinction is wishful thinking at best.

For Fremson, who analysed veiling practices in South Asia, these performances operate to signify 'a moral way of life', one where families are paramount in the organisation of communities with the home being associated with the sanctity of women. Fremson narrates a powerful comment by a young female street vendor in Pakistan: 'If I did [wear the *burqa*] ... [they] would tease me because the *burqa* is for good women who stay inside the home' (Fremson, 2001: 14). Abu-Lughod has analysed Fremson's encounter with the street vendor as an instance where the street vendor's status in local society is associated with her decision to not wear the *burqa*: 'Here you can see the local status associated with the *burqa*—it is for good respectable women from strong families who are not forced to make a living selling on the street' (Abu-Lughod, 2002: 786).

Tayyaba's identity and class politics in Canberra are reflected in Rawalpindi, Pakistan too. Ayesha Farhat is a young student at an elite military engineering college in Islamabad. While she was in senior year at school she started attending Farhat Hashmi's lectures but had to discontinue after some time as her mother was disturbed by the visible changes in her. She says she does wear the *hijab* when she can, though initially she was a bit hesitant. But over time she felt 'Allah gave me confidence and support to continue with it', even though initially she had to have 'discussions even with my own self as to what I was doing'. She describes herself as being quite the social and popular student in high school (due to her good looks, she says); even then her proudest moment in high school was one after taking up the *hijab* when a junior approached her and expressed her admiration: 'I was very happy as this girl was not just looking at my face.'

However, as she quickly clarifies:

> Covering my head is not a compulsion, so I will not cover my head during family function, when I go to weddings for instance, as I don't want to hurt my mother's/family's feelings. You know how people from our village talk. What will they say about me?

So when does she cover her head and why? I asked her. Ayesha replied:

> In my college EME (the military engineering college) women have to cover their heads as male cadets also study with us. They come from all kinds of families, all status. You know there are drivers there, plumbers—all these village people, the way they look at you, you can't control their eyes. Now they look at me as their younger sister. If I cover my head in public, I feel more secure, I feel people like me and respect me more. Boys might not tease you as often. There is an attitude [and] it calls for respect.

So, one way to show her social standing is by covering her head in certain contexts. She decides from whom it is appropriate to veil, which she feels gives her some kind of control over her surroundings.

# Liberation from Within

Rabia's family background is professional and upper middle class, and her father works with the Pakistan Foreign Service. She represents a tendency among young, upper-middle-class, urban women who are seeking to assert their identity within the more formal strictures of their faith. She mentions that she went through an identity crisis as a young teenager and had problems adjusting to the school and her colleagues in middle school in Canada: 'The kids there can really get to you, you are a straight A student, they get jealous of you, you are an outsider but you still speak better English than them, the teachers like you more.'

She describes trying to get a grip on her teenage angst by looking for answers within her cultural identity and within Islam, and one day deciding to take up the *hijab*. She explained:

> It took a lot of guts and courage ... people looked at me ... even my teachers started commenting ... then this Canadian teacher gave me a pat on my back and said, 'Like this girl had a lot of courage, she has changed herself

a lot.' Initially, I used to go to her crying, 'Oh they don't understand me, they are giving me a hard time, what do I do?'

Her mother and sister have not followed her in her decision to take up the *hijab*. She explains that she can understand her mother's predicament:

See, I understand my mother's reasons for not taking it as she is an Embassy wife and would have to totally cut herself off from day-to-day social affairs ... the hijab is not just covering your hair, it prepares you for so much more ... she told my father, 'Can you see me wearing the *hijab* and minding the drinks table for you at embassy functions?'

Rabia felt that it became very difficult to explain herself and what she believed in when she went back to Pakistan from Canada, and later on to relatives and family friends in Canberra when her family moved to Australia:

Pakistan was a Muslim country ... and they were like, 'You are coming from Canada, why do you look this way?' They used to ask why I have a *hijab* on, and I said, 'Why can I not wear a hijab? What do you mean by all this?' I was so hurt that these, my relatives, they are supposed to be more religious. I have non-Muslims patting me on my back and giving me respect ... and I come back to my own country and get told off.

Rabia expresses the predicament for a particular generation of young Pakistani women. Knott and Khokher's study of young South Asian Muslim women in the diaspora saw this particular generation distinguishing between 'religion' and 'culture'—'a distinction between what, for their parents' generation were largely indistinguishable realms' (Knott and Khokher, 1993: 596).

Further these young women are gradually rejecting their parents' conformity to ethnic traditions while wholly embracing a Muslim identity in and of itself—to give up, as I have mentioned earlier, the ethnic customs affiliated with 'home cultures' and adopt more shared and normative Islamic practices from what they have seen after observing other Muslim families living in the diaspora. Among these young women there has been a gradual self-conscious exploration of their religion, which was not relevant to the previous generation (ibid.: 596).

In the interviews Rabia continually voiced her frustration with the global Muslim in general and the Pakistani community of her parents' generation in particular, for failing her generation. She felt that most

Pakistanis of her parents' generation could not control today's 'wayward youth' as the parents themselves could not understand the intricacies of their faith and identity, being too confused as they were in their own ethnic and cultural interpretations of faith. She explained:

> The Pakistani [Muslims] have brought it upon themselves. There was a time in history when we Muslims were the strongest nation. How the hell are we weak now? We had all of the Middle East, there were more non-Muslims who fought against the war in Afghanistan, stopping evil, than us ... what you did to yourself, so this is what you get! I had arguments with my family when I visited Pakistan about the way they prayed, dressed. They think it's Islam but it's actually culture.

After taking up a particular style of *hijab*—the headscarf, Rabia felt more comfortable hanging around with her own 'clique', as she describes her group of Egyptian and Palestinian friends. She feels these young men and women can 'hang around together, talk about our different cultures and Islam, we became pretty close ... and there was a point when it was not just about our particular appearance [of wearing the headscarf].'

The veil has acquired a new symbolism in countries where it is not mandated. Many women choose it both as a reaction to the failed bourgeois nationalist programme of the post-independence era (although there is still a great deal of male coercion) and as part of the mainstream, middle-class rejection of the secular ideologies that have dominated public life. Veiling cannot, in these historical circumstances, 'be constructed as regressive' (Majid, 2002: 71) and must be seen as the younger women's recuperation and affirmation of their heretofore-marginalised identity. Islamic dress is the 'uniform of arrival'(ibid.: 72), the latest stage in a long struggle against colonialism and the post-colonial elites who, although politically secular, continue to impose a false Islamic orthodoxy on the people they govern. The veil is a reminder that most Islamic societies are still part of the global neo-colonial order and that the collective process of liberation through the recuperation of a mutilated identity is far from complete. The response the veil elicits is thus, to a large extent, a symbolic statement about the continuing class struggle in the Islamic world (ibid.). The early feminist lifting of the face-veil was about emancipation from exclusion; the voluntary wearing of the *hijab* since the mid-1970s is about liberation from imposed, imported identities, consumerist behaviours, and an increasingly materialist culture. Further, a principal aim has been to allow women greater access to Islamic literacy. Embedded in today's *hijab* is imagery that combines notions of respectability, morality, identity, and resistance (Guindi, 1999). Rabia feels that it is difficult for friends and family to understand her as she is still seen as 'modern' rather than someone who has sidelined herself from mainstream life totally. Her relatives and the immediate social circle see her as playing with ambivalence, being both 'Muslim and modern' without wanting to give up one for the other:

> I'm like, [I would say] we can go to the movies, and they say, *can* you go to the movies? Like I say yes I think I can. God gave me eyes, and I'm like, I am wearing the hijab but I don't want to kill myself. I can still carry on with my life; I still laugh, I still joke, I still talk to boys. Why do I have to choose?

Of course the classification between what qualified as spaces a good Muslim like Rabia could frequent with her new appearance or not was all her friend's and family's. Perhaps, Rabia's new 'sacred appearance' (where a 'sacred appearance' as Guindi explains was once the preserve of more senior members of the Muslim community who attained a special status from completing a Hajj pilgrimage (Guindi, 1999)) had now become the standard for Rabia's generation. It was no longer the status earned by one's grandmother and grandfather in their later years. Rather, as Guindi explains, these young people are forging their own permanent status of sacredness, thus, challenging the life-cycle rhythm that most (Pakistanis in my case) were familiar and comfortable with.

## Personal Choices

Zarmina has been in Australia for 10 years now and is a senior director at a humanitarian aid agency. She describes herself as always being a 'ritualistic Muslim', yet she says she is able to separate 'the ritual' of her personal faith from the 'divine' of a 'revealed faith'. While not letting go of her belief in Islam as personal faith and the Quran as the word of God, she is able to step back and observe her religious belonging with all its contradictions. In fact she accepts the contradictions of her faith as a necessary part of the whole. At the personal level, however, she finds her faith and her identity located very specifically within Islam. She says that there have been periods in her life, such as the recent events in Iraq and when she lost her brother, when her colleagues suspected that she had lost her faith in God. Her own perspective on this is that she has never questioned the existence of God, but she does question 'His day-to-day management of affairs'. As she describes it:

> There is a difference between questioning and being angry. I never once questioned the existence of God. Okay fine, I did not have a lovey-dovey relationship, so if that's wrong I don't know, for I know we are not supposed to question God, but we are human beings and we do have a mind. I can't be a good person and not a good Muslim ... having a good human spirit is number one, a good faith.

God, she believes, has always given her strength and support, while religion gives her the discipline that she feels all human beings need. She says that she wants to adopt the basic tenets of the faith, and does not want to get into the rules and regulations and laws. She feels that she is more attracted to and respects the basic tenets of the faith.

For instance, she says she wore the *chadar* in the comparatively conservative city of Peshawar in Pakistan, and that she did it out of choice. Her mother and her immediate family and friends never wore one. As she explains:

> Lots of people didn't wear one, and I wore one because I didn't mind wearing one. I used to go to a lot of villages as a development worker, it was sort of like a sneaky way of getting an entry to these villages, speaking to the men and women, and having that sort of way to meld in, of giving them a feeling I was one of them, so never had a problem.

Over time she saw that societal pressure in the province she was working in started increasing for women to cover up. Every day she says she saw more and more women taking up the *chadar,* and more women compelled to cover their faces. If they didn't, they would be taunted and in more extreme cases there were incidents of men slashing women's arms with blades, or molesting them. And this is what started making her feel uncomfortable, that women's decision to take or not take the *chadar* was not the informal option it had been for her:

> I am uncomfortable when I think of the element that is creeping into Peshawar. I am fine wearing the *hijab* if I want to wear the *hijab*, and it's my personal choice ... the way I interpret religion is my personal choice, but if a system is imposed on me, I will rebel. Iran is the only country I have lived in where it is the law, I was very uncomfortable with it, and that's what I am.

This was corroborated by my own visit to Pakistan during my field research. Lingerie shops had put up fresh notices that they were now 'also' catering for 'sisters' needing *hijab*, and 'the sisters' may enter the premises to place their orders. Advertising billboards featuring female models were doused with black paint. Some shops for women's apparel had illustrations of oysters pasted at their entrances, a closer inspection showed these oysters shielded a pearl with the inscription '*hijab tahuffazhai*' [*hijab* is security]'. The shop owners disclosed that a group of men had been putting them up in the area and they left them there as they approved of the sentiment.

Zarmina feels that one has to revisit the Quranic verses and she is quite sure that their interpretation would be completely different from what has been going on recently. She explains:

> *Hijab*, the way I read it, is not just the specifics of what should be covered and what shouldn't be, but rather the whole message is the spirit of modesty and how one should conduct oneself. How do we want to interpret that? Modesty here means something else. Somewhere else in Australia there will be different elements of society and for them modesty will mean something else. For me even wearing skirts or even jeans will not attract a lot of attention and be interpreted as immodest.

I asked her whether she believed the veil would be liberating for some as it would give them mobility to move out of segregated living spaces, along the lines of what earlier respondents had claimed as 'portable seclusion'. She was not persuaded: 'No, I don't take heart in these views, I'm not the sort of person who says it's liberating. No, I don't think it's liberating, and it has this protectionist element.'

As Moghissi has debated, many arguments made in support of *hijab* as a tool of women's empowerment suffer from a myopic view of the practice. In writings which view the veil as a tool of empowerment, the element of choice is taken for granted, while, more often than not, the element of coercion, be it in the form of using brutal force or intimidation, or social, cultural and political pressure, is not even mentioned (Moghissi, 1999: 42). *Bud hijab* (improperly veiled) women are subjected to harsh legal and extra-legal punishment in Iran (ibid.: 43) How can these realities be reconciled with ideas of the veil as a conscious and well-considered choice by 'Muslim women' designed to facilitate entry to previously barred public spaces? One must give equal weight to the experiences of larger sections of the female population who either refuse to wear the veil altogether, or do so for very practical reasons like avoiding men's aggressive sexual comments in the streets.

As Nawal El Saadawi remarks, women in Islamic societies are caught between the globalised image of femininity or female beauty as a commodity in the West and the Islamic notion of femininity 'protected' from men and hidden by the veil. In fact 'veiling' and 'nakedness' are two sides of the same coin. Both mean that women are bodies without a mind and should be covered or uncovered in order to suit national or international capitalist interests (El Saadawi, 1997). Studying Egypt's newly veiled lower-middle-class women, Arlene Macleod found that for some the veil represented a turning back to a 'more authentic way of life'(Macleod, 1991). After a century of modernisation driven by the West, the choice for many remains between the security and protection that the Islamists promise, and the cruel exploitation of a corrupt and mismanaged market economy. In other words, it is the crisis of third world-style modernisation that defines women's choices, not the spiritual and ideological attraction of Islam and the veil (Moghissi, 1999: 43).

# Analysing the Quranic Verses

While being against a single interpretation of Islam, Pakistani Muslims have internalised an Islamic identity and seen themselves as Muslims. The question of Islam as a reference point for everything has in the last two decades seeped into the life and thought of Pakistanis in a distinctly different way than it had done before. It is this core that visiting religious lecturers are able to tap, and it is this identity that makes it difficult even for progressive movements to move outside the Islamic debate. In Pakistan for instance, the women's movement, and the Women's Action Forum in particular, initially used the strategy of using progressive interpretations of Islam to counter the interpretation of the Pakistani state. In other words, it used Islam against Islam, and was reasonably successful in sometimes pushing the state into a difficult position, but even more successful in mobilising women who identified with Islam, and who would not have gone along if they felt that what they were doing was against their religion. Even while resisting religion, Pakistani women have been internalising a lot of the philosophical and ritualistic aspects of what they have been more familiar with. Though I may be personally uncomfortable with the 'strategic use' of the Quran, of the mindset that it is only through the

Quran that we can resolve our conflicts, it is important to go back to the particular Quranic verses that deal with veiling, which more often than not have been interpreted in a very restrictive way.

For Riffat Hassan, who has researched extensively on gender and Islam, in the context of proper attire and conduct, the Quran lays down one basic principle, which may be described as the principle or law of modesty. In Verse 24: *An-Nur*, in lines 30–31, modesty is enjoined upon both Muslim men and women:

> Say to the believing men that they should lower their gaze and guard, their modesty, that will make for greater purity for them, and God is well acquainted with all that they do.

> And say to the believing women that they should lower their gaze and guard their modesty, and they should not display beauty and ornaments except what [must ordinarily] appear thereof; that they must draw their veils over their bosoms and not display their beauty except to their husbands, their fathers, their husband's fathers, their sons, their husband's sons, or their women, or their slaves whom their right hands possess, or male servants, free of physical needs, or small children who have no sense of the shame of sex; and that they should not strike their feet in order to draw attention to their ornaments. (Hassan uses here the translation by Yusuf Ali.)

The verses raise a number of questions. The Quranic injunctions enjoining the believers to lower their gaze and behave modestly apply to both Muslim men and women, and not to Muslim women alone. It has to be noted here that there are no statements in the Quran which justify the extremely rigid restrictions regarding veiling and segregation which have been imposed on Muslim women by some Muslim societies or groups (e g , the Taliban in Afghanistan). For those who dispute this view, scholars like Riffat Hassan put forward one brief question: 'If the Quran intended for women to be completely veiled, why then did it command the men to "lower their gaze"?' (Hassan, 2002)

Ayse Saktanber, who researched women and the politicisation of Islam in Turkey, concludes that:

> I never came across any woman who implied that women were the source of *fitna,* that is, social disorder and anarchy. On the contrary they all asserted that it was not only women who had to cover their *awra* (private parts) and act in accordance with Islamic *adab* (respectability), men also had to follow the same rules and be modest. However, they did not elaborate upon

why women's hair, necks and arms are considered to be private parts but men's are not (Saktanbar, 2002: 221).

I believe that the interpretation of the verses have always signified men as the 'agent of the gaze' and women continued to be viewed as 'the object' with the interpretation focused on insisting that women avoid attracting the 'explicit gaze' of men by veiling practices.

Muslim women are enjoined to 'draw their veils over their bosoms and not display their beauty' except in the presence of *mehrem* (their husbands, other women, children, eunuchs and those men who are so closely related to them that they are not allowed to marry them). Although a self-conscious exhibition of one's *zeenat* (that which appears to beautify, embellish or adorn one) is forbidden, the Prophet's wife Ayesha has been credited with the interpretation that it is women's personal decision as to what they consider part of their normal routine/dress code and what is 'attractive'. This allows for Zarmina's interpretation of the *hijab* as reflecting one's personal code of modesty and how one should conduct oneself. This particular Quranic verse can also be interpreted as saying that if the display of *zeenat* is unintentional or accidental, it does not violate the law of modesty. Here I am reminded of how students at the Al Huda campus would whisper a prayer of forgiveness if they found that they had been slow in covering their faces when a male visitor passed by.

Riffat Hassan believes that a number of women-related Quranic laws, which are interpreted by some critics of Islam to be restrictive of women's freedom, are in fact meant to protect what the Quran deems to be a woman's fundamental rights. For instance, in the Surah 33 (*Al-Ahzab*): 59 it is written:

> O Prophet! Tell thy wives and daughters, and the believing women that they should cast their outer garments over their persons [when abroad]. That is most convenient that they should be known [as such] and not molested. (Translation by Yusuf Ali)

Hassan believes that the reason why Muslim women were instructed to wear an outer garment when they left their houses was so that they may be recognised as 'believing' Muslim women and differentiated from 'street-walkers' for whom sexual harassment is an 'occupational hazard'(Hassan, 2002). For Riffat Hassan, in diasporic communities where there is no danger of believing Muslim women being confused with 'streetwalkers' and 'the outer garment' is the sole mark of identification for a 'believing'

Muslim woman, the mere wearing of 'the outer garment' would not fulfil the true objective of this particular Quranic decree. It is worth noting that older Muslim women are not required to wear 'the outer garment'. Surah (Verse) 24 (*Al-Nur*): 60 reads:

> Such elderly women are past the prospect of marriage. There is no blame on them if they lay aside their [outer] garments, provided they make not wanton display of their beauty, but it is best for them to be modest, and Allah is the one who sees and knows all things. (Translation by Yusuf Ali)

Hassan has reflected on the last-cited verse as the Quran giving women leeway in situations where they might not require 'the outer garment' and there is a possibility that women may continue to be modest even when they have discarded 'the outer garment'. Most Muslim societies, in general, have mainly disregarded the basic intent of the Quranic statements which regard women as autonomous human beings capable of being righteous *as an act of choice*.

Riffat Hassan's explanation of these verses, that women who on account of their advanced age are not likely to be regarded as attracting the male gaze are allowed to discard 'the outer garment', reminded me of an altercation I had witnessed between a mother and daughter in Canberra. The daughter had been an avid supporter of Al Huda dictates regarding 'proper dress codes', much to the dismay of her mother who took a liberal attitude towards her religious beliefs. On her daughter's query as to why her mother refused to veil and persisted on wearing 'Western style' dresses, the mother snapped back saying, 'because I'm post-menopausal now and can wear anything I want.'

Shaheen Sardar Ali places *hijab* as discussed in the Quranic verses in a specific context (Sardar Ali, 2001). She clarifies that the particular verses were revealed on the night of the Prophet's wedding to his cousin Zainab. Some ill-mannered guests lingered on after the wedding feast to the consternation of the Prophet who was impatient to be with his new wife. Anas Ibn Malik (a companion of the Prophet) informed him that the guests had finally departed. It was while Anas Ibn Malik was in the room with the Prophet and Zainab that the verse was revealed. It is significant to note that at that point the Prophet, while reciting these verses, let down a *sitr* (curtain) between himself and Anas Ibn Malik. So, in actual fact the *hijab* descended to place a barrier not between a man and a woman, but between two men. The connotations of this barrier were far-reaching and all-pervading for women, as it was she, the woman, who was left behind the *hijab*, symbolising her marginalisation from life. In addition one should note that the verse of the *hijab* was revealed during Year Five of the *Hijra* (AD 627), which was one of the most disastrous years for Islam, militarily as well as politically. While these incidents undermined the morale of the inhabitants of Medina (the city where the Prophet migrated to), the Prophet was pressured on all sides, by friend and foe alike, to retrace his steps towards equality between the sexes and not to involve women in all fields of life. They accused his wife Ayesha of adultery and harassed the Muslim women on the streets of Medina, creating a state of insecurity and chaos. When challenged by the Prophet, they argued about the difficulty of knowing a slave from a free woman, a virtuous one from the 'others'. They emphasised that were the Muslim women to venture out properly veiled, all would be well. In the circumstances of the military crises in Medina in Years Five to Seven of the Islamic calendar, the Prophet did not have many choices for coping with the insecurity in the city. Thus, as Sardar Ali explains, the *hijab* descended upon Muslim women. It incarnates, expresses and symbolises the official retreat from the principle of equality that the Prophet was so eager to enforce (Sardar Ali, 2001: 147). Fatima Mernissi poses the question thus:

> Is it possible that the *hijab*, the attempt to veil women that is claimed today to be basic to Muslim identity is nothing but the expression of the persistence of the pre-Islamic mentality, the Jahilliyya (ignorance) mentality that Islam was supposed to annihilate? (Mernissi, 1991: 46)

The veil was, by all accounts, not an original concept introduced by the Prophet but a pre-Islamic one that was re-introduced by force of circumstance on Muslim women. The compulsory veiling of women seems to be integral to the defining of a politicised Islamic national identity, as has been the experience in Pakistan, Iran or Afghanistan. For instance, there were few veiled Palestinian women before the *Intefada*. Women in nationalist struggles are configured as embodying the community/ nationality's distinct superior tradition and cultural identity. The graphic representation of women's subordination as symbolised by the veil exposes the gendered nature of the process of constructing a nationalist identity. In many contexts women are expected to be the public signs of Islam by their dress and deportment and, beyond that, to master and practise distinctive Muslim teachings. This suggests a shift in the boundaries of public and private from an ideal long held in Islamic societies: women are, ironically, now part of public life. It is talk about women that fills public space (Metcalf, 1994).

Werbner points out a particularity of Muslim politics, evident particularly in the diaspora, which is concerned with the defence of the legitimacy of Islamic symbols. Veiling, for example, becomes inherently political when transformed into a public symbol:

> Islamists, disillusioned with pusillanimous, corrupt Muslim regimes, call for a global ummah and a return to a pristine political Islam, an idealized ethical order in which veiling becomes part of a larger symbolic complex which imaginatively re-enacts the foundational moment of Islam (Werbner, 2002: 20).

Symbols which abide over a considerable period of time, because they have an affective element capable of 'holding' a particular emotion or idea—the veil, the Kaba, Hercules, mother—can never be fully explained and will always have an element of mystery—an individually unknowable, transpersonal element. As Henry Cobin remarked, 'Symbols: that which cannot be said in any other way' (Cobin, 1987: 41).

# 4

# On Gendered Spatial and Ritual Politics in Canberra and Islamabad

## Alleys without Name

*There's a street in Karachi that follows the moon…*

*Near an Imam Baragh, there's a line of houses, with back and front doors and no boundary walls. When the lunar calendar enters the month of Muharram, Shia women make their way to the Imam Baragh daily.*

*There is a back door to the Imam Baragh for them, for the ones in purdah, and to reach that back door without being gazed upon by strangers in the open streets, they walk through the neighborhood houses.*

*Back and front doors are flung open, and the women walk through from the hallway of one house to the hallway of another until that alley within houses takes them all the way to the door of the Imam Baragh.*

*It is an alley without name, it is an alley that ceases to exist when the moon disappears, but it is an alley all the same and one that says more about Karachi than anything you'll find on a street map.*

—(Shamsie, 2002: 330)

Ritual observance among Muslims has primarily centred around two focal places: the mosque and the home. The mosque perceived as purely the men's sphere of influence has served as a backdrop for the performance of communal rituals and festivals, for theological punditry and for political-cum-ethnic organisation both at home in Pakistan and in the diaspora (Werbner, 1990). Domestic rituals like the reciting of the Quran, convening for scripture reading and group prayers have customarily been held in the home, involving the participation of women, and in most cases organised by them. But in the recent past, one has seen both in Pakistan and in the many spaces that host Pakistani diasporic communities, the introduction of 'subversive and transgressive' (Bhabha, 1994: 8) practices and spaces. These can be, for instance, the International Islamic Centres in a community that host Muslim populations, open to both men and women, or the women's seminary Jamia Hafsa in Islamabad, which provided a formidable challenge to the Pakistan government's support for the Coalition Forces and then President Musharraf's project of 'enlightened moderation' for practising Islam in Pakistan. Though still constituting a space recognised as 'Muslim', these spaces are seen as contesting the hierarchal boundaries between mosque and home.

Al Huda's 'living room seminaries' abroad (domestic spaces that hosted scripture groups) and the Al Huda campuses in Pakistan and abroad were these new emerging religious spaces that Pakistani women were either allowed to access, or they struggled to be allowed access to them. From the networks they formed through their *dars* (lecture/scripture meetings), I could see these cities being mapped similarly to how Shamsie approached Karachi, Pakistan in the excerpt above. Women's *dars* meetings created religious and diasporic spaces 'previously non-locative' if I had looked them up in the street directory, reflecting the 'imagined maps of diaspora Muslims' (Metcalf 1996). The *dars* [scripture reading] patrons spinning their webs of influence had geographically divided the city of Canberra into zones that hosted (or not) their contacts. Comments like 'Oh the Tuggeranong group, no they are not with us', or 'you mean the *milad* group' started to come up in conversation. At times women would reside in one suburb but be identified as 'honorary residents' of another due to their affiliation with a particular network, and slowly a parallel streetscape took shape for me. From observing the networks of Pakistani women in Canberra I wanted to learn more about how they were redefining and appropriating space in the midst of the tensions of culture, religious identity, ethnicity, gender and diaspora. Metcalf proposed, '[I]t is ritual and sanctioned practice that is prior and that creates "Muslim" space… which thus does not require any juridically claimed territory or formally consecrated or architecturally specific space'(Metcalf 1996: 3).

Vertovec (2000), Metcalf (1996) and Werbner (1996) have explored these spatial symbols by researching the associations and communities created by the encounter of diasporic communities and religious identities, the 'cultural space' that emerges as Muslims interact, and the 'physical space' of residence and community buildings founded in new settings.

Werbner echoes Metcalf's 'imagined maps' by suggesting that Muslims in diaspora connect via a 'global sacred geography'.

## Living Room Seminaries

The Al Huda phenomenon is a road map to how Pakistani women negotiate social relations—whether they be belief systems, generational change, ethnicity, class, gender, sexuality, or whether they choose to veil or not (among other life choices). Al Huda is their positioning of the self. As discussed in the previous chapter, Werbner (2002) has declared the process of positioning of the self as sited social 'boundaries'—that is identity markers of inclusion or exclusion highlighted situationally.

Al Huda's popularity illustrates how generational change in the Muslim communities has influenced religious practices in the Pakistani community particularly those of women's. Young Pakistani women like their sisters elsewhere in the Muslim world are building upon their growing interest in religious studies. Unlike their grandmothers who were content to read the Quran in Arabic (for many this was the only form of 'literacy'), they exhibit great enthusiasm about learning how to translate the Arabic of the Quranic verses. Not content with the traditional explanations of the Quranic verses offered to them by their mothers' generation, they explore alternative commentaries for the religious texts. This can be phrased as the 'engendering of religious literacy'.

However, what is particular about Al Huda's appeal for Pakistani women? This question was imperative as I unpacked the analytical moment of social geography and class for the Pakistani community at home and in the diaspora. Why was it that Al Huda appealed to particular 'living rooms' in Canberra, Australia and Dubai in the Middle East but not in Brunswick, New Jersey or Manchester, United Kingdom. Why was Al Huda overwhelmingly popular with the 'high ranking military officer wives' of Islamabad and the residents of Wanniassa, Canberra but not with the housewives of O'Malley, Canberra? Issues of class, power and aspirations towards dominance of social networks is central to understanding the Al Huda phenomenon and what is particular about the Canberra Pakistani community. What Al Huda's supporters have in common is their need for a support system and their exclusion from certain networks traditionally dominated by 'old money'. Al Huda tacitly acknowledged this particular community's 'moment of arrival.' Therefore, the conversations in these living room seminaries revolve around exhibiting wealth and being seen as doing well for themselves, of consumer goods, designer kitchens and of affluence; any mention or analysis of Pakistan's poverty or the needy is missing. Al Huda is how particular Pakistani families can network. These families are, as I interpret, a bourgeois group doing the 'right thing' by being part of this particular organisation and attending the Al Huda lecture sessions, and thus achieving what they perceive as social status.

Al Huda, on its part, concerns many in Pakistan and beyond, finding as they do, advocacy material for it in the offices of controversial organisations like the Jamat-ud-Dawa. For instance, the website for Jamat-ud-Dawa, when I was exploring the organisation, offered a hyperlink to Al Huda's and Al Huda reciprocated this by promoting Jamat-ud-Dawa through its electronic resources. At the time there was no evidence of any other inter-relationship between the two organisations that could have worried the authorities. However, matters may have changed after the 2015 incident when an Al Huda alumni along with her husband were allegedly involved in a mass shooting in California, and recent reports of Pakistani women who have studied at the institute accompanying their husbands as ISIS recruits in Syria. At the time, I could deduce that the 'good Muslim technocrats' (male) that the Jamat-ud-Dawa produces need a cadre of 'good Muslim', skilled, professional women to complement their project. I see here strains of the 'Home Economics' school project that the British introduced to South Asia—the 'local elite' returning to a household where the woman of the house had been socialised to repeat the colonial project.

## On the Ties that Bind

I had moved to Canberra in 2002 to explore the tangled networks of gender, class and religious interpretation between communities in Pakistan, and the Pakistani diaspora in this particular city (particularly in the light of the events of 11 September 2001)—tied as the two communities were through spatial and ethnic realities. But I soon realised that the Pakistani community in the city had been influenced more by the emergence of a particular religious network for women based in Islamabad with supporters in the Pakistani diasporic communities in North America, Australia, and the United Arab Emirates. Despite the events of 11 September, it was the growing popularity of a particular transnational religious network (the Al Huda movement) that was discussed in the city. Rather than the influence of 11 September in their lives, I would hear their views regarding Farhat Hashmi (the founder patron of the movement) and whether they approved of her supporters' activities. If certain families were to comment on the events of 11 September, they would turn it into a critique of the repercussions of an 'overzealous religiosity', a popular refrain that was applied to Hashmi's supporters as well. A discussion on whether to patronise this network divided the Pakistani community in Canberra on matters relating to religious, self, and community identification.

Al Huda conducts Quran classes and diplomas in Islamic studies for women in Islamabad and certain cities hosting Pakistani diasporas. Hashmi herself pursued a degree in theology from the United Kingdom and aspires to find a discursive space to assert her identity within the more formal strictures of her faith. She does so while critiquing the control the (male) clergy has over religious debate in Pakistan. She is ill at ease when certain women's groups consider her and her students as siding with religious right-wing groups even though they may tend to take stands similar to these groups on certain issues. She still faces a lot of opposition from the Pakistani clergy both in Pakistan and in the diaspora communities, as she and her colleagues at Al Huda are seen as neither the 'good local Muslim' nor the 'Western other'.

I had first heard of Farhat Hashmi in the late 1990s. Rawalpindi, home to the General Headquarters of the Pakistan Army, had a bevy of army wives who liked 'doing good work'. One of the general's wives had decided to host Farhat Hashmi's lectures during the month of Ramadan at a local hotel. This was a time when the religio-military nexus in Pakistani society was strong, and to be seen at her lectures seemed the 'right thing' as all the high ranking military officers' wives were there. Hashmi was a visitor from the business city of Karachi, Pakistan, and didn't seem very controversial for our military cantonment. My cousin from next door had attended a lecture with her mother and updated me on her return. They didn't find anything meaningful in the lectures that answered their queries, and eventually stopped attending the lecture sessions. But Hashmi might have come up with satisfactory responses for others in the congregation, for over the years her popularity grew with the gradual mushrooming of Al Huda campuses everywhere. This was accompanied by rumours about the source of her funding, as people deliberated, among various theories, whether it was the Pakistani military that was backing her or was it Saudi money wanting to spread Wahabism (a school of Islamic thought) in Pakistan. I was re-introduced to Hashmi's organisation when a family friend brought along some of her organisation's print material on one of my visits home: 'You are away from Pakistan, Aneela, and I'm sure you might be questioning Islam now.' The material included a book of *duas* (supplications) that I was to recite at dawn and evening for 'protection'. '*Invocations for Morning and evening with Invocations for Protection*', read the cover. On the first page Hashmi explains that it is necessary for women to recite these prayers early in the morning when laziness and sleep overcome them so they can start the day feeling empowered. Similarly, in the evening, when the dusk light makes them feel melancholic and depressed, remembering these prayers allows their hearts some 'peaceful respite'. The other was a brochure for enrolling in the diploma classes at the Al Huda campuses. The front cover had the Al Huda monogram and the street addresses of the main campuses. On the back cover was a *Hadith* (tradition attributed to the Prophet):

> The example of guidance and knowledge with which Allah has sent me is like abundant rain falling on the earth, some of which was fertile soil that absorbed rainwater and brought forth vegetation and grass in abundance. (And) another portion of it was hard and held the rainwater, and Allah benefited the people with it and they utilised it for drinking (making their animals drink from it) and to irrigate the land for cultivation. (And) a portion of it was barren which could neither hold the water nor bring forth vegetation (then that land gave no benefits). The first is an example of the person who comprehends Allah's religion (Islam) and gets benefit (from the knowledge) which Allah has revealed through me (the prophet S.A.W) and learns and then teaches it to others. The (last example is that of a) person who does not take Allah's guidance revealed through me (he is like that barren land) (*Sahih-Bukhari*) [compiled by Imam Bukhari] (as quoted in the *Taleemul Quran* diploma brochure, Al Huda Publications, 2002).

The onus of appreciating and understanding what Hashmi was offering us was left to us. Were we to challenge and critique what she had to offer and let our minds stay a barren field, as she refers to it? On my field visits to her campus in Islamabad I grew to realise that her organisation and the growing evangelist missions in the diaspora were moving towards conversions within Pakistan and in the Pakistani diaspora. For them, the faithful have to return to the realm and comprehend the true message rather than introducing their 'true message of Islam', as they described it to communities other than the Pakistani Muslim.

My attempt to interview Farhat Hashmi educated me in the walls erected around Al Huda and her personality. I began by interviewing students of Al Huda in Islamabad, who in turn introduced me to their teachers who put me through to those identified as Hashmi's inner circle. After a fortnight of introducing my project and myself to Hashmi's colleagues, I was able to get an appointment to see her for an hour at Al Huda's Islamabad campus. Her colleagues explained Hashmi's hectic travel schedule commitments and how she conducts lectures in Karachi and Islamabad in Pakistan every week in addition to her international travel commitments. During the interview I sat on a chair opposite a *divan* where Hashmi replied to my queries resting against pillows. Her colleagues sat in a tight circle of chairs around her *divan* while a group of younger students sat on the carpet avidly taking notes. The meeting and the setting of the room emphasised Hashmi's status as the 'charismatic leader'.

Hashmi explained the background behind setting up Al Huda and the opposition she has faced along the way. She was of the opinion that there were few women in Pakistan who were trying to interpret Islam for the common people:

> I am just trying to make religion simple for people, and that's what I am accused of most of the time, that I am making religion approachable for the average people. People criticise me, as there are so many illiterate children in Pakistan, why don't I instead start children's schools. Well, children learn something here and then go back home and their parents teach them something else, it's very disorienting for the child. With relatively mature girls I feel they are in a position to judge for themselves. I believe, with my classes the young women are more confident, there is calm and centring in their life, they know about their status in society and I feel that now their sense of right and wrong has been awakened.

She felt women were drawn to her courses as her approach is, in her words, 'more *hamdardana* [caring]', and that in her lectures she can sympathise with and discuss personal experiences in matters 'of mutual interest' that the male clergy could not. In the interview Hashmi started out by positioning herself as having feminist sensibilities and insisting that Al Huda was inclusive in its outreach, as it includes evening classes for working women and students. But gradually she shifted towards how she felt women's primary role as homemakers should not be compromised for personal ambition:

> My point of view is that a woman's primary responsibility is her home. After she has fulfilled that, it is up to her to go into whatever field suits her best. I have no agenda to take away women's rights. Al Huda holds evening classes especially for working women. But peace in the home depends on the woman and that aspect should not be ignored at the cost of working outside the home (Interview with Samina Ibrahim, Newsline, February 2001).

I left the interview still uncertain about where to place Hashmi. Though I admired her for challenging the hierarchy that controlled religious spaces, in many ways she had stayed complacent over the gender-biased legislation prevalent in Pakistan and Muslim communities. She explained everything as the 'wisdom of a just God' and it was only the 'passion of one's misguided youth' that struggled against what God had ordained best for women. She believed if I were to listen to her lectures on audio cassettes covering religious matters that women like me critiqued the Hudood Ordinance[1] for, my opinions would change for 'the better'. Though I had personal objections to her advocating the 'merits of compliance', I could not deny her appeal for a growing group of Pakistani women who subscribed to her networks as an aid to overcoming the unequal ethnic and class distribution that they have inherited. Particularly for Pakistani women living in diasporic communities, being involved in these networks could ease the pressures of living life in the diaspora, and assist them in their

---

[1] The *Qanoon-e-Shahadat* (Law of Evidence, based on a very subjective interpretation of Quran's Surah 2 (*Al-Baqarah*) was proposed in 1982, and became a law in 1984. The particular verses of the Quran interpreted for this legislation dealt with economic transactions, but as we will see they were adapted for all legal cases requiring witnesses. *Hudood* Law (which designates adultery, rape, prostitution, theft, armed robbery and alcohol consumption as crimes against the state subject to Islamic punishments) diminishes the personal status of women, who, although otherwise recognised as *sui juris* agents, are thereby deprived of the legal capacity to bear witness in legal cases coming under the jurisdiction of the *Hudood* Law. The law requires the testimony of four adult Muslim male witnesses of good character; women and non-Muslims are not considered 'reliable witnesses'. Under the Majority Act both boys and girls are considered adults upon reaching the age of 18, but under Islamic laws a girl is presumed to be an adult when she enters puberty. This means that while the value of her evidence in civil matters is only half that of a man's, and is totally discounted for the purpose of 'hard' punishments, she is adult enough at puberty to receive 'the maximum punishment under law'. This law has not only legally reduced women's status to half that of men, but has also meant that if only women are witness to something, nothing can be proved. Originally, it was proposed that this would cover all laws outside of *Hudood*. In the end, after much protest and lobbying, particularly by women's groups in Islamabad, it has been limited to 'financial and future obligations'. This has meant in practice that in the event of future and financial transactions being reduced to writing, the acceptable testimony would be that of two men or one man and two women. Its effects are hazardous for working women, especially in the impact in the banking profession on the promotion of women officers. Since the Shariat Bill was passed, in a number of cases of official registration the government authorities have refused to accept the signatures of women attesting documents, demanding that male witnesses be produced. These laws have an effect on rape cases, where women victims are tried and convicted for adultery instead, as they can seldom produce the 'four male witnesses' required.

quest to acquire the 'desired stage/status' where they can be recognised and gain distinction within the community. The meteoric rise of Farhat Hashmi and the organisation's success in building a base amongst the professional, urban, and upper-middle-class Pakistani groups has confused the traditional as well as the modernist/ secular groups in the Pakistani community. One can borrow from Göle in analysing the 'ambiguity of signs' posed by the mass appeal of Hashmi and the Al Huda movement. She has studied the surprising crossovers between 'Muslim' and 'modernity', and between secular and religious practices taking place in Turkey, which have unsettled the fixity of positions and oppositional categories. Göle's work catalogues the new social imaginaries being shaped by these circulatory, trans-cultured, and crossover performances (Göle, 2002). As her study of Islamists in Turkey shows, though these groups are in an oppositional political struggle with the modern secularists, they often mirror them and search for public representatives who speak foreign languages and belong to the professional and intellectual elite. This was reflected in Al Huda's move to recruit students who belonged to similar elite backgrounds.

In Pakistan both the feminist and Muslim fundamentalist movements have attempted to define and deal with individual and communal identities in global and local conditions. Both groups have attempted to find the means to control the mechanisms of cultural representation. In the case of Pakistani women, feminist groups had tried to introduce 'progressive interpretations' of Islam to counter the interpretations of more conservative groups. As Moallem describes for experiments elsewhere, both feminism and fundamentalism are major factors responsible for and responding to the 'crisis of rationality' as well as the crisis of 'masculinity' and 'femininity'. Both arose inside the problematic of modernity as it deals with relations between men and women with respect to the universal and in particular, the public and private, family and state, and individual and community space:

> [B]y using mainstream feminist concepts and ideas such as patriarchy and male chauvinism. In the case of feminists, they might import fundamental-ist components into feminism by depending upon a form of essentialised nurturing femininity associated with women's nature and the construction of a glorious matriarchal past (Moallem, 1999: 324).

In addition to the lecture (*dars*) network formed by Hashmi and her colleagues, there is also the very successful Al Huda 'Institute of Islamic Education for Women' in Islamabad and Karachi (and in the past few years in Ontario, Canada) that run diploma courses. Hashmi's and her colleagues' lectures are also available on the internet in Urdu and English, making them very attractive for young Pakistani women in diasporic communities who might not be so fluent with the Urdu text. Many of the Pakistani residents attending Hashmi's lectures in Pakistani cities belonged to the professional, urban, and upper-middle-class groups and were now looking for answers within Islam. Al Huda's educational prospectus and publicity literature list the following programmes being conducted under the institute's patronage:

1. *Taleem-ul-Quran* (Quranic Education) Course: a one-year certificate course offered to students after A-level/O-Level/ Matriculation examinations so students could study for a year and continue with their regular studies in the next academic session. Al Huda offers this academic course 'to equip young women with Quran norms so they can proceed with their life "with a calm heart and at peace with themselves", and meet the challenges of modern life as confident Muslims [and] to recite the Quran with a proper Arabic pronunciation' (Al Huda Publications, 2002).

2. Ilm-ul-Kitab (Knowledge of the Quran) Evening Programme: Hashmi declared that this was designed keeping in mind a particular Quranic verse which the brochure refers to: 'Actually Allah has bestowed such a big blessing on the faithful that amongst them He raised one of their own as a Prophet who recites His verses to him, betters their lives and educates them in the Book and its knowledge though the same people were lost in sinful lives earlier' (Al-Imran: 164).

The course description clarifies that the module has been designed keeping in mind young women who might be studying or working in the morning and could not participate in the morning classes. The evening classes are of shorter duration and concentrate on translation and commentary of the Quran 'from word to word' (as the prospectus describes it), Sunnah-traditions of the Prophet and guidelines for the proper upbringing of Pakistani women.

The programmes mentioned above and the other diplomas offered at the 'Al Huda Institute of Islamic Education for Women' in Islamabad were offered in Urdu and in some cases English (which was desirable for the expatriate population and the professional cadre that Al Huda targeted). The institute claimed reliance on an 'advisory board' that reviewed the curriculum, the use of 'up to date' audio and video aids and multi-media presentations, and access to 'international visiting scholars' on campus. The brochures also announced the provision of hostel facilities for visiting students on Al Huda premises. The academic prospectus also gives details of the different branches of the 'Al Huda School of Islamic Studies' in Pakistani cities that also offer certificate courses, short summer courses, special courses offered in the month of Ramadan, 'simplified training courses' for students from rural backgrounds, 'Reality Touch' programmes for teenage girls to have a proper Islamic upbringing, the 'Colours of Islam' programme for children, and special classes for men.

The concept of the weekly *dars* (religious lectures) programme was described in the prospectus as,

> Two weekly programmes are held for women from all ages and schools of thought, on Mondays at Hotel Pearl Continental in Rawalpindi and on Wednesdays at Hotel Pearl Continental in Bhurban. Besides these two hotels, women who have attended Al Huda courses hold weekly sessions at their residences (Al Huda Publications, 2002).

Of particular interest for me were the 'correspondence courses' in Pakistan and the 'international classes' offered by the organisation, as I could now observe for myself the growing influence of its transnational religious networks. Hashmi had a strong support base in the Pakistani diasporic community and it was this 'constituency' that funded Al Huda's activities through outreach programmes and financial donations. Regarding this programme, the brochure explained:

> Individuals who are desirous in participating in the Al Huda courses but due to certain circumstances cannot attend any of the campuses can participate through correspondence. For students separated by distances can study at home through cassettes and pamphlets. Registered students will give written examination on completion of every Quranic chapter. Successful students are given certificates.... Al Huda graduates settled all over the world are busy in spreading religious knowledge. These countries include United States, Canada, Australia and the United Arab Emirates (Al Huda Publications, 2002).

Finally, there was the 'Al Huda Information Service' that included the Al Huda website, radio programmes, and audio cassettes, publications of books, pamphlets, and greeting cards with 'Islamic prayers for the appropriate occasion.' The brochures would end with a summary of community services provided by the Institute that involved:

[H]elping the destitute, providing dowries to young women in need, scholar-
ships for students, meals for needy families during Ramadan, and in certain
centres women are taught home economics so they can provide for their
families. Al Huda also arranges for the digging of wells in rural Sindh (Al
Huda Publications, 2002).

Through the 'Friends of Al Huda' welfare programme, friends and family
of current and former students could provide to this fund. The brochures
specified how one could contribute amounts set aside for *sadqa* (charity)
and *zakat* (a specific amount of annual charity compulsory for Muslims).
The details for a Pakistani rupees account and a foreign currency account
for Al Huda would be mentioned. However, those who had attended
Hashmi's lectures would come back with tales of the charity boxes set
at entrances overflowing with contributions. The donations would be
collected at intervals to see the boxes quickly full of offerings all over
again. Hashmi had struck a chord with her audience and they were eager
to help her in her mission.

It was at Al Huda's campus in Islamabad that I was introduced to the
groups of 'overseas students', young women from Pakistani families in
Australia, UK and the United States who were participating in the 'summer
programmes' that offered diplomas in Islamic studies on completion.
These women stayed mostly in the hostel accommodation provided on
campus and maintained the strong networks developed in Islamabad on
their return to their families. It is these networks that form the basis of
the transnational web of Al Huda's influence in Pakistani households in
diasporic communities over the world. This was the theme I witnessed
for myself in the *dars* classes organised by former students and extended
families in Canberra and attended diligently by women's congregations
in Canberra's living rooms. They kept their connections with Islamabad
through the exchange of audio-cassettes containing Hashmi's lectures,
accessing the Al Huda website (which kept audio and print files of her
lectures to be downloaded), and watching the recent telecast of her lectures
on the satellite TV channel 'ARY-Digital' during Ramadan.

While at Al Huda's campus I had quizzed women applying to the
institute about what brought them to the institute. One applicant who was
going through a trial separation from her husband and attending classes
said that the institute would give her the space to do something without
raising any controversy at home. Another disclosed she felt guilty as she
found herself getting addicted to watching 'English' films on satellite
television and wanted to save her soul. A frequent visitor was a former

student who having now set up a study group in her local area had queries posed by neighbourhood women; she was not sure whether her classes would be successful as the women attending had a lot of personal problems posed by family conflicts. Hashmi had asked her protégé to impress upon the women coming to her as students to recite the 'prayers of protection' she advocates to suppress the growing doubts in their mind. Most of the women at the campus confided that they were tired of being labelled the 'idle rich' of Islamabad and wanted to 'do something good.' Riffat Hasan, who draws from a discourse of human rights and theology when analysing the Quran, criticises Hashmi's followers:

> Many women who have become the followers of Dr. Hashmi come from the elite classes and had plenty of money and time, much of which was spent on worldly pursuits. Dr Hashmi made these women aware of the importance of fulfilling their religious obligations. She also told them that doing whatever was pleasing to their husbands was good. If, for instance, their husbands wanted them to dress ornately or in any other way, it was their duty to be compliant. It is interesting to note that a number of women who follow Dr. Hashmi still wear rich and gaudy attire beneath their '*hijab*'. It is likely that they are still spending a lot of money on their appearance but now their husbands appear to be happy because they are told that whatever the wives are doing is for their pleasure. It is not surprising that Dr. Hashmi's message is irresistible to the privileged women in her 'target groups.' These women had all the material things and comforts they wanted when they came to Dr. Hashmi. In addition to that Dr. Hashmi showed them the way of attaining paradise (by doing what was pleasing to God) as well as marital bliss (by doing what was pleasing to their husbands) (Hassan, 2002).

I had concluded as much from my interviews with Hashmi. As she spoke to me, I felt that she steered clear of any message of bringing social justice to Pakistan. She declared that she was often accused of concentrating on the 'educated and privileged classes'. As she says in her interview with Samina Ibrahim:

> Well, some of the ladies who attend my classes previously spent their time at coffee and lunch parties. At least now they are coming here. That is the first step. The next step is to go out and help those less fortunate, if I can motivate the educated and privileged section of society to go out and also spread the message of the Quran. I teach in Clifton because by chance this is where I was given the facility. And I hope that those who are coming here will be inspired to go out and help others. It is a reality that if I had started with the under-privileged my message would have been restricted

only to them; they would not have been able to influence other sections of society. The women of the rural areas cannot come and educate women in the city, it can only work the other way round. If I am not holding classes in the rural areas, my cassettes are available there. It has not been my intention only to teach a certain segment of society. I teach, and like a river runs through whatever channel it finds, in the same way what I teach spreads in whatever way it can. Ultimately my goal is to reach as far as I can through those who come to my classes (Newsline, February 2001).

Al Huda's print literature and audio resources are frequently distributed in Pakistani community meetings long after Hashmi has left. While Hashmi's husband, who accompanies her on these visits to Pakistani diasporic communities, also lectures the Pakistani men at meetings, he has not managed to get as prominent a profile (nor raised as much controversy) as his wife. Al Huda, though based in Pakistan, operates as a transnational network in the United States, the Middle East and Australia, so that even if Hashmi loses her audience in Pakistan she has enough support in the Pakistani diaspora to allow her to go on enjoying her current prominent profile. The phenomenon of her success where others have failed has been discussed at various forums among Pakistani academics and within the Pakistani communities.

As Bhattacharjee (1997) explains, leaders of the community, predominantly male and wealthy, often invite 'cultural/religious' experts from South Asia to come and confer their expertise and 'authenticity' to transplanted cultural activities. These 'experts' are mainly from the dominant cultural tradition and a consequence of such an essentialised definition of 'home' is a homogenisation of national culture, marginalising any support or acknowledgement of movements for social change (Bhattacharjee, 1997). The Pakistani diaspora in Canberra has consistently hosted such speakers from Pakistan over the years. My interviewees spoke about Babar R. Chaudhry of the Arrahman-Arraheem foundation from Karachi, of international scholars like the Canadian Jamal Badawai of the Council of American Islamic Relations and Tariq Modood from the University of Bristol. However, none of these speakers have created as much nervous energy as Farhat Hashmi and her organisation Al Huda. In interviews few could remember any of the other speakers by name, just by which religious school of thought they belonged to, or who had sponsored the visit.

For many women, attending Hashmi's lectures is a part of their effort to consciously involve themselves in the religious reawakening of the Pakistani community. However, Hashmi is careful not to upset the patriarchal structure of Pakistani communities, though she does challenge the fact that traditionally it has been men who have mediated with religious scholars or interpreted the religious discourse. In her lectures she cautions women from using their new-found economic independence to challenge the men of the family or the patriarchal structures of the communities they live in. For instance, when I queried one my interviewees in Canberra regarding an issue arising over gender relations in Islam, she played back an audio lecture of Hashmi to address my arguments. This again signifies how Hashmi has captured the religious imagination of the Pakistani women, for any religious or cultural concern in the community is debated purely on the grounds of whether one agrees with Hashmi's explanation or opposes it—thereby clearly dividing the community between her supporters and others. My query to the homemaker in Canberra was regarding whether it was possible that Pakistani women challenge their gender roles, and Mrs Anwar played back the following words of Hashmi:

> No matter what you do, or how many vitamins you eat, you can't build up your body like a man's…If you take pills to stop periods, playing with your cycle, how many diseases can happen…if you are playing with your nature, forcefully changing your structure, your personality, you are being cruel to yourself, forcing yourself…not suitable for anything, can't become a man and won't even stay a woman, so don't have an inferiority complex, ask for God's goodwill. You can't proceed in life, progress if you spend time in addition and subtraction of religious merits… If you are getting the same *sawab* (religious merit) raising children as participating in a *jihad* (holy struggle), then what is the need? God is wise, He kept these differences as He has a higher purpose, He knows best… the *ayat* (verses) where women get angry at God… *qawwamun* means guardian, protector, administrator, the one who nurtures… men are custodians! Why are you getting angry? You have a servant…if he is responsible for you this means they, the men, are carrying your burden…men are earning merit because of earning for the household, protecting, providing for the house, and women earn merit from being obedient, listening to their husbands, co-operating. If a woman dies with her husband happy she will go to heaven… at times after marriage women listen to their parents, want to visit them frequently—that's wrong, as where your life is concerned listen to your husband. A woman shouldn't even keep *nafali* fasts (to fast other than for the month of Ramadan) without her husband's permission (Taleem-ul-Quran Parah, Audiocassette of Hashmi's commentary of the Quranic Surah 4 Al-Nisa, 2002a).

Hashmi employs a discourse of 'biological determinism' supported by religious inferences so any angst at the growing realisation of the inequality of distribution of resources in Pakistan and the gendered reality of the Pakistani community and family is suppressed by her arguments. In her lectures she refers to 'scientific' proof that confirms what she has been lecturing her students about all along:

> I am quoting now from *Man, the Unknown*. This is by Alexis Carrel (she proceeds to spell out his name), and he has received a Nobel Prize for his work. He says that in his work he researched the differences between men and women and... the difference was not only of the sexual organs, the womb, it was of level of comprehension, the difference was in their tissues, the chemical balances, each cell, its secretions was different. Now how can we go on ignoring these differences? These women's liberation people asked that remove differences between the genders, give same kind of education to everyone. This is wrong, for even in each cell of a woman she has femininity; it's in her nervous system. You cannot change it all now by providing same education and all that they are asking for, can you? So women I feel should develop themselves according to their biology, and whatever they can contribute will have as much to do in developing civilisation. Now a lot of problems, mental and physical, occur because women are fighting their physical constitution and try thinking like men (From Hashmi's commentary on the Quranic verse Surah 4 (Al-Nisa), 2002a).

Pakistani women who derive their class and legal status from their husbands may potentially move to an undesirable status if they decide to upset the status quo for it may plunge them into further obscurity. So they might keep quiet and say that they are doing well by God by not challenging laws that are 'God-given'. Mrs Qayyum, who had set up a women's *dars* (religious lectures) group patterned on Farhat Hashmi's lectures commented:

> When you talk about the Law of Evidence and whether it's unjust or not? Who is the most just? It is Allah, He is the most just. If He has created the entire solar system, which operates in such a just manner, if there is discipline in everything we see, if there is balance in all you see, then why do you doubt His system? It's in the Quran. How can you argue against that? When you talk about something being fair or not, ask yourself first who is the most fair? Then why doubt that?

Her group was comfortable in saying that they wanted to assert their identity within the moral formal strictures of Islam, as God protects the good Muslim women from the evil of the outside world.

# Competing Voices: Assuming Moral Responsibility for Canberra's Pakistan

The Pakistani community in Canberra witnessed the daughters and extended family of the *dars* organisers returning to the city after participating in the 'summer school' and 'diploma programmes' organised by Al Huda in Islamabad. A section of the prospectus for the 'diploma course' (and which was quoted by Shakeela—one of the students who had just returned from a programme in Islamabad) quoted a verse from the Quran's Surah 9 (*Al Tawbah*):

> And it was not important that all of the Faithful stood up… but it might have happened that from every one of their communities rose and left to get an understanding of the Faith and returned to the inhabitants of their area to warn them so that they did not adopt non-Islamic attitudes and refrained from [such] activities. —Surah 9 (*Al Tawbah*): 122

I was fascinated by how the organisation could integrate a religious sanction into their transnational network by strategically using Quranic verses. Shakeela went on to explain:

> [the value and basic aim of the course] equipped us as Al Huda states to create a Islamic character and attitude and such people whose knowledge and behaviour should not be for their own personalities but take it to any corner of the world, inside the house or outside, with our full effort and pure intention to better the lives of other people and this is only to gain Allah's goodwill. I liked it as they used modern audio, video aids and multi-media presentations to make everything effective and interesting.

Shakeela and her colleagues could keep in touch with each other and refresh all that they had learned via the Internet website maintained by Al Huda. The Al Huda website emerged as a public space which enabled a new class and generation of interpreters of the faith who are facilitated by this medium. These competing voices provide a commentary on Islamic texts for those like themselves and others who visit the website. Shakeela could extend the conversations, expressions, and representations of and about Islam that she conducted and learnt from the website and e-mail lists she had subscribed to, to her immediate family and their networks in Canberra. The website hosted a translation and a brief commentary on the Quran in Urdu and English, lectures on various topics, 'prayers of protection, for understanding the Quran, for travel, for pursuing a good education and for an obedient and good Muslim offspring free to download' (www.alhudapk.com/reading-material/). Her family or their circle of friends would direct their queries to her and ask her what her colleagues had to say, thus giving them the 'moral responsibility' of interpretation and direction to their religious behaviour in Canberra. These transnational networks of 'moral responsibility' once again operated from what was understood as 'home', therefore, defined as the private space arbitrated only by women. These conversations 'of and about Islam that were previously confined to coffee houses, university dormitories, factions, peer circles' and the mosque had moved to sites of 'discussion and debate' (Anderson, 1999: 48). Towards the end of my field study, Al Huda was holding online lectures through their website where 'live lectures from Hotel Falletti in Lahore would be broadcast', as the organisation's website claimed. These were followed by Shakeela and her contemporaries wherever they were (in Australia and Pakistan). Therefore, even within the *dars* congregations one can see a change in consumption of media (from the audio cassette lecture sessions in the living rooms to now virtual congregations) as well as the focus of the Pakistani women groups.

These young women would counter what they saw as 'Pakistani Islam'—the get-togethers on the Prophet's birthday, enjoying music and dance at weddings, celebrating *chand raat* (the celebrations on the last night of fasting and prior to the Muslim festival of Eid)—what Werbner calls the 'fun' element of South Asian culture. These celebrations are condemned as wasteful by them and regarded as un-Islamic. The celebration of New Year's Day was a particular target because of its association with the Christian rather than the Muslim calendar. Al Huda in particular had arranged lectures that disapproved of the celebration of such events. The *dars* congregation introduced me to two such lectures (which are also available for purchase in specially designed CD packages) titled 'Expression of True Love: Valentine's Day or Sacrifice' and one deriding April Fool's Day (Images 4.1 and 4.2).

# Conclusion

Al Huda differs from other religious networks in the Pakistani diaspora in that it is reflective of a particular 'women's world' that is purely mediated, organised, targeted towards and funded by women's contributions.

**Image 4.1**

*Valentine's Day Lectures CD*

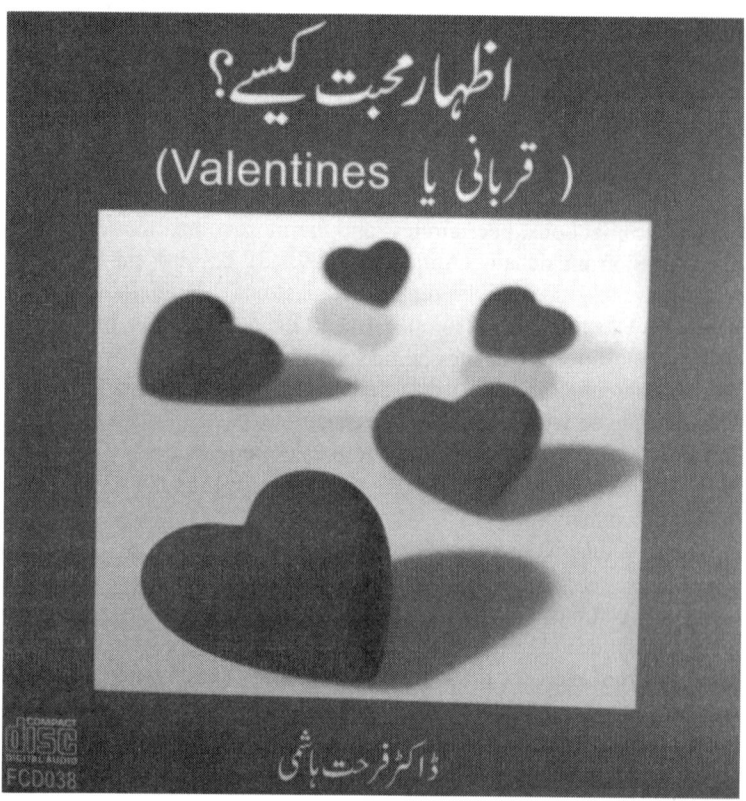

*Source*: Al Huda Publications.

Farhat Hashmi and Al Huda as an organisation could be sustained by
the support structures they have formed in the Pakistani diaspora, even
if they lost their current popularity in Pakistan. What had started in the
Pakistani cities of Karachi and Islamabad had been taken over by the
networks maintained by Al Huda students globally. Over the years the
organisation has managed to fashion, among other developments, a set
of psychological devices about self-empowerment in Pakistani women
where they could 'make themselves at home' anywhere in the Pakistani
diaspora in unfamiliar as well as familiar surroundings. They could be
at home without perhaps even knowing the language or the culture of
the host community—as long as they could have access to Al Huda

**Image 4.2**

*Friendship Lectures CD*

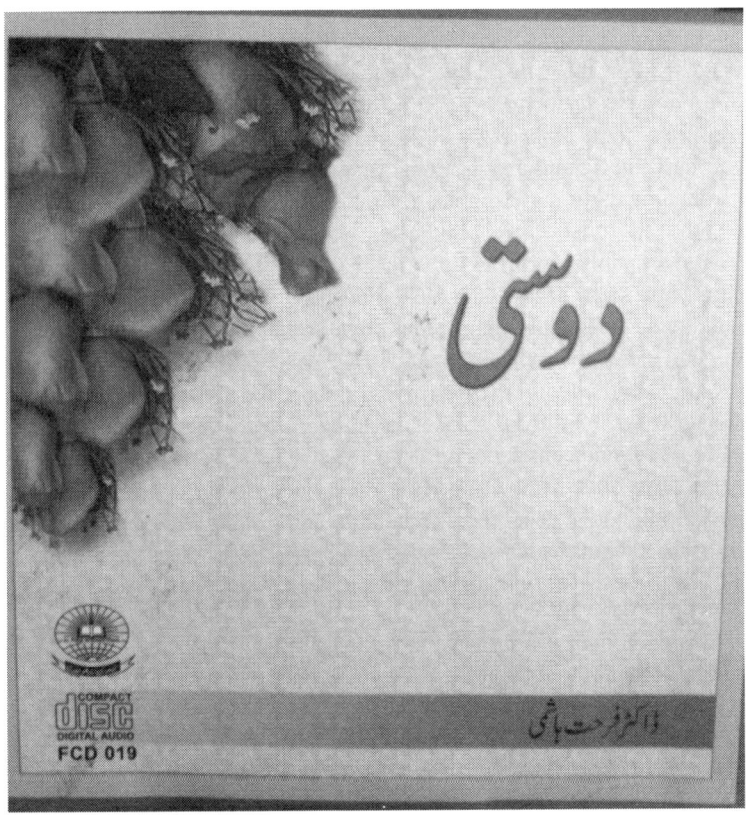

*Source*: Al Huda Publications.

resources. Just as Al Huda describes it in its brochures, they have been able to host the particular *dars* sessions where Pakistani women 'of all schools of thought and background' were encouraged to congregate and situate themselves in reference to their 'sense of belonging' to Al Huda. Was this then the beginning of a particular 'crossroads culture' where women representing the diversity of belonging (of ethnicity, class, spatial and temporal privilege that is indicative of Pakistani communities) could acquire a common set of religious values and interpretation? And through Al Huda, deliberate upon the conceptions and mechanisms for implementing these values?

And how far could Al Huda challenge the particular relationships of power in the Pakistani diaspora as it discussed, interpreted, and demonstrated this process? It was not only the Pakistani cultural elite in diaspora communities that had been displaced through the recent developments; I frequently wondered how the male relatives treated the growing involvement of their families in the *dars* networks. Some of the members of the congregation I had spoken to in Canberra spoke about how they had to constantly reassure their husbands regarding what was discussed in the lectures as 'essential in maintaining religious traditions.' But it is obvious that the movement has long moved from the level of inter-household networks, and has gradually entered the public world of Canberra's Pakistan. Therefore, over time there were confessions of how a particular husband was 'not very comfortable with the developments and made it obvious that he didn't appreciate this decision'. However, what is remarkable is that the students were still desirous of continuing with these activities despite the opposition they faced. Young women would declare that through these networks they had discovered a newfound confidence and have been able to assert their heretofore marginalised identity. In Canberra a young student was quick to emphasise that enrolling in the congregation had brought 'a calm and centring in her life', that Al Huda had made her aware of her status in society and she now felt that her sense of right and wrong had been awakened.

> My parents think that what they do is enough. They feel that for them their relationship with God and Islam is personal. It's not just my parents, and I see most people are following the same path. That's because we are always concerned with how others look at us, do they think we are backward? At times I feel I am alien to my family, that I am a misfit. Everyone has such low purposes and concerns from their lives; there are no high aims. I feel I am doing something now by teaching others about Islam. I don't judge what I do by what am I gaining monetarily, what are [the] benefits, as others in Pakistan do [see them] before doing anything.

Would the Pakistani community at home and abroad continue to accommodate this movement now that the *dars* practitioners had so clearly challenged the 'perceived wisdom' of age enjoyed by the parents' generation? And what about the hierarchy of status and control in the public space threatened by this new class and gender of 'religious mediators'? Farhat Hashmi had been asked similar questions some years ago by the Pakistani media who were of the view that the *Ulema* (the male religious clergy) had tolerated her, as they had not seen Hashmi as a threat since her target audience was so small. Hashmi had replied in her usual emphatic manner in an interview with Samina Ibrahim:

> I did not start my mission with anyone's approval and I will not end it because of anyone's disapproval. I do not fear the Ulema. I do not fear anyone. All I am doing is spreading the message of the Quran. If somebody objects to that, then their fight is not with me, but with God (Newsline, February 2001).

The energy created by the 'living room lectures' and the introduction of new 'moral communities' had led to tensions as prescribed roles throughout the Canberra Pakistani community were changing. The 'transnational gendered religious networks' had also struck at what Rahman has declared as the 'secularist cliché' that religion be 'relegated internally to the position of a private creed' and ritual, as 'being something merely between a man's heart and his God' (Rahman, 1984: 227–28). The challenge of pursuing modification in practice and rituals, while not outright confronting familial structures, has been prominent in the years the *dars* congregations gained popularity. This is true for other Pakistani communities around the world as well who find themselves in the new political, economic, and cultural settings of the West.

Has the element of cyber–consciousness introduced through Al Huda's 'online congregations' contributed to the ways women now maintain and expand the transnational networks in the Pakistani diaspora? The globalisation of religious information and images through Al Huda-sponsored networks had contributed to a state of affairs where sharing the same geographical place, or any of the controls and restrictions over the mobility of women did not matter anymore. Through advances in telecommunications, through sharing and mastering these networks, women were able to build their own coalitions and find support structures that might not have been available to them earlier under the traditional class and power divisions of the Pakistani diaspora. What is particular about these alliances is their gendered nature, and the consequent reaction in Canberra's Pakistan ever since these new groupings have gained a prominent profile emphasising that. The energy created by the 'living room lectures' and the introduction of new 'moral communities' have given rise to tensions as prescribed roles throughout the Canberra Pakistani community are seen to be changing.

What is problematic for Al Huda critics is the constant calls of Hashmi and her organisation 'to homogenize the structure, religious behaviour and responses of women's groups to enforce a rigid Islam' without allowing

any space for the diversity of cultural and ethnic belief that had characterised how Pakistani women had interacted with Islam earlier.

I found much of the Al Huda discourse worrying especially when I read
about Hashmi describing the 2004 earthquake in Kashmir and NWFP as
God's punishment for 'immoral activities'. According to Hashmi, 'The
people in the area where the earthquake hit were involved in immoral
activities, and God has said that he will punish those who do not follow
his path.' Opinions such as this are problematic considering the Al Huda
Foundation had turned its attention towards the education sector in the
earthquake-devastated region of Northern Pakistan hoping to redress the
void created by the collapse of government schools (International Crisis
Group Report, 2006).

This brings me to another feature of the Al Huda discourse that made
me nervous about being part of the congregation. I fear that over time
Al Huda would enforce a 'uniform guide' to religious interpretation that
does not allow any competing discourses. Did Hashmi's lectures becoming the 'one truth fits all' remind me of all that was troublesome about
religious belonging in Pakistan during my childhood years? Growing up
in Rawalpindi, Pakistan, my neighbourhood friends and I had discovered
that we recited our evening prayers differently from each other. When I
went to my grandfather who had taught me my prayers, and was the 'wisest
person about religion' we could think of, he tried to simplify sectarian
and ritual differences between us by stating the fact that 'my neighbours
are Punjabis'. That seemed adequate to my friends and myself, and their
longer prayers could be slotted somewhere alongside other facts like why
they could tolerate spices, could watch TV long after my bedtime, and
spoke better Urdu. There were no winners or losers about who prayed
correctly, and we were at peace. Maybe when they went back home,
their parents might have deplored my family's religiosity. But during
the short period of religious fervour of our school years, whenever we
prayed together after evening play time we were comfortable with our
differences. Years afterwards, when I narrated this episode to colleagues
at university, they weren't so tolerant. Times had changed, they said,
and wouldn't it be more prudent for me to harmonise my prayers with
theirs, 'for I did want to be a good Muslim, right?' Maybe it was around
this time that I stopped praying in front of others, as I was getting tired
of being corrected constantly. Roughly around the same time I withdrew
from engaging in what Pakistanis call 'drawing-room debates' over my
religious beliefs. I had resigned myself to the discomforting knowledge
that terms like Islam and Muslim were neither straightforward nor without

controversy, so it was best I kept quiet rather than antagonise my friends' parents. It is this that kept me hesitant to participate more actively in the women's congregations in Canberra. I was reminded of this episode when I read Rushdie's personal debate on his relationship with Islam:

> *I am not a Muslim,* that's what you meant. No supernaturalism, no literalist orthodoxies, no formal rules for you. But Islam doesn't have to mean blind faith. It can mean what it always meant in your family, a culture, a civilisation, as open-minded as your grandfather was, as delightedly disputatious as your father was, as intellectual and philosophical as you like. Don't let the zealots make *Muslim* a terrifying word, I urged myself; remember when it meant *family* and *light*....I reminded myself that I had always argued that it was necessary to develop the nascent concept of the 'secular Muslim', who like the secular Jews, affirmed his membership of the culture while being separate from the theology.... I told myself, you can't argue from outside the debating chamber. You've got to cross the threshold, go inside, the room, and *then* fight for your humanised, historicised, secularised way of being a Muslim (Rushdie, 1991: 435–36).

It made me nostalgic for a time when I too was comfortable with being Muslim, when I didn't have to be apologetic to my neighbours about my family's particular 'ethnic relationship' with being Muslim. However, if I was so eager to reclaim this lost relationship, wasn't it time that I too started grappling with the contentious issues of differences within our religious faith? I am glad I started this process, for I realised quickly that for some time I had my own prejudices and stereotypes about Muslim women, the same ones that others are so familiar with. Over the months the picture I had in my mind was at odds with the actual fears and hopes, anxieties and aspirations of the Pakistani women. These women were challenging the assumptions that, if they were treated as equal members of the community, the community would risk erasure due to a loss of difference from the 'conquering other'. Why has it been that Muslim women continue to be perceived as passive members of a monolithic community sitting morosely apart, when they could very well be active participants in multicultural cultures whose perspective they too shared in their daily lives? My interviewees took their commitment to Islam not only as one among many moral and spiritual values, but also as something which was itself interpreted and exhibited differently in their relationship with Canberra society. However, what worries me is whether Pakistani women's connection with Al Huda would gradually move them away from the 'multiple dialects' they spoke of culture, ethnicity and politics to one of a single language of belonging and interpretation. This plurality is what I fear we will miss.

However, I hope one's endeavour to explore a history of Pakistan with the Pakistani women as narrators would not only identify a different gender, but also a new generation and class of interpreters for Islam. There had been a growing need to document the experiences and instances of resistance, solidarity and agency disseminated through alternative voices, activist movements and channels in the transnational and regional forums, those that have remained sceptical of hegemonic discourse. The experience of diaspora had encouraged and facilitated the process of Pakistani women being able to address and thereby reframe the power framework of who has the authority to interpret religious texts. This could lead to a fresh medium of expression on matters to do with religious belief and diversity, not only for themselves in their personal lives, but also for others in the community.

The growth of the gendered transnational networks of religion mediated exclusively by, and focused towards and funded by, women's contributions challenges the way the male elite have traditionally controlled religious spaces in diasporic communities. This could only happen if one applies alternative means of seeing not only the socio-political practices of diasporic communities but also how one views the religious behaviour of the women living in these communities. Though women may explain their religious involvement and social performances as moral obligations and religious responsibilities, in many ways they are challenging the authority of others to define and interpret religious duties for them.

# 5

# Texts of War

Try as I might to ignore the images of the Jamia Hafsa students and the accompanying flood of memories, I do keep returning to those photographs. The image of the *burqa*-clad women as they pose with their batons; when they first appeared, stirred within me a compassion that initially made me very apprehensive. I would ask myself why I viewed these images with empathy, and how best to label the affinity I felt with these veiled students. They remained faceless for the world, but I could definitely recognise the frame of mind and resolve with which they had posed for the photographs. Perhaps this book project was aimed at unpacking this feeling of comradeship.

Decades ago I too may have exhibited quasi-similar life choices as theirs when I signed up for a postgraduate degree in Defence and Strategic Studies (albeit I perceived my role in 'organised violence' as a planner, a strategist, not as one who would actually take up arms herself). It says something for the Pakistani mindset that in all the years since I completed my degree, the pursuit of organised violence continues to hold its attraction for young Pakistani women—whether it is a young grad student seeking 'liberation' from the perceived drudgery of pre-determined gender roles when it comes to a 'safe' academic degree for women, or a means of identifying with the dominant Pakistani discourse valorising the Soldier of Islam.

There have been seminal studies on women and the national question in Pakistan, and whether framed in the lens of knowledge, religious texts, history, work or class, they all in their own way aim to provide road maps to the creation of knowledge and identity in Pakistan. But what about the other performances in Pakistan's history, those that may have been archived as part of military annals, but which have left a far greater impact on the national psyche about how gender roles and relations are defined by the Pakistani state? In this chapter I will catalogue instances where certain definitions of gender identity were promoted in Pakistan to encourage a societal sanction for violence. Now for my generation, a watershed moment arrived in the days leading up to the nuclear tests in May 1998—this particular period can very well form a case study as to how gender identities were reinforced through a nexus of religion, militarism, and societal discourse.

The seeds of this chapter lie somewhere in 1999, in the days leading to the first anniversary of Pakistan's nuclear tests conducted on 28 May 1998. The first anniversary was celebrated as *Youm-i-Takbeer* (literal translation: Day of God's Greatness) and the Pakistani public was asked by the then government to celebrate the day in a befitting manner. This included national rallies and parades, thanksgiving prayers, and country-wide festivities. On occasions such as these, Pakistani citizens who have opposed the nuclearisation of South Asia are reminded of forever being on the margins of nationality tests. I could draw parallels with the struggle Pakistani feminists go through most days—at ease with their Pakistani identity but still challenging the gendered expectation of duties towards the state. The process of categorising identities, of discerning the self from the 'other', leaves some of us feeling like 'others' in one's own nation. A particular type of world-view has been presented in Pakistan with male and female roles exacerbated, which is compounded with Pakistan being very close to a Praetorian state. At the best of times and definitely the worst, every time the Pakistani state has faced a crisis, the military dictatorship emerges as the hyper-masculinist authoritative figure considered the final decision-maker for which course of action to follow. In a situation such as this, amity or harmony is taken as a sign of submissiveness if it is not on one's own terms. A hostile state of affairs with active conflict held at bay would be more acceptable than reconciliation or pacifism (read as a feminine peace) approached through dialogue. The latter state of affairs will be perceived as being spineless and encouraging the enemy to trample all over one. This could be a significant reason why the Pakistani public in May 1998 seemed more comfortable with the status of deterrence brought about by conducting nuclear tests rather than pursuing a policy of restraint and dialogue. I have referred to this episode elsewhere (Babar, 2001) as 'the grand symphony: when all the performers came out to play', a time when a cacophony of discordant notes came together in the crescendo of war drums.

But first, an overview of engendered duties towards the Pakistani state and how the 'good woman' is constructed in the national idea.

# Pakistan's National Idea: Articulation of the Women's Question

What have we learnt so far from studies on the women's question in Pakistan? That it is just not Islam that is the sole determinant of the gendered expectations reigning over Pakistani women and their life choices. Like societies elsewhere, we acknowledge the big role class, ethnicity and interpretations of cultural traditions play in defining women's life options and gender experiences in Pakistan.

However, one has to agree with Moghissi that although different interpretations and traditions exist within Islam making it hard to generalise, it can be said that Islam is a sex-affirming cultural and religious tradition (Moghissi, 2001). Basing its world-view on the creative and procreative balance of nature, it enjoins a strict separation of the masculine and the feminine principles. The two together represent qualities of a desired whole. As Boudhiba has argued, in Islam the unity of a bipolar world can be achieved only in the harmony of the sexes:

> The best way of realising the harmony intended by God is for the man to assume his masculinity and for the woman to assume her full femininity… anything that violates the order of this world is a grave 'disorder', a source of evil and anarchy (Boudhiba, 1985: 156).

Within parameters that make sacred the sexual dichotomy by positioning a divinely ordained, bipolar universe, any violation of the different roles and functions assigned to the female and male acquires a cosmological significance. And this, as Boudhiba points out, is the reason why Islam condemns those who overstep the limits enjoined to them by sexual difference. As the details of daily behaviour are indicators of deeper and less obvious prejudices, it is not surprising that chief amongst those who incur the anger of God are 'men who dress up themselves as women and women who dress themselves as men' (Boudhiba, 1985). Beginning with the nineteenth century which Kandiyoti (1992) has marked as the start of the articulation of Muslim nationalism in South Asia, the period led to a spate of literature being produced regarding the 'nature', role and function of Muslim women in society. In order to cope with their own exclusion from the wider field of economic and political power, the Muslim orthodoxy focused on the domestic enclosure and declared women's service within it as the 'ultimate and inviolable repository of

Muslim identity' (Kandiyoti, 1992). This attitude towards women prevails even today in current-day Pakistan with Pakistani policymakers viewing their world as an insecure space divided between the Islamic (home) and non-Islamic (world). The home/world divide in religious ideology and nationalism has led to the ideal woman commonly portrayed as a good caregiver serving the family and home, supporting the nation through self-sacrifice, dressing properly and remaining virtuous. The home was not only a shelter for the besieged self, but a spiritual centre which women were expected to guard by means of high standards of virtue and morality. Added to this is the fact that the emphasis on exercising spirituality and morality is an oblique reference to the control of female sexuality (Saigol, 1997a). Good women were those who were either married or who remain secluded, taking care of husbands, in-laws and children. Rita Manchanda (2001) highlighted the paradox:

> It is precisely at the time of dramatic shifts in gender roles, brought about by the societal upheaval attendant on conflict, that the impulse to promote women's social transformation and autonomy is circumscribed by the nationalist or communitarian project itself. For these projects need to con-figure women as the guardians of the community's accepted and acceptable distinct cultural identity and tradition, thus circumscribing the process of desirable change and even pushing back women (Manchanda, 2001: 13).

Saigol (1997) refers to Syed Ahmed Khan, who is often regarded as the founder of Muslim modernism, advocating as he did the merits of Western education and technology to Indian Muslims as a way to retain class power and prestige. However, he did not abandon the nationalist project of portraying Muslim women as the repository of Muslim identity and urged Indian Muslims to prevent their daughters from getting a Western, modern education. He instead urged them to give their daughters exactly the same domestic education which was designed to create the 'ideal Indian Muslim woman'.

> I cannot approve of the modern system of education devised for the education for women. Developing institutions for women's education and fashioning them along the lines of European women's institution is inappropriate for contemporary conditions in India. Therefore, I strongly oppose these measures. I am also not in favour of the kind of knowledge being imparted to women as it does not suit our conditions and our women do not need this knowledge for centuries to come (*Khutbat-e-Sir Syed* as quoted in Saigol 1997a: 167).

There is a great deal of emphasis on the idea of difference between 'our women' and European women through phrases such as 'our conditions' and 'our women'. In the same speech, Syed goes on to describe the kind of education he feels Indian Muslim women should acquire:

> [G]irls who attended cooking classes were taught all the things that are necessary for women to know, for example, they were taught the manners and etiquette necessary for family life. Their education did not consist of the knowledge that some are trying to introduce in our women's institutions in an attempt to imitate the West. Given the social conditions of Europe and America, that knowledge may be required for their women. It is possible that women in these countries can become postmasters, telegraph officers or members of parliaments. But in India the conditions are different and will remain so for hundreds of years.
>
> ...
>
> Girls in earlier times used to study the Quran and its translation, they learned about prayers and fasting and issues related to religious rituals...this was the best method of education as it produced virtue, kindness, sympathy, love and a good moral character. Such an education was useful both for worldly and spiritual matters and to this day it is the most useful education. I cannot understand what is to be gained from teaching women the geography of Africa and America, Algebra and Trigonometry or about the battles between Ahmed Shah and Mohammad Shah, wars between the Marathas and those of Delhi (*Khutbat-e-Sir Syed* in Saigol, 1997a: 168).

As Saigol points out, for Syed Ahmad Khan the only reason for the attainment of knowledge is a utilitarian one—its practical application. Practicality is defined implicitly as the performance of gender roles, that is women's domestic duties and men's public role. So the citizenship that the nationalist poet Iqbal espoused as integral to his political philosophy was to be available primarily to men. It was men who were to conceive ideas; women's role in history was to remain loyal wives, sisters, and mothers, helping implement their ideals (Rouse, 1997).

When I interviewed Saigol in 1999 for my postgraduate research project on a feminist reading of militarism in South Asia, she shared with me her work on the educational curriculum in Pakistan and how the state encouraged a gendered reading of Pakistan studies and South Asia's history:

> Within Muslim nationalism women cannot have equal citizenship...if your sense of self and nation and space comes from Islam then it is very difficult for women to be equal. If you read commentaries of Surah Nisa

and Beheshti Zever, there is a clear demarcation of man being superior to women, that man is dominant, superior and higher, it clearly says that do not consider yourself equal to men… so the rhetoric of equality, modernity, democracy it is loathsome to religion. So when your nationalism and sense of citizenship is based on Islam, how can you project gender equality? Women's citizenship will suffer as a result.

In Pakistan the debate about control of women's mobility by the religious elite in Pakistan remained marginal up until 1977 when President Zia's government made a conscious use of Islam as a political weapon and invested in the right wing lobby. This was the Pakistan my generation was born into. For Mumtaz (1994) the controls on women's mobility reflected their (the religious elite's) perception that middle-and upper-middle-class women were threats to the existing order.

> Built largely upon differentiation, it has led to the politicisation of gender whereby those advocating women's emancipation are viewed as modern and as such opposed to Islam… but it intensified after 1977 with the military government's use of religion to legitimise its stay. With the weight of the government behind them the position of male antagonists of women's rights was bolstered, as were the efforts for cultural hegemony. Women as the supposed carriers of cultural values became central to their political project. On the one hand there was a relentless running down of women's rights activists, their 'otherness' being singled out for attack, and on the other hand active mobilisation of women belonging to the emerging middle class was undertaken (Mumtaz in Moghadhem ed, 1994: 229).

Similarly, Pakistan's foreign policy towards Afghanistan and the Cold War adventure through the 1980s promoted the seclusion of women and put in place a narrow public space for women. Most women in the Khyber Pakhtunkhwa were forced to don a *chadar* (shawl), and sending girls to school continued to be actively discouraged. The majority of women in the NWFP enjoy little reproductive freedom as reflected by the fact that birth rates are highest in the province as well as deaths in childbirth. Afghan refugee women were not allowed to venture out of the camps. It might be argued that these trends existed before the development of gun culture, to which one might say that the comparative improvement in other provinces of Pakistan indicates that retrogressive tendencies have kept positive social change at bay in the NWFP (Khattak, 1994: 35).

Gardezi (1997) has elaborated on how Zia decided to secure his regime through the propagation of an explicitly anti-woman ideology and proclaiming a mission to 'revitalize society by correcting the immorality of women' (Gardezi, 1997: 101). In doing so he ushered a convoluted, and as Gardezi identifies it, 'a distorted version' of the relationship between Islam and the origins of the nation. Thus women's groups such as Women's Action Front (WAF), who challenged controls on their mobility and encroachment of their rights as guaranteed by the 1973 constitution, were seen as that what is not considered to be Pakistani.

During the same period Pakistan's Muttahida Qaim Movement (a political party with a strong base in Karachi's Urdu-speaking population) was on its part mobilising women, and had included them as party workers in numbers unprecedented since 1947 (Haroon, 2001). A significant reason behind this could be that MQM drew its support from the urban middle class in cosmopolitan Karachi. However, as Haroon elaborates in her analysis of women associated with MQM, the women workers could not challenge patriarchal structures. MQM, at the time of her research had more than 7,500 women workers with not a single nomination for a party ticket at the time of general elections. During a particularly difficult period for MQM, when most of the party leadership had gone underground and male workers were targeted, women workers were called upon to take up more responsibilities (and allegedly provide cover). However, at no time did they challenge their gendered roles or the militant ideology of the MQM that was taking their loved ones' lives and putting their families at peril with the security forces. Haroon conducted an interview with MQM's only female senator Nasrin Jalil, where she asked of the senator whether she found anything problematic with their subservient (to the party leadership) role.

> Women in our party perform all office chores. They clean, sweep, make tea, make calls, receive messages and attend public meetings when they are asked to. They are not involved in decision making because politics is not their field. Most of them are not educated and do not understand the complexities of the situation (Haroon, 2001: 187–88).

Haroon concludes that the role of the (mostly lower-middle-class) women workers has remained passive and it is only in crisis situations where they take up previously unprecedented tasks such as protecting the militants, taking out funeral processions, in some cases, washing and burying the dead, conducting *Quran khwani* (reading of the Quran—which was used allegedly as a forum to pass on information and messages to the militants), encircling police stations and at times passing on arms. But at no time did their membership in the MQM provide them with a forum where they could explore women's agency. They were not part of MQM's mandate or discourse unless it was as victims of state terror—the party leadership would then call on 'good boys' to marry and rehabilitate these 'victims'. In interviews they could not deliberate on what '*Mohajir* identity' meant beyond better jobs and life choices for their men in their families.

By the end of the 1980s Benazir Bhutto was winning political mileage by her 'dramatic entry into motherhood'. Inayatullah has read the situation as one where the image of Benazir Bhutto as a single woman had her being situated by her critics 'in the land of female archetypes, that of the Amazon or hero, and later as the daughter of a Great Man, her father Zulfiqar Bhutto' (Sohail Inayatullah in Bahri and Vasudeva 1996). This as Benazir Bhutto had initially portrayed herself as a dutiful daughter who only stepped out of the home to avenge her father's death. But it was only as a mother that Inayatullah sees her as finally finding political success. Ironically, after her death, Benazir Bhutto appears reduced to the mother-figure who ushers a new chapter of dynastic politics with her son as her political heir. And perhaps this is this how the Pakistani populace will be finally comfortable with her legacy—the brave mother who laid down her life trying to bring democracy to her electorate family and who 'bequeaths' the Pakistani nation her first-born to carry on her mission.

# Our Razia Sultana Moment

In my school textbooks amongst the paeans to Khadija (the ideal wife), Fatima (the ideal daughter) and Fatima Jinnah (the ideal sister) there lived the enigmatic character of Razia Sultana. Razia was mysterious, neither wife nor mother. How did she sit with all the demure women who had been elevated to a pedestal, the ideal of Islamic and Pakistani consciousness? Razia Sultana has admittedly been an 'anomaly'. As Saigol (1995) explained in her analysis of the creation of 'gendered' knowledge in Pakistan (through school curricula), Razia Sultana had dared to give up the confines of *purdah*, she trained in horsemanship and the arts of war and would appear in court in male clothing. Our textbooks may have dealt with this by bringing readers' attention to how she was serving and protecting a Muslim dynasty, dealing with her good Muslim woman 'ambiguity and category violation…by placing her neatly into the masculine category'(Saigol, 1995: 241). We are told that Razia lived such a life to protect an 'Islamic dynasty', which gave us, female readers too, a 'divine' sanction to dream of one day taking up arms to protect the Pakistan state. And as I viewed the images of the young seminary students of Jamia Hafsa in Islamabad, I wondered whether this same discourse of women defying gender dictates in the service of Islam also influenced them in justifying their own disobediences, stepping out of the sacred *chardevari*.

Coming to my Razia Sultana moment as a graduate student, getting a degree in War Studies was the closest I could get to be part of Pakistan's war machine. In Pakistan, societal values place a premium on military service or aspirations for pursuing it as a career option. Stephen Cohen, in his profile of the Pakistan Army, describes our situation as 'A Pakistani who cannot share equally in the obligations and rewards associated with such a central institution as the military is not truly a citizen in the full sense of the word'(Cohen, 1990: 50).

And how can one ignore the other reminders—this time the pressure to fulfil the dream of Jinnah, the founder father of Pakistan! Remember the 'Unity Faith Discipline' motto I refer to earlier in this monograph? The Pakistan Army had interpreted Jinnah's three principles of 'Unity Faith Discipline' in a newspaper advertisement as follows:

> The weak and the defenceless in this imperfect world invite aggression from others. The best way in which we can serve the cause of peace is by removing temptation from those who think we are weak, and therefore, they can bully or attack us. That temptation can only be removed if we make ourselves so strong that nobody dare entertain any aggressive designs against us (Jinnah, address to H.M.P.S. *Dilawar,* 23 January 1948)

Spare a thought for the young Pakistani woman growing up under the Damocles Sword of 'half a judgement, half a personhood',[1] to which one could add a grave crisis of citizenship if the women are not seen as active participants in combat. It is important to acknowledge this particular 'condition of citizenship' for there has often been the argument that the entry of women in male bastions like the military is the precondition for women's achievement of full citizenship rights. I will not, at this stage, deliberate whether this statement could be the precursor of a party of women with masculinist minds. What I will do instead is share my memories of a Pakistan where one grew up idolising the image of a valiant warrior hero forever in combat to safeguard Islam. Young women

---

[1] The infamous Law of Evidence.

like myself, secretly fantasised about a career in 'organised violence' (or designing strategies for) when we too could aspire to achieve similar glory. There is also the intriguing question of milbus (military business interests), which has made joining the military a lucrative career for Pakistan's young. Milbus is the internal economy of the armed forces that is established primarily to bring personal advantages to military personnel, especially the senior echelons of the officer cadre. Ayesha Siddiqa (2007) defines the term as parent-guardian militaries, which though attempting to exhibit that they have withdrawn from the centre stage of politics, continue to ensure their control of the establishment and government through a legal and constitutional mechanism. They do this not only out of a fear of leaving the state to civilians but also because they have developed huge financial stakes in the business of running a state which must be protected at all costs. Such militaries are classified as primary predators and, are in fact, a source of kleptocratic distribution for their own members and cronies (Siddiqa, 2007).

Pakistan's social transformation (that we all bemoan today) where young women grow up dreaming of the gun and where a significant section justifies religious violence cannot be understood without identifying and calling out the existence of a religious-military nexus in the country. As I have acknowledged elsewhere (Babar, 2001), key religious actors in Pakistan have vocally supported militarism and the two entities together have sponsored religious revivalism and an understanding of political Islam where a generation of young Pakistanis (along with their political and religious leaders) are no more interested in studying whether religious texts of Islam that they speak of following even justifies their use of force.

We are all aware that Pakistan's ruling elite at the time of independence consisted of an alliance between landlords and the nascent industrial bourgeoisie, backed by the military and bureaucracy. The gradual erosion of social infrastructure, endemic poverty and growing inequality between the regions undermined civil society and accelerated the trend towards militarisation (Hussain, 1993). Hussain explains that while there has been a rapid deterioration in the level of professional competence, and in institutional procedures for decision-making and an absence of effective methods of in-service training in the bureaucracy, the military has by contrast seen a significant improvement in each of these spheres. Thus, the military as in several other developing states exercised a decisive influence on state policy, either by directly taking over the structures of the government or indirectly by controlling and/or manipulating the civil ruling elite (Hussain, 1993: 39–49).

The process of creating a superior military class was further augmented by the 1977–88 military rule of Zia-ul-Haq. Over the years not only has military rule become extensive, it is also intensive in terms of the ideas of their superiority that the military men brought to their 'civilian offices' that they were literally as their recruitment material assured them 'Men At Their Best'. Khattak (1997) elaborates that

> while there was some resistance, many ideas were internalised by the people so that many reproduced themselves as the colonised, and accepted the denial of rights and equality as a result of the inability of the civilian politicians to rule and the corruption of the civilian institutions (Khattak, 1997: 48).

Perhaps this is why Pakistan's former Chief of Army Staff, General Aslam Beg, when interviewed by me took pride in sharing:

> There are not many people who come up to our level of motivation....the man sitting here has different level of commitment for a country for which people living there (at border) are fighting for. (There is a) Difference in level of commitment between you and us towards the cause (of Pakistan), pertaining to one's beliefs, personal causes.[2]

His colleagues shared his vision.

> Military has discipline, army are men in uniform, taught that way. Even an army sepoy working as batman is the safest (man servant)—polished, disciplined men, complete gentleman. Never an untoward incident when we evacuate families (in case of emergencies). Only when we interact with civilians that we may revert to original, regress.[3]

The supremacy enjoyed by the soldier as hero has been extended to the level of the symbol. General Beg justified it as Pakistan needs 'militaristic symbols in the public space (which are there) to prevent a state of conflict. Didn't Allama Iqbal write "*Shamsheer o sana awwal, taoos or rubab akhar* (the sword and dagger first and music and lute last)?"

The eternal presence of a supreme 'militaristic' mindset has been 'an enabling factor of governance' in Pakistan over the years. Mubarak Ali

---

[2] Personal interview, April 1999.
[3] Capt AB, personal interview, May 1999. He was referring to the 1971 war crimes in the then East Pakistan—a case of events brought about by (according to him) the army living in close proximity to civilians and their corrupt practices.

refers to Anatole France as he explains, 'A people living under the perpetual menace of war and invasion is very easy to govern. It demands no social reforms. It does not haggle over expenditures on armaments and military equipment. It pays without discussion' (Ali, 1995: 59).

Rubina Saigol in her definitive work on the educational policies of the Pakistani state has pointed out that for a significant portion of Pakistani history its policy-makers have operated under a declared principle of 'Now everyone of our young persons will be trained to rush to the battleground at a moment's notice' (Saigol, 1995: 257). Other Pakistani academics, such as K.K. Aziz, Dr Nayyer and Ahmed Salim have conducted pioneering work in analysing Pakistani textbooks and how they privilege a militarist discourse. To date any attempt to change this text has met with a lot of hostilities lest the essential 'Pakistani' national spirit be diluted.

Even a cursory look at the keepsakes and tokens in the public space can inform us about a Pakistani political and urban sociology that privileges the military. Consider for instance the ubiquitous car stickers used by taxi-cab and (civilian) private car owners in Pakistan. They bear religious verses strategically aligned with stickers praising and cajoling one to join the ranks of members of the Pakistan military. My colleagues would joke about this juxtaposition as further evidence that the taxi drivers believe that it is Pakistan's religio-military nexus rather than the car's engine that guarantees the car's smooth running! Perhaps the driver's unwavering faith has shifted to gods more earthly, therefore, in addition to his supplications to Almighty Allah at dawn and dusk for granting him a secure livelihood and good health, he thought it wise to pray to the khaki defenders of the faith as well. He now invests in 'charms' and 'invocations' not only to express his gratitude in the Master of the Heavens but also in the wonderful men who are but executing God's word across Pakistan every day!

Chaudhry Tufail, the former *amir* (head) of the Jamat-i-Islami, who in the 1980s was also a member of Pakistan's legislature, when interviewed, had no doubt about advocating a militaristic reading of *jihad*. In a personal interview conducted as part of my postgraduate project, he shared,

The real task is to conduct *jihad*, to propagate the word of Islam everywhere…God has instructed us to spread His law all over the world. Therefore, if we have to use power or force to convince the people it is justified. We have been instructed to put our lives in the path of God as it is the cause of truth.[4]

---

[4] Personal conversation with Chaudhry Tufail at Mansoorah, April 1999.

The commentaries of Maudoodi, the founder patron of Jamat-i-Islami in turn have been strategically employed to justify the world-view that the philosophy of non-violence is not practical. The only way to overcome any opposition to one's ideology is to annihilate it, rather than debate and/ or argue. The following Maudoodi quote has been particularly popular among Maudoodi and Jamat-i-Islami followers:

> [I]n reality they are a poisonous sore on the body of society which if allowed to remain, will kill us, so our mind and reason tell us that the logic demands the cutting of this poisonous part. It is quite possible that there are such intellectuals in this world who believe it is a sin to kill such cruel people and their timid souls tremble at the thought of the flow of the tyrant's blood (which is the only way to remove the source of evil). But such an intellectual cannot correct this society. He can stay in solitude and calm his soul in the forests and mountains but his teachings cannot keep the world free from wrong, from evil and anarchy (Maudoodi, 1996: 36). (The translation from the Urdu is mine.)

Pakistan's military on its part has also been very adept at using the sayings of the Holy Prophet (*Sahee Bukhari Hadees*) to promote recruitment. Imagine if you are an impressionable teenager growing up in Pakistan and being accosted with the following *Hadith* (tradition attributed to the Prophet) reproduced in the public space in the form of billboards, flyers, newspaper advertisements:

> And it has been said to stay awake for one night in this just war is better than to spend a thousand nights in prayer, and to stand steadfast in this war for one day is better than to spend sixty years in prayers. The fires of hell have been banned on the eyes that stay awake in this war. The feet that have grown dusty in this war have been promised that they will never be dragged into the fires of hell. And those who have escaped war to stay at home and have hesitated at the call of war have been admonished in the sternest tone (Saheeh Bukhari—practice of Prophet compiled by Bukhari).

And

> Let not those who disbelieve suppose that they can outstrip (Allah's purpose). Lo! They cannot escape. Make ready for them all thou canst of (Armed) force and of horses tethered, that thereby ye may dismay the enemy of Allah and your enemy, and others beside them whom ye know not Allah knoweth them. Whatsoever ye spend in the way of Allah it will be repaid to you in full, and ye will not be wronged (Al-Anfa, 59–60).

Paying no attention to the need of coming up with a definition of the 'just war' mentioned in the religious tradition they quote, the words appear as part of recruitment material circulated by the Pakistan army. They also appear in the literature distributed by problematic *jihadi* groups to justify their militant struggle in Kashmir. The *Hadith* is also quoted by religious right-wing groups as they side with martial law regimes in Pakistan and defend the decision that a larger share of resources be given to the Pakistani military.[5] And *Hadith*s just like this one also become part of the discourse of resistant groups in Swat and Waziristan—as I witnessed for myself with stickers of the *Hadith* prominently displayed in rest houses in Swat.

Pakistan's texts of war—the tale of the religio-military nexus has also given birth to a discourse that firmly puts in place gender identity. In the Pakistan I grew up, societal and nationalistic discourses were very much a gendered construct with the stakeholders informed by patriarchal and gendered ideologies. The Pakistani military has ensured that martial values predominate and the militarised rhetoric remains a part of popular culture and religious symbols with the masculine as privileged. If one looks at the articulation of cultural and national identity in Pakistan as expressed in the visual form, from public spaces to public monuments, the cultural spaces, signs and iconography, all reflect the national ideology of a predominantly Muslim, masculine identity and consciousness (Lalarukh, 1997).

## 'It is Not Discrimination but Discretion'

Yuval-Davis (1997) in her seminal work on women and militarism elaborated how militaries and warfare have never been just a male zone, women have always fulfilled certain vital roles within them, but predictably 'not on an equal, undifferentiated basis to that of men'. She has outlined how the sexual division of labour within the military has often been even more formalised and rigid than that in the civil sector. So in the case of Pakistan, the military had been content for some time with recruiting women as doctors, nurses, and teachers, they were content in keeping them in reproductive roles so as not to shatter any stereotypes. They felt that they were doing so to save 'our women' the 'indignity' that

---

[5] Personal interview with Maulana Saleemi (former Naib Amir Jamat Islami), Mansoora, April 1999.

women in the West were facing (as in sexual harassment from colleagues). This conveniently absolves them of any responsibility as 'the source of temptation', i.e., the female is removed. It is important that I revisit the conversations I had with certain members of Pakistan's military elite in 1999, for I, like many others, continue to doubt the sustainability of the project of 'enlightened moderation' and Pakistani women's recruitment in armed forces and the air force that the mid-2000s brought about. For it is only when we are sure that mindsets have changed can we as Pakistani women believe that women may have a secure, sustainable tenure as members of the Pakistani military.

I grew up in a Pakistan where women were yet to participate in 'active combat'; their inclusion in PAF as fighter pilots and elsewhere was yet to become a reality. At the time it would only have been a hypothetical question whether the inclusion of women in South Asia's militaries would lead to a more 'humane' world as they would bring their 'peace-making' skills to the fore (and force).

When I set out to conduct my interviews with the military high command, it was 1999. Female officers had just been inducted in the Indian military and the Indian Air Force (Pakistan's bête noir). At the time my interviewees were vehement in their opposition to recruit women in the 'fighting arms', as they put it, of the Pakistani military.

General Aslam Beg, a former Chief of Army Staff, who later decided to set up a think tank on matters of national defence and security, thought the following:

> Highly regard hundreds of women in the medical corps, they are respected, doing a wonderful job...but to accept that our women can be inducted in the fighting arms, I think we should learn from the mistakes which more liberal countries like the United States, like the United Kingdom have made by inducting these women. I mean I would prefer that women should not be degraded the way they are being degraded. Instead of just by the sake of giving them a job in armed forces and damaging the dignity of women, it is better to put them in other professions where they can do better rather than going in armed forces and trying to find equality in a profession where it is very difficult to find it. There are certain things which are just not considered proper in our society. We cannot accept the kind of indignity for women, men and women sitting in the bunker in the battlefield... they can't tolerate it over there, we cannot.

The whole argument comes down to the inside/outside debate that Chatterjee (1993) had put forward as to how women and the conduct of gender relations become the 'markers' for societies. The good general in the interview kept on referring to the 'here', i.e., Pakistan (virtuous values, control of female sexuality) and the 'over there', i.e., the West (its allegedly loose sexual morals). Pakistan seemingly triumphs in his discourse over the 'more liberated' West as Pakistan keeps women in segregation, and the West is left repenting over its mistakes.

General Beg's colleague entered the room just then and added,

> I think women provide the peace of mind that the armed forces need, whether it is the officer, soldier or jawan. The credit goes to women. In the house, during the household work, she is taking the man's mind off from all the worries which a man carries when there is no peace. I think women do share a lot in all acts of bravery the man performs and commits. So to say that the credit of such bravery and chivalry goes to the menfolk is not true, it goes to the womenfolk who stand behind and provide all the support. *Jihad* is not fought with just a gun or sword in your hand. If I go to war, my wife stays behind and looks after my house and my children.

Dietrich (1997) recognises that the one powerful fix that codifies the ambiguity of women as powerful yet under control, is the symbol of motherhood, which in many ways is cross-cultural. There are a great many variations in the extent of patriarchal control but what has been common all over is that these mothers have been merited, have been valorised by the 'greatness of their sons'. Motherhood has been used by the various educational, political and religious elite in society to establish ideological control over women, to keep them out of education and professions and to reduce them to their reproductive roles. At the same time they were glorified for their ability to sacrifice, and conceptualised as mothers of the nation (Dietrich, 1997: 44–45).

A psychologist working with the Pakistan Army (he had retired to work with General Beg as a member of his research institute) was very helpful with his input during our interview:

> If women have been kept in non-combat positions like doctors and nurses, one way of looking at it is discrimination, but the other way to look at it is protecting the honour of women. That she should not be forced in a situation where embarrassment becomes a way and she cannot even openly say what has happened to her, and yet damage is done.... I personally feel that army culture intends to create conditions where exploitation of women or taking advantage of them are avoided. It is not discrimination, I would call it discretion.

# The Creation of the Good Mother: Pakistan's Military and Electronic Media

*Alpha Bravo Charlie* was a popular Pakistani television serial telecast through 1998 in the period leading to the nuclear tests. It was a private production co-produced by Pakistan's Inter-Services Public Relations (ISPR). With high production values, it was a hit with the audiences, and DVDs of the serial still enjoy good sales.

The woman's domain in Pakistan Television Company plays had been limited for years to that of wife/mother/sister/daughter. The characteristics of the 'good woman' are as follows: self-sacrificing, self-abnegating, virtuous, domesticated, religious, traditional, dependent, conservative in dress, emotional, rational, brave for others, and honest in poverty (Malik and Hussain in Hussain, 1996: 32–34).

The female lead in the ISPR production *Alpha, Bravo, Charlie* was hailed as the 'new woman' who had her own identity, rather than being someone's wife or sister. However, two episodes into the serial, the male protagonist is quick to remark that even though she seems 'modern' and has been educated abroad, she is not as she seems, for she is a good Muslim who prays five times a day. In later episodes the female lead upholds her 'Pakistani-ness' by adopting the veil when she visits her husband's family and declares that she finds the *burqa* very liberating as she can view everyone but no one can see her. Her character is a teacher in a school for special children, and fights with the school administration which treats teaching as a mere 'occupation'. She takes her missionary zeal into the marriage as well, declaring that among her suitors she chose one who was most 'in need' and whose life situation she could change for the better. She also makes it clear that she wanted to fall in love after getting married. After getting married she leaves her job and only goes back to work when she becomes a widow and moves back to her family. So an independent career is shown as something that women should take up when the husband— 'the provider'— is not around. When her husband passes away, an old paramour proposes marriage but she turns him down in favour of someone who has become a quadriplegic in war and has recently been dumped by his fiancé. However, the army officer turns her down declaring that she was a fellow officer's wife, and one does not covet the widow of a colleague and a war hero at that. For the rest of the serial she is portrayed busy raising her son and the drama ends with her son graduating from the Pakistan Military Academy.

# On Divine Divisions

The military's elite anxiety regarding women's entry in Pakistan's military was echoed by their counterparts among the religious right. The former Amir of the Jamat-i-Islami (Chaudhry Tufail) declared:

> Women have mostly been instructed to nurse. When there is a total war, a *nafeer awam* (national call) and everyone is commanded to participate, then women too can come out to fight without taking the permission from their menfolk... it goes to women's courage that they manage the house when the men are away. And as they cannot leave the housework, they cannot participate in combat. But they will receive the reward for this labour. They will receive the same level of *sawab* (religious merit) for their work. You see not everyone participates in the same profession. In wars it's the same. Not everyone becomes the general or the commander, does he? It is according to his capabilities. God has not created men and women equal to each other. For women is the task of reproduction, of taking care of the education of the young, to take up the responsibilities of the house. Even in current times the responsibilities are not equal. God has himself made such divisions among men and women.

Hence the emphasis is on the view that if there are any objections to this then their fight is not with the Pakistani military or with their particular sect but with God himself, that these were divinely sanctioned gender divisions of labour.

The year 2006 was therefore remarkable for a reason. At the time the religious right had broken off ranks with the Pakistani state and in particular Pakistan's military (though this could be a moot point for at the time the Head of State, President Musharraf, was a serving army officer). Their relationship had cooled off in the wake of the Musharraf regime's support of the Coalition war effort. The post-11 September world had asked for Pakistan's government to reign in the radicals and stop supporting their jihadist effort, and for all purposes President Musharraf was complying. So in 2006, as an attempt to secure the Pakistani state's secular credentials, female cadets performed the prestigious duty of guard of honour at Jinnah's tomb on the founding father's birth anniversary. The year also marked a Sikh officer graduating from the Pakistan Military Academy—he performed duties along with the female cadets at Jinnah's tomb. There were announcements in the media that the coming year would see female-only regiments graduating from the Pakistan Military Academy in Kakul. Do bear in mind that it was a military regime and the particular nexus it had formed with Pakistan's religious right in the 1970s had used women as a symbol of their particular project. From the late seventies on, General Zia's regime used a narrow reading of Islam and societal values to curtail Pakistani women's personal liberties and social mobility. When the same military wanted to make a show of breaking off ranks with the religious right and pursuing a policy of 'enlightened moderation', it used the Pakistani woman (and this time one in army uniform) as a powerful symbol.

In 2010 I had contacted the ISPR offices for details on this development. They responded with the following information:

> In Pakistan Army women joined as doctors and nurses way back since 1947. If u are asking women officers other than medical corps yes, they joined army on 11 november 2006 and passed out from Pakistan military academy on 14 april 2007. This process still continues and other details are with you.
>
> *Total lady officers in Pakistan army are 2949. the breakdown is as following*
>
> *doctors 576 and 2230 in the nursing service*
>
> *143 on other branches of the army.*
>
> Women cadets also performed guard duties at the moselium of Quaid on 25 dec 2006. They are participating as part of their training in routine military exercise and firing various weapons. (Atique Rehman, email communication, 26 April 2010)

Clearly a case of 'The Military Giveth and the Military Taketh Away'.

Khattak (2010) has a very interesting take on this issue; she identifies the Pakistani army's moves to integrate women and the developments in the last five years as 'the look good syndrome' (Box 5.1).

However, the years 2006 and 2007 marked twin developments for both the friends turned foe; the paths of the (now perceived as) diametrically opposite were overlapping and the warring twain did meet. Ironically the same time as when the image of the Pakistani woman, a woman dressed in khaki at that, was employed to signify the changed direction of the Pakistani state, the Red Mosque female cadre was also readying itself. In their case the Jamia Hafsa student was shown as a symbol of the final step, when the *nafeer aam* (all out call to arms) was about to be sent and when even 'meek'(read good) women were asked to step out of the security of the *chardevari* (four walls). Describing the state of Pakistan as one where Islam lay in dire peril, the Jamia Hafsa students declared that they had no choice but to leave the sanctity of their educational institutions to protect their seminary and other mosques in Islamabad.

**Box 5.1**

*The 'Look Good' Syndrome: Women's Commission in the Pakistan Military as a Foreign Policy Explanation*

[A]cceptance in the international arena. Although civilian regimes also violate human rights and may adopt anti-people policies, military regimes are under comparatively more pressure to build their international image by making symbolic gestures toward women's and minority rights. These moves are thus viewed as being closely tied to foreign policy.

(With women's) greater awareness of their rights and are articulate in protesting and resisting military dictatorship, which has become harder to impose in its tyrannical form. To make such rule palatable, the military introduces some policies that make its acceptance as a fair and democratic force compelling. This strategy is especially helpful to the military as it puts the civilian regime that it has replaced appear undemocratic and unjust. In contrast, the military appears to be a champion of the marginalised thus diluting the issues as well as creating distrust of popularly elected governments.

This explanation is based on the conception that realpolitik and pragmatism inform the military's moves. Given that women are a large untapped political constituency, the military tries to win their support through offering limited political change. Such change is not restricted to the political realm alone; it is extended to other areas as well to create a positive image for the armed forces. For instance, when employment with the armed forces was opened up for women candidates under equal opportunity, it meant that they would be eligible to be recruited as commissioned officers and not be restricted to being doctors and nurses in the armed forces. Even with regard to the latter, the military advertised and projected the positive image of women when Dr Shahida Malik was promoted to the rank of a General in the Pakistan military in 2002. Similarly, women are now allowed to enrol in the Pakistan Airforce aerospace, engineering and fight pilot programs. Many analysts assert that by taking such steps the military as a whole believed that it was projecting a progressive and liberal image within and outside the country.

From all appearances one can infer that the military is comfortable with the presence of women; however, when this group begins to assert itself and insists that its demands be met, the picture changes. Ultimately, they need to fit in with cultural practices, not bring about drastic change into their lives. If change needs to be incremental while retrogressive attitudes are indirectly encouraged, it only indicates that the military is comfortable with the presence of women but not their demands. Ultimately, they need to be camp followers, much like their sisters living in the cantonments. That women have proved to be more politically astute in the long run is a tribute to women than to the military that propped them (SDPI, 2005).

*Source*: http://www.democracy-asia.org/casestudies_studies_saba_gul_khattak_ p2.htm Accessed 19 November 2010.

Other parties from the religious right wing had provided tacit support to the feminisation of the Red Mosque movement, however, they were also deriding in public that the Pakistani army had resorted to deploying women to defend the Pakistani state. I believe what they found objectionable was that a female Kakul graduate was seen as having social mobility; serving the state seemed like a personal life choice and one that was taken as a step towards self-empowerment. It was not the 'final step' when poor defenceless women have to resort to the shame of stepping out of the *chardevari* to defend a home in peril.

Khawar Mumtaz of Shirkat Gah (a research institute working on women living under Islamic laws) has narrated elsewhere how after the creation of Pakistan there were efforts to start the National Voluntary Guards where 'women guards' would be given some military training in return for a monthly stipend. There was a lot of hue and cry as the religious leaders could not tolerate women marching like soldiers. There were religious edicts against women 'parading with their heads uncovered and bosoms exposed'. They protested that these women would be staring into men's eyes and would have no shame and dignity. During the same time, some women's social service groups came into being as well. They did not fare badly as the women working in these were viewed as doing what was 'their kind of work.' These women did community work in a voluntary capacity without any salary. In contrast, the 'women guards' were getting remuneration for their services, which would have given them some degree of economic freedom. This did not go down well with the Pakistani public. Three decades later, in 1971, Pakistan was faced with a tumultuous state of events. The country fought a bitter battle with India, and saw its eastern wing separating to form the independent country of Bangladesh. However, even at this stage, or perhaps particularly at this stage when they feared that the chaos of civil war may change how gender relations were controlled in the country, the religious elite defined the role of women in national reconstruction as follows:

Since participating in person in war or outdoor work is not incumbent on women, it may be concluded that they will get 700,000 coins in reward for each coin given. [I assume here the Maulana is referring to women giving charity as part of the war effort.] Same also about time, energy and skill spent.

Now that the war is over, the duties of women are not so much in the battlefields as these are in the hospitals, help-centres, camps for the bomb-stricken, etc. What most demands their particular attention is the care and rehabilitation of the family members left by our soldiers, many of whom are now in East Pakistan. It is the education of their sons, marriage of their daughters and general care of their wives and mothers and sisters. Nature has given special gifts to women for the service of nursing. According to the dictates of Islam, even giving encouragement or inspiration, giving comforting and grief-effacing talk, smiling and making others smile, has been listed as Jehad. Praying for the sick and the dying, for the needy and the destitute, for the success of those engaged in national reconstruction—all those also constitute Jehad, so apt for women. Let our women folk take to the habit of regularly offering Salat and make their men folk do the same (Maulana Asadul Qadri, in Dawn, 7 January 1972, p. 4).

That our religious elite are fond of impressing upon women the effac-ing power of prayer after every calamity has not lost its charm. Pakistani women were asked to pray over the loss of their nation in 1971. In 2006 again local MMA representatives in NWFP chastised women asking for justice after the sexual and communal violence in the region to just 'pray over it'. They fail to realise that perhaps Pakistani women might be get-ting tired of praying after every crisis and desire a more proactive role.

Keeping in mind the chauvinistic mindset of the Pakistani military, one couldn't help wonder about the scenario when the Prime Minister of Pakistan happened to be a woman. Pakistan's problematic civil-military relations aside, there were reports that the military high command were uncomfortable with the Prime Minister visiting the General Headquarters, for in such a situation they would have to salute her. Matters came to a head at the Joint Services Parade on 23 March 1989, as she was sure to be present at the dais to take the salute. When I inquired of the Chief of Army Staff (General Beg) about the issue, he explained:

The Joint Services Parade is meant for the President. So we are saluting the President. The Prime Minister is present there and stands by the President on the dais... we gave her (Benazir Bhutto) all the respect that was due to her. Whenever she was in her individual capacity, there was no hesitation giving her a guard of honour.

An officer who was a member of the military top brass at the time was more candid when he said to me, 'Yes, we did salute her but you have to understand that the elation was not there in the heart of the soldier.'

If I look back now to the period of my life when I (like many young women of my generation) was enamoured by the thought of a life in the military, I wonder whether I would have been as enthusiastic if I had known of the misogyny that lurked within. Though even at that time the Pakistani military had a track record of carrying out a coup in every decade of the nation's existence, but we still continued to carry an image of the military officer as one who was polished and disciplined with no inclination to delve in the murky world of politics and corruption (as civilians are wont to do). And though the Pakistani military, when I was growing up, displayed the self-righteous attitude (like militaries elsewhere) of knowing best how social and gender relations should be organised—for example, in the 1980s, the Director of Education for Federal Government Colleges got instructions from the General Headquarters (of the Pakistan Army) to make the *chadar* a part of the uniform for the girl students[6]—we continued to believe that a career in the military would be a space where we could rise beyond our gender. It was a living contradiction that though certain personalities in the Pakistani military put considerable stock in its Islamic credentials and ability to control the decorum of the Pakistani woman in public, at the same time the institution itself wanted to keep its image as a secular and professional organisation untainted by religious rituals and symbols. This led to episodes such as the following (which was shared with me by Maulana A. Saleemi, the former *amir* (head) of the *Jamat-i-Islami* in a personal interview in 1999):

> In the times of General Zia, all the doctors had to serve some time attached with a military unit. There was one female medical student who was a member of the student wing of the Jamat-i-Islami. When she was sent to the military unit, the commanding officers told her that she could not take the veil as it was against military policy. Obviously she complained and we requested President Zia to look into the matter. She was exempted from military duty for the military feared that if she is allowed to take the veil then other girls would be encouraged as well.

However, a decade after this interview (and two decades after the 'waiver' narrated in the incident above), one read of women gaining membership to what had been a traditionally male bastion—the Pakistani army. One read accolades in the newspaper of how proud Pakistani women marched in separate contingents at the passing out ceremony at Kakul and that they were led by a young girl in a *burqa*. I have yet to understand whether this

---

[6] As a student in a Federal Government college administered by the Pakistan Army, I had to sign a pledge that makeup/cosmetics are contraband, the *chadar* is an integral part of my uniform, and I will 'resist' (sic) from political conversation. All college students were required to sign such a pledge if they wanted admission to a Federal Government college. That this episode was followed by a four-year charade as young girls played their own 'citizen politics' by stuffing their *chadar* in school bags to take out on a day when the kindly college watchman would warn us of a 'surprise raid' is another story. Suffice to say I grew up believing a woman's chastity lies in her school bag.

was an instance of the Pakistani military high command being able to accommodate the crossover performances of the new Pakistani woman, or that the Pakistani military had a new demography, one that did not find the *burqa*/veil alien to its institution.

## Texts of War: Militarism and Gender Identity in Pakistan

We return to May 1998. Pakistan conducts nuclear tests. I revisit this particular moment in Pakistan's history as it has formed the 'habitus' for the present generation of Pakistanis. These are the young people that one witnesses eagerly adopting the language of violence—whether it is the Red Mosque contingent which is out there in the public domain or those among the country's young that provide tacit support to militarism in South Asia. The events of the summer of 1998, and the discourse produced and circulated at the time to a great extent formed their particular mindsets, moulded their receptivity towards militaristic values, and contributed to the passion with which they embraced certain life choices.

A year later when I started my project of archiving national attitudes towards the nuclear tests, I began by speaking to school children. These were Pakistani students aged between 13 and 16 years. They belonged to upper-middle- and middle-class families and studied in English medium schools. The interviews were conducted in the port city of Karachi. My research questions at the time were regarding their attitude towards the nuclear tests. However, during the course of the interview they shared with me how they understood the images of valour that were being disseminated via the educational curriculum and popular media, their perceptions regarding gender roles and career expectations. For instance, the young men who were interviewed were quite emphatic in their idolisation of the military as a career choice.

The army is so disciplined, punctual, brave.

Gallant life, courageous job, the officers are so disciplined. They are heroes. It is an ideal job for men to be in the military, whether it is Army, Navy or Air Force.

Benefits attract us. We watch PTV dramas about them, so idolise it—love tanks and rifles, firing in the air.

The young women interviewees echoed these statements, however, their responses reflected that they were aware of the limits to such aspirations.

Forces are the best way to serve the country. It is a separate issue that they don't allow the women to defend the country. It's only the forces that protect the country. What we can do is not the same as defending it.

I really like the army and its discipline. I like their lifestyle and their uniform. I admire it a lot. I know I cannot join it; maybe I can marry an officer.

The students confessed that they could not recollect any reference to famous women in Pakistani history and that all the heroes in their Pakistan Studies textbooks were the male recipients of the military gallantry award *Nishan-i-Haider*. When asked what made them feel secure and confident, the boys declared that their idea of security was to have a gun, whereas for the girls their (moral) character and whether they took the veil or not was more important. One of the young women interviewees shared with me how she had vowed to her brothers that she would become a martyr (in the cause of Islam) and gain religious merit until she was 'corrected' by her peers in school that female *shaheed* (martyrs) have half the status of a male so she should give up competing with her brothers.

What also stayed with me was the young adult interviewees' earnest belief that some amount of physical violence is necessary to keep children on their toes. They believed that most children can only understand the language of violence. Their debate over corporal punishment exhibited the 'common sense' notions that young Pakistanis have about their community, and their 'inherited' perceptions regarding the power of the stick over dialogue. One could study their statement as a case study of Cohen's theories regarding 'perversions of inheritance'. Cohen (1988) elaborates on 'racist common sense' notions in school children about themselves and others, and how these perceptions are sensitive to articulations of race, sex, ethnicity, age and other constructions (Cohen, 1988).

As part of this project I was also exposed to the social texts of the time, and was reminded that when nationalism regenerates (and in the case of Pakistan the religio-military nexus did so with great force), a process of othering will also usher in the feminisation of the other, and not in very complimentary terms. So during the 1965 Indo-Pak war, for instance, there were sly digs at the Indian Prime Minister (PM Lal Bahadur Shastri) regarding his height; there were war songs where he was declared a devotee of the flute-playing Lord Krishna: *Jan Diyo Tussi Murli Bajaane Wale Ho* and *Maharaj Khel Diye Bandooq De Nal Jang Khed Nahee Zananiya*

*Dee* (war is not a game effeminates play). In 1971 Pakistani newspapers ridiculed the Indian Prime Minister Indira Gandhi as a 'poor orphan girl given to telling vicious lies'. This fits in with Saigol's (1995) thesis that the hero in most knowledge constructions in Pakistan is brave, valiant and morally superior with positive and 'masculine characteristics', whereas the 'other' is portrayed as fickle, inconsistent, and treacherous (the same characteristics which are used for women in Pakistan's social texts). So, underlying the hero/villain theme is the masculine/feminine conscious-ness of the other.

In an interview conducted with Dr Saigol, she explained to me:

I looked at social studies textbooks from grade three onwards to grade eight. I looked at the government, mainly Punjab Text Book Board, social studies textbooks... and page after page is filled with Two Nation Theory, which is basically analysed as Pakistani nationalism. And it is replete with gendered constructs, ideas of how the representation of Hindus and enemy as weak, as vegetable eating, feminised... feminising the enemy as those who cannot fight, those who attacked us in the middle of the night, therefore, how can they be brave? And how we always defeated them, and they were the ones who always started the war. That's interesting, how when they are constructed as weak enemies, they are feminised, in how we can beat them easily and one of us is equal to ten of them... binary oppositional terms that are dropped off... complete opposites of each other, there is absolutely nothing overlapping in them, they are weak, we are strong, they are cruel, we are kind. This was to me a very gendered look in terms of binary oppositions.

The 1998 nuclear tests were a particular episode in South Asia's history when all the paranoia, fanaticism, hostility and banal nationalism created and nurtured by the two countries came together in perfect harmony. This ranged from the ridiculous as in the cartoon strips appearing in the Pakistani and Indian media—nuclear tests proving to be a 'viagra' for the allegedly 'impotent' Indian nation and one of the Indian PM lighting up a nuclear warhead as a cigar asking the world leaders to finally talk to him 'man to man'. In Pakistan, following the Indian tests there was obviously a great deal of flurry as the Indians had pre-empted them in conducting the nuclear tests. The print media through editorials and other write-ups pressed upon the Pakistan government to conduct the tests as well. There was a cartoon strip in the Urdu language daily *Jang* (18 May 1998) showing an Indian (the Brahmin's pigtail was there to identify him as a Hindu) stripping in front of the American President who has covered his eyes in dismay to depict how the Indians flaunted their nuclear tests despite strict American surveillance. The cartoon is captioned '*Hindu baniye ney dhoti khol dee*' (the Indian shopkeeper flashes himself). The editorial for the day was built around the theme of this cartoon striving to drive the message closer home:

> If we have continued to cover ourselves (as in kept our nuclear programme discreet), it does not mean that our manhood is in doubt. The power that we have is there, we have that capability down there, it's there. We have it by the Grace of God...now if we were to become peace supporters should we be singing sweet songs and lullabies and pat children's cheeks to go to sleep (*Jang,* 18 May 1998).

The Freudian references to nuclear capabilities and manhood aside, it was hard to overlook the feminisation of peace and derision towards what are seen as female traits.

The same editorial page had also prominently displayed a *Hadith* that valorised exhibiting *ghairat*—male pride.

> Hazrat Saad bin Abi Waqas told the Holy Prophet that if I see my wife talking to a man who is a stranger for her, I will finish her off with a sword. The Holy Prophet announced that you people may question Hazrat Saad's *ghairat* as strange. By God, I am more *ghairatmand* than Saad, and Allah is more *ghairatmand* than me. That man is a big *beyghairat* who can tolerate shamelessness in his own house (*Sahee Bukhari Hadis*).

This re-emphasised the not-so-subtle references to defending Pakistan's honour by conducting nuclear tests. By this stage it had become a task sanctified by a personality no less than the Holy Prophet. How long could a valiant Pakistani view the motherland at the mercy of a rapacious neighbour?

The references to defending the nation's *ghairat* were raised by the political elite as well. The 23 May 1998 issue of *Jang* had a photograph of a determined Chief Minister of Punjab with the tagline, 'The Punjab CM Shahbaz Sharif declared India has challenged our *ghairat.*'

> Religious groups constantly urging Sharif (the Prime Minister) to be a real 'man' and explode the nuclear bomb because it is a matter of national pride. Anyone familiar with the feminist discourse would interpret Pakistan's test as a petty pursuit of masculine muscle flexing (Foqia Sadiq Khan, *The News,* 29 May 1998).

The government of Pakistan continued to be pressured to conduct the tests employing highly gendered terms: 'Why this silence? I fear they are busy counting the money they received from selling our mother? It is famous about Pakistanis that they will sell their mothers for a few dollars' (Abdul Qadir Hasan in *Jang*, 24 May 1998).

The editorial of the same resource person was punctuated with the following terms in the period immediately after the nuclear tests of 28 May.

The well-off can be prostitutes and their pimps as well but dignity is only given to those whom He (God) wants. Those who were opposing the tests because of some principles, they are welcome to stay here. But those who were opposing it because they feared the loss of their daily bread, their destination should be a prostitute's *kotha*. Spare these the upright and honourable country, as this country is not for them (Abdul Qadir Hasan, *Jang,* 30 May 1998).

Others reiterated the theme.

*Traders Association President Muhammad Imtiaz:*

I feel a sense of relief. There was no other decision that Pakistan could take. When you push a man against the wall, he has no option but to fight back and defend himself (*News*, 29 May 1998).

*Ulema should prepare nation for challenges: President Tarar*

Speaking to a 15-member delegation calling on him at Aiwan-e-Sadar, President Tarar said that ulema could play an important role in molding public opinion adding that 'we must make it clear to all those having nefarious designs towards Pakistan that this nation is capable of protecting its honour and dignity. We stand like an iron wall to protect our national honor' (*News*, 6 June 1998).

The construction of divine sanction for the nuclear tests could be gauged by the images of the thanksgiving prayers being offered on the Friday following the nuclear tests in Pakistan's major mosque (Faisal Mosque). The photographs were carried on the front pages of all national dailies and video footage was telecast as part of the news bulletin on national television. Some of the clergy declared the Comprehensive Test Ban Treaty as against the spirit of the Holy Quran as it would violate Verse 60 of Surah Anfal of Holy Quran which enjoins the Muslims to keep the war horses ready for the enemy (*Friday Times*, 9–15 July 1999).

The media also shared images of men marching in public rallies and firing in the air. The editorial pages of *Jang* had a photo of workers of the Muslim League Youth Wing participating in a rally and posing with Kalashnikovs. 'Nawaz Sharif has proven with the blasts that Pakistan is a land of *ghazis, ghairatmand, janbaz, jan nisar* (conquerors in battle, honourable and courageous men willing to sacrifice their lives) (*Jang,* 30 May 1998). In direct contrast the women were shown veiled with the caption accompanying their photograph reading: 'Pakistan Muslim League Women Wing's procession where they thank the government for exhibiting its *ghairat* (honour, pride) in protecting them' (*Jang* 29 May 1998).

Qadeer Khan, the scientist responsible for the tests, was portrayed as a warrior hero and christened 'the father of the space and missile programme' (*Jang*, 23 May 1998). None other than the President of Pakistan in his address to the nation declared: 'He (Qadeer) is the one the Poet of the East (*Iqbal*) declared *mard-i-momin* (the ideal Muslim man), he is the renowned *sapoot* (male progeny) and true son of Pakistan' (*Jang*, 13 May 1998).

There were posters and car stickers of Qadeer with the caption 'Soldier of Islam' everywhere in the aftermath of the tests. In the press there were articles praising him for being a good Muslim. In fact the good Muslim theme was liberally used for all the scientists associated with the tests. The public was told about how the scientists recited the Quranic prayer before pressing the button, about how after the explosion they immediately prostrated before God, about how the air vibrated with the calls of *Allah Akbar* (Allah is Great).

The nuclear tests conducted by India also threw up the particular conundrum of Abdul Kalam—the scientist responsible for the Indian nuclear programme was an Indian Muslim. Pakistan's media, which usually drums up public sympathy around the cause of the Indian Muslim's deplorable condition, was caught in a dilemma. They got around this issue by doubting the religious commitment of a certain section of the Indian Muslims and that too in terms that reinforced our patriarchal mindsets and the myopic perceptions about inter-communal relationships.

**Sajjad Anwar:** *Jawan mardee* (gallantry, chivalry), *zinda dilli* (large heartedness), *dau tauk bahadri* (bravery) have become a legend of the past for the Indian Muslims (*Jang*, 18 May 1998).

**Saleh Zafir:** Muslims are taunted in India and if some Muslim is at a high post in India it is not because of his skill or wisdom but definitely because he has some relationship with a big Hindu family... they have 'sold' their girls to the Hindus. Someone's sister is in a Hindu's house or someone's daughter is married to a Hindu (*Jang*, 18 May 1998).

**Box 5.2**

*May 1998 also brought a friendly blast from the past as war songs from the 1960s were recycled*

---

**Song: *Jang Khed Nahee Zananiya Dee* (War Is Not A Game Effeminates Play)**
**Artist: Rasheed Anwar**
**Year: 1965**

*Maharaj Khediye Talwar diye*
*Jang Khed Nahee Hondee Zananiya Dee*
*Asee Puttar Punjab Dey Pani-ya Dey*
*Asee Nasal Mehmood Dey Ghazia Dey*
*Doodh Peetey Maa Pathania Dey*
(Kings play with swords
War is not a game for effeminates
We are the sons of Punjab's rivers
The descendants of Mahmud and conquerors
We have had the milk of Pathan mothers.)

To this was added a ditty penned by Raees Amrohvi and published in *Jang*.

**Jang, 18 May 1998, Raees Amrohvi**
*Sirf Uljahn May Tera Pak Padosee Hi Nahee*
*Cheen o Nepal Ko Hai Aur Bhee Uljhan Tujh Se*
*Hum Hi Do Chaar Muhalley Mey Nahee Shikwa Tera*
*Har Parosee Ko Shikayat Hai Paddosan Tujh Sey*

A nagging female neighbour, India, troubling the very masculine, sober neighbourhood, amity of China, Nepal and Pakistan.

*Source*: Author.

---

In war songs popular in Pakistan (see Box 5.2), the female voice is always shown as inciting the man to save her, her honour, her dignity, or she appears as an extension of the patriarchy-property nexus in the form of the 'good woman' who is willing to sacrifice the menfolk for the war effort. Rahman has described verbal behaviour as part of socialisation. One learns one's role in life, including one's place in the power structure from the way one speaks or is spoken to (Rahman, 1998: 1). If this is true, the future does not bode well for young Pakistanis who grow up listening to the following metaphors being used to describe them in nationalist songs. For instance the hero is praised in terms such as: *mard-i-mujahid* (warrior hero), *shujaat* (bravery), *jawan mardi* (gallantry), *jyala* (headstrong), *daleyr* (courageous), *sarfaroshi* (willing to sacrifice his life in the cause), *mader-e-watan kay aabroo kay muhafiz* (guardian of the chastity of the mother/land), *jurrat* (courage), *sheyr-i-bahadur* (lion hearted), and *mardangee* (manliness). Women however have to contend with highly gendered terms that put a premium on the good Pakistani woman playing at modesty and chastity: *shama-i-aman* (lamps of peace), *tan pak* (pure bodies), *deys ki izzat* (nation's honour), *aabroo* (chastity), *paykar-i-haya* (embodiment of modesty), and *varee jaana* (unrestrained emotions of love).

Pakistan's educationists whom one assumed might have employed a language of ethics were equally virulent. 'It is a symbol of power and exhibiting your manhood,' declared the head of the department of Urdu, Punjab University, Lahore to me. He further added,

> I can quote Shehzad Ahmed, a colleague and an intellectual who said that if there is any change in the pre- and post-28 May 1998 period, it is that the writer's community spirit and morale received a boost and their identity was defined. Writers, poets may write of peace but there are more instances of war material. Byron delivered *ghairat* to his people by writing that if we don't rise to the occasion then the damsels with black eyes will suckle slaves…that the coming generation will be slaves.

Though a significant number of stakeholders I interviewed for the research project provided wholehearted support to violence as a political weapon, and it was also evident that the print and electronic media were active participants in supporting the project (and quelling dissenting voices), it was heartening to see that there were still some dissenting voices (albeit marginalised) that criticised militarism developing into a national project.

There were groups in Pakistan who had been pressing upon the government to follow a policy of restraint and to refrain from conducting nuclear tests. They made a case for disarmament, and questioned whether the tests could resolve Pakistan's real problems such as safety from police brutality, corruption, economic violence, bad development policies, and freedom from deaths caused by possible disease and radiation the tests would usher. These groups heavily criticised state discourse, print media and policymakers for using highly psychosexual metaphors while promoting the cause of the nuclear tests.

> These were couched in terms of taking over, penetration, very phallic, of proving our manhood, virility and strength, the ability to hit out. All were sort of conflated. There was a very monolithic interpretation of courage, in terms of power to attack, defeat, take over, demolish. Courage in terms of the ability to sacrifice or the ability to remain silent, that has gradually disappeared from the lexicon. In the wake of the nuclearisation, one felt

that society was getting more violent, the aggressive male in the public space. In the bazaar, men are getting more aggressive, one feels there are more instances of sexual aggression, and demonstrations of violence are on rise (Khawar Mumtaz in a personal interview with me).

Could we then blame the Indian politician nee rabble rouser Bal Thackeray for declaring that Indians should celebrate 'not being eunuchs any more'.

India should adopt a tit for tat policy. We need real bombs and not diwali crackers to take on neighbors such as Pakistan and China. We had to prove that we are not eunuchs. Now we are a more powerful nation (*Pioneer*, 12 May 1999).

Mr Thackeray had to contend with the former Pakistani Foreign Minister Sardar Assef Ali who too was debating delivering a 'castrating reply to the Indians'.

For one we behold the masculinisation of mindsets in the region. Fearing the thesis of biological determinism (that women can only be the pacifist voice in society rather than being aggressive like men), a significant section of women in South Asia (especially those in senior positions in the bureaucracy) act as agents of the state. The 'tougher' they are seen in the masculinist sense and supporting militarism, the higher they believe they can reach when it comes to the echelons of power. Therefore, I was not surprised when certain female academics and media personalities pointed out that it was unfair when people questioned their being pro-nuclear.

I think nuclear weapons are efficient weapons and if one country feels they are rational to use, why shouldn't the rest of the world have the same option, and my being a woman has nothing to do with it or my being a man or my being a Pakistani in the way I look at it.

Dr Shireen Mazari, a senior defence analyst and media personality was very candid:

If you don't like war, if you are cowardly, then it suddenly means that you are a feminist. *O tau zanani hai* (she is a woman after all), she will not fight. This is a wrong image of women also. For me women are no less aggressive, or less competitive, or less prone to using violence given half an opportunity. I don't buy it at all…women have themselves chosen to become subjugated to male dominance. It is not because religion and culture has decreed that. It is not that they were ignored. It is not denying the fact that in most cultures men have ruled, because women have let them rule.[7]

# Conclusion

Pakistan's national idea has involved the propagation of myths—myth of a glorious past, of an imagined community, of demon enemies, of what the 'good men' and 'good women' of the state can do or not do. Discourses continue to valorise a belligerent rather than a more rational and pacifist attitude towards each other. As critics in both Pakistan and India point out, in order to justify the militaristic agenda of the two governments (Pakistan and India), the people are likely to be fed with images of militaristic heroism. The myths are present within the educational discourse where knowledge is constructed to suit the powers that be. They continue with the media where there are strict images and roles for the men and women of the state. The religious elite who one would have expected to employ a language of ethics have actively incited the public with inflammatory speeches. One should also keep in mind that there is no separation of the church and state in Pakistan; members of the religious elite happen to be members of parliament as well. Therefore, they can easily quell any opposition to the militaristic project by proclaiming eternal damnation for anyone challenging the status quo and also assure that no legislation is passed that may attempt to do so. With Pakistan's crisis of governance and the military establishment running a state within a state, it is very difficult for anyone to challenge their supremacy within parliament as well. With the executive and legislature towing the line, it is only rarely that the judiciary has challenged their writ and in any exercises where it has dared to defy the military (case in point the 2008 lawyers' movement that took up the question of kidnappings by military personnel) the movement soon changed direction. As long as Pakistan's citizens regard the valorisation of militaristic values as natural, it is impossible to envision a society where an alternative discourse can develop.

---

[7] Personal interview, 28 March 1999.

# 6

# Our Lady of Lal Masjid

In the smouldering remains of the Lal Masjid in 2007 rose the spectre of Pakistan's difficult tomorrows. One has to investigate what transpired at the site all those years ago to comprehend the crisis that engulfs Pakistan today.

The then Pakistani President, who also happened to be the Chief of Armed Services (COAS) and who had taken upon himself the nomenclature 'Pakistan's Chief Executive', Pervez Musharraf has always maintained that Operation Silence was a course of action forced upon him by a belligerent Lal Masjid administration. While a concerned Pakistani civil society had implored of the government to tackle the menace of a 'state within a state' that Lal Masjid posed (ironically this continues even today with the current avatar of the Lal Masjid and its administration), but even the most strident of the infamous mosque's opponents had baulked at the state-sponsored violence unleashed during the fateful week in early July 2007. After the operation was over, with the dead buried and the mosque repaired, many of us viewed the flickering images on our TV screens of a Friday congregation walking through the mosque with great sorrow. I mention sorrow as those were some heart-rending moments when former students and members of the prayer body broke down in tears and kissed the walls of the mosque. We still struggle to find words to articulate best our dilemma. The Pakistani nation had grieved at the time and even now continues to bring up the sheer waste of human lives during Operation Silence. I too could understand the anguish of the gathered students and congregation; this was after all their alma mater and their misery was genuine. However, at the time I was also aware and continue to acknowledge (like many others in Pakistan) how vehemently opposed we are to the world-view of Lal Masjid and its patrons. So you could not help but shudder at the premonition of the dark days to come as the Friday congregation clambered to repaint the mosque walls in the defiant red of its former glory.[1] In the following pages I chart the trajectory of the actors of the Jamia Hafsa (the seminary affiliated with the Lal Masjid and its benefactors), as they built a constituency for their socio-political movement. Despite the government cracking down on their official website and publications, or perhaps because of this censorship, their discourse appeared in a variety of ways that might have not been used earlier. Emulating the very same urban Pakistani and his/her consumption of the computer-generated world that they had condemned in the past, the seminary and its well-wishers replicated Jamia Hafsa and the Lal Masjid in cyber space. During the course of my project I have come across file-sharing websites that host photographs, scanned images of their publications and daily journals. Others like youtube.com have videos of the infamous *Shariah ya Jihad* conference and odes to the Lal Masjid martyrs. I have come across 'web logs' that give updates regarding Maulana Aziz and his wife Umme Hassan who survived the Red Mosque operation. And concerned citizens in the country have drawn attention to CDs containing disturbing eyewitness accounts of the siege that circulate, despite a ban imposed on them. In the following pages I will identify the 'war of words' originating from the Lal Masjid and how the protagonists of the uprising chronicle their own version of the events of Operation Silence.

The testimonies of Operation Silence survivors pinpoint to the Pakistani government's policies in the post-2001 world as the first breach of trust they experienced, with 19 July 2005 marked as a black day in the seminary's history. On this day a police raid was conducted at the Jamia Hafsa, their students were arrested and female students baton-charged. The Jamia Hafsa website (jamiahafsa.org) contains scanned images of newspaper reports that describe the incident and published images of the injured students being treated in hospital (accessed 21 August 2009). This is followed by a temporary lull when according to Umme Hassan 'they went back to the business of study'. The first rumblings to shatter this temporary peace appear with the emergence of a list of mosques to be removed by Islamabad's Capital Development Authorities (CDA) as part of an urban development project.[2] The students occupy the ill-fated

---

[1] The mosque had been whitewashed by the city administration before 'returning' it to the mosque patrons. It was painted a defiant red by the patrons, repainted again by the authorities, and the paint wars continue.

[2] The mosques had been built on government land including areas in the Green Belt where any kind of built construction was forbidden by the town planners. At times these plots were

Children's Library, but in the course of a month this action unravels into kidnappings, harassment of video shop owners and barbers in the neighbourhood of the Lal Masjid, and alleged threats to female drivers and women who did not observe *purdah* in the vicinity of the mosque. In brief, the administration and students of the Lal Masjid very cleverly employed the strategy of brinkmanship in order to push the government's hand and to stop CDA from continuing with their anti-encroachment drive. It remains to be seen whether the gruesome end was part of their calculations (that is students being held hostages and losing their lives was the price they were willing to pay in order to create sympathy for their cause and build a new constituency among Pakistan's youth which was already dissatisfied with government policies) or whether matters just spiralled out of their control (Image 6.1).

## Enter the Red Mosque

Zafar Abbas, writing in the English language daily, *Dawn*, narrates the activities of the Red Mosque's women's wing of the early days.

> Hundreds of *burqa*-clad and baton-wielding students, occupied a children's library in the federal capital in January. Now both the men's and women's wings of this emerging brand of the Pakistani Taliban have started to impose new rules of morality by forcibly shutting down video and music shops in Islamabad, and by abducting women whom they believe are engaged in immoral activities. But who are these people, and why are the government and the security services finding it so hard to enforce the rule of law? Is it that the government really wants to avoid bloodshed because hundreds, if not thousands, of women are part of this violent brigade? Or is it a reflection of some kind of infighting in the establishment where one faction has a soft corner for their former Islamic allies? (*Dawn*, 31 March 2007)

Pakistan's tricky relationship with its *madrassahs* is reflective of the crisis of governance that has befallen the state. In Pakistan the growth of militaristic values and rise in the numbers of non-state actors eager to usurp a democratic and secular political process has led to a world-view

---

'gifted' illegally by sympathisers in previous regimes. On their part the Capital Development Authority and other officials did try to bring in sayings of the Holy Prophet, edicts that justified removal of mosques as part of public work.

**Image 6.1**

*Jamia Hafsa students taking to Islamabad roads, 2007*

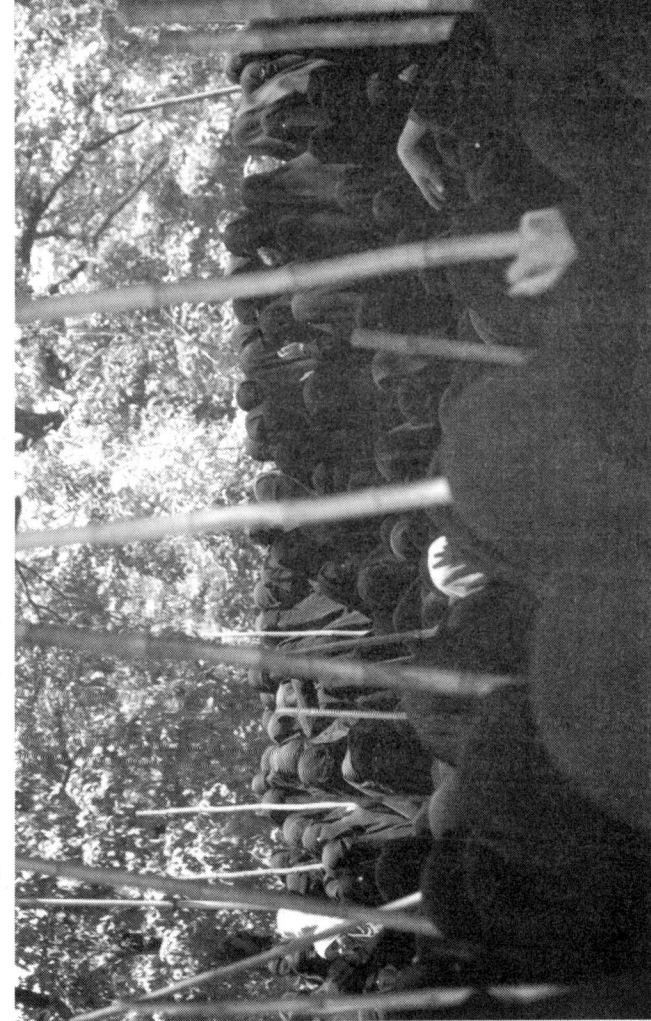

*Source:* Tanveer Shehzad.

justifying violence in the name of personal faith. With the paucity of debate and the state brutally repressing dissent—it was ironic that it was primarily the problematic religious lobby that managed to mount a credible challenge against the Pakistani state regarding its crisis of legitimacy. These groups provide a forum to critique the government's political policies and challenge global forces perceived by them as 'out to get' Pakistan. *Madrassah* groups and their benefactors declare their agenda of ushering in social justice and reform in Pakistan. 'We want our rulers to be honest people'—they claim in interviews, perhaps a thought shared by many silent spectators in Pakistan who now lean towards the far-right and militant groups, believing that other groups have abandoned them. Abdul Rashid Ghazi, the patron of the problematic Red Mosque, declared, 'We are only a student protest. We do not want to overthrow Musharraf as such. We want to overthrow the entire Pakistani system, which serves only one per cent of the population.'

How did the infamous kidnapping episodes unfold? One morning certain Pakistani citizens opened their email inboxes to receive the following missive. (I have translated the flyer from Urdu to English.)

G-6 Residents Call for Unity with Jamia-Hafsa!

There was a wave of happiness running through the residents of the area on news that they were free of the notorious and disreputable Madam 'Aunty Shamim.' Numerous residents rushed to the Lal Masjid to express solidarity with the male and female students of the seminary. The residents of Sector G-6 were effusive in their praise of the students of the Lal Masjid. According to details received, the notorious and disreputable Shamim, who had the backing of powerful individuals, was running a den of vice in G-6/1–4, a locality close to the Lal Masjid. Those living in the proximity of Shamim's den were worried and harassed by having the den in their neighbourhood. They had complained to the police a number of times and demanded legal action against Shamim but no one paid heed to them. They then requested Maulana Muhammad Abdul Aziz to free the residents from this problem, so on the request of the residents, initially the students of Jamia Hafsa tried to make Shamim understand. But when instead of refraining from her activities, she threatened the students and expressed her intention to continue with her nefarious activities, the students of Jamia Hafsa had to take her hostage and closed her den of vice. The residents supported and praised the steps taken by the students of Jamia Hafsa. The residents came in large numbers and congregated at the Lal Masjid today (28 March) at nearly 4:30 p.m. They, in front of the media, openly declared that the police didn't have the guts to apprehend the Madam, they supported the act of valour and bravery of the male and female students of the Lal Masjid, and they were free of Shamim. The residents of G-6 criticised strongly the government's arrest of the respected and virtuous teachers of Jamia Hafsa for the sake of a wrong woman's security. On this occasion the head of the G-6 Federation, Raja Shaukat Sultan along with other office holders reiterated their full co-operation with Maulana Mohammad Abdul Aziz and expressed their thanks for resolving a long-standing problem of G-6.

At the same time the police representatives were issuing the following statements: 'Both sides resolved to maintain peace, respect the overall law and order and avoid the recurrence of incidents that occurred during last couple of days.'

Qamar Abbas Cheema of the Punjab Police Rawalpindi and Constable Hammad Raza of Islamabad Police said they were not tortured by the students. They said they were captured when they were passing by Lal Masjid. 'They have not mistreated us; they have served us tea and allowed us to keep our mobile phones. We are in touch with our officials and we are not facing any problem,' Raza said. 'We are told that negotiations were underway and we hope the matter will be over soon,' he said.

At this stage the city administration and the supporters of the seminary administration in the government were hoping that they could broker a 'peaceful' resolution to the issue. So the standoff continued as the government continued to set several deadlines for surrender and the *madrassah* students continued to skirmish with the security officials.

Images of veiled women holding Kalashnikovs within the seminary compound, raising slogans against the government in one instance, then the next moment being photographed raiding CD shops, burning their merchandise and issuing edicts against government ministers and common Islamabad citizens, held the Pakistani nation captive over the coming weeks. In the earlier days there were debates in Pakistan's drawing rooms, in the opinion editorial columns in newspapers whether this was the Talibanisation of Islamabad? As a significant population of the seminary were from areas that were now under the sway of the Pakistani Taliban, there were questions whether the socio-political revolution had now moved to the nation's capital. The situation could also be viewed as an issue of class and migration—a concern that had come up with other seminaries. The expatriate population of Islamabad and a cosmopolitan upper-middle-class and middle-class population worried these new arrivals. As Saigol has written elsewhere:

> The commercial, consumerist, Westernised and, in their view, depraved morality of the societies inclines them to react against everything perceived

as Westernisation and modernisation. The city represents moral degradation, loss of cultural values and spiritual emptiness. The fundamentalist call to return to a state of Islamic purity and clean moral values, appeals to them (Saigol, 1995: 86).

That the students came from impoverished backgrounds could not be denied. As events unfolded and news came of military forces closing in on them, some of the *madrassah* students left the compound. They were given some money by the government and were told to go home. However, there was the problem that many had no homes to go to, so they lingered on in a state of flux.

It is important to identify this moment as one where the empire of the fringes strikes back at the centre. What one had here was a whole new generation of people, and a class and gender that had been to date disenfranchised from doing politics in Islamabad. Has there been any other occasion in Pakistan's history when a 16-year-old woman from rural Khyber Pakhtunkhwa had a chance to have her voice heard in the nation's capital?

We have seen the phenomenon of women taking up weapons in South Asia before, and tried to explain it as religious feminism. In the 1990s, members of the Rashtra Sevika Samiti (the women's wing of the paramilitary Hindu nationalist organisation, the Rashtriya Swayamsevak Sangh) were given training in martial arts. Their 'heroine' was Uma Bharti who had spearheaded the Hindutva revolution (until of course her wings were clipped by the party establishment). And though at the time there was the same spiel of perhaps religion liberating women, it was only when one asked the important questions that you discovered that the exercises were explained as giving women healthy sons.[3] There was a massive effort to rope women into the social revolution 'without questioning patriarchal family ideology'. Indeed, the RSS was perceived to be an extension of the family and thus, women's involvement in the movement considered acceptable—but again, only in gendered roles, quite similar to what I was now observing in the case of Jamia Hafsa. Jamia Hafsa's Principal was affectionately called *Apa* (it is not within the scope of this chapter to get into the discourse analysis of the vernacular of *Apa* compared to the Anglicised Aunty of Shamim). The students did not fear criticism or antagonism; no one chastised them for their public activities, nor were they seen as undermining the Lal Masjid family. The female students approached and counselled 'Aunty Shamim' in an act that is read as quite feminine, they 'try to make her understand'.

---

[3] Tanika Sarkar, personal interview, May 1999.

However, as the said Aunty doesn't stay within her prescribed limits, the students have to act the way they do. The students feel they are gaining status, power, and great capabilities, though any analysis of the text of the Jamia's press release makes it very clear that the *pater familias* remains Maulana Muhammad Abdul Aziz. After all the residents of the Islamabad suburb approach the Maulana and express their gratitude to his person— definitely not the young women who were responsible for saving Aunty Shamim's soul and the morality of the neighbourhood.

Aliya Salahudin, a filmmaker, in her contribution to a July 2007 issue of the English language Pakistani monthly *Newsline* describes her discussions with the students and their principal as veering from the tricky question to relatively 'safer topics of economic inequality in society, the moral corruption of those in higher ranks and the country's puppet regime working at the behest of the much despised United States of America'. However, the discussion always managed to return to 'western indecency' for this remained the only issue that the students deemed important enough to rise against. The student's mission to rescue Pakistani women from decadence and a life of indecency is reminiscent of the arguments used by nineteenth-century Muslim reformers in South Asia. Reformers like Thanvi (author of the seminal *Heavenly Ornaments or Beheshti Zevar*) had seen the solution to the Muslim community's decline (among a range of other moves) in reforming and guiding women in the community. This was because they were viewed—paradoxically—as both the principal executors of wasteful and 'impossible' customs and as the chief victims of such customs (Werbner, 2002) Umme Hassan (the principal of Jamia Hafsa) and her students also framed their quest for the purification and rectification of the Pakistani nation's religious life in a discourse suggestive of the struggle of the Prophet's companions in the early years of Islamic history. There are references to Jamia Hafsa's life mission of imposing Shariah in Pakistan—though rather than a reading of the Shariah which may introduce an equitable distribution of resources, good governance and security for the Pakistani citizen, the institution remained obsessed with a version of Shariah that can eradicate 'the increasing immorality of Pakistani women'. There were also their ultimatums that the Jamia Hafsa student body was willing to be martyred in the cause of purging Pakistani society of all its evils and to bring back morality. The Pakistani media commentators at the time were also struck by the naivete of the students, as the young women declared that it was not their colleagues who held the public library hostage, but rather angels dressed in *burqa* (cloaks). The students also claimed that *ababeels* (the tiny birds referred to in the Quran as siding with valiant Muslims) circled the sky as their classmates took on shopkeepers who sold evil CDs and DVDs and that the students had been encouraged in their valiant mission by dreams of the Holy Prophet. The references to the angels and birds could be explained as either extreme gullibility or what is more probable as a cover/sanction to their public activities, for some might censure them for transgressing the 'religious limits' set upon their gender. This was when many among them were facing criticism that they had been sent by their families to learn good morals in the seminary and not to challenge the Pakistani state and wage a religious war.

The young women's relationship with the state authorities was con-flicted as well. There were the instances of kidnapping police officials and their defiance against the Pakistani government as they snatched assorted rifles and walkie talkies from the police personnel deployed near the Red Mosque. Geo, the private Pakistani TV channel had telecast images of one of the Jamia Hafsa teachers addressing her students with 'Students! Are you ready to challenge the government, the army and the police?' The students are vocal in their support. 'Students, will you chase away the government, the army and the police?' They all passionately reply in the affirmative. However, there are also instances where they address the Pakistani military personnel as brothers and ask of them to side with them—perhaps in reference to a time when their institute was a protégé of certain powerful officials in the Pakistani military!

The Jamia Hafsa protagonists viewed themselves as the 'true feminists'. In a letter to the public posted on the (now banned) website of the Red Mosque they ask of well-wishers like Dr Amir Liaqat from the Ministry of Religious Affairs to come out of his house and defend Islam so that they can return to their homes and the seminary. The author of the open letter is Saiqa Kanwal (there is also an email address for her), and in the 'open letter' to 'Uncle' Amir, she tauntingly writes:

> Use the names of the Ummal momineen (wives of the Prophet and mothers of the Ummah) and refer to instances when the female Sahaba (companions of the Prophet) participated in battles and tended to the sick, to propagate talk of women's rights… and the spectacle of (men and women running together in) marathon races… are now using the discourse of referring to the same holy personalities to convince us to return home… the very same TV channels who were busy propagating the so called Women Protection Bill are now busy putting us through a media trial.[4]

---

[4] Accessed from Lal Masjid.org (20 August 2009).

Could this be what Moallem (1999) had referred to when she spoke of fusions of feminism and fundamentalist elements? Could there be fundamentalism with feminist elements? This is debatable as we see none of the essentials of feminism (from any school of thought) when it comes to the students of the Red Mosque. There is no talk of equity of the genders, of class politics, of biological determinism, or of a more feminist interpretation of religious texts. The students come from a background where they are well-versed with the deteriorating socio-political situation of the country, they are aware of the inequitable distribution of resources in the community and how gender, culture and family play a role in perpetuating these inequities; they are aware of the problems of governance and insecurity their region faces and that they could have used the platform of the Jamia Hafsa to bring about some essential changes. However what one witnesses instead are students being used as pawns by the administrators of the Red Mosque. First to bully the government into taking back their decision to raze the illegal seminaries and mosques, and then by their threats of conducting a moral *jihad* to blackmail certain actors within the state who were threatening to withdraw their political patronage.

When the military operation against Jamia Hafsa ended, the women once more withdrew to the anonymity of the veil. As the Pakistani state and the families of those missing or dead challenged the headcount (with families also hesitant to disclose any names or association), it was the discourse of weapons discovered or the militants who were holed up in the complex that overpowered any other conversation. We never find out what happened to the veiled women with sticks. How many of them died as martyrs? What happened to their movement? Will they ever return? They had been reduced instead to passive statistics of 'government atrocities'.

My journey in patching together a piecemeal history of the bloody July encounter begins with the Jamia Hafsa website lalmasjid.org. (The website has seen multiple reincarnations, over the years I have seen it blocked, then reappearing in another avatar.) In its August 2009 avatar it included scanned newspaper items of the 2005 police raid. The website had live updates as a sidebar that you could scroll through to get numbers of the day for (formerly errant) video shop owners who have given up their 'heinous' mode of earning a living to embrace a life of good Muslim practices. Next to that was an icon of a flickering torch—one that linked to incident reports for audio-visual material being put to fire by righteous Muslims.

The website also contained an 'open letter to Quaid-i-Azam University's Vice Chancellor' by the (now deceased) Maulana Rashid Ghazi. The letter was in Urdu, and it is unclear whether it was published in any of the Pakistani newspapers. It is important to pursue this material as it is an instance of the Red Mosque administration reaching out to forums other than the pulpit and their mosque in Aabpara, Islamabad. In his letter Ghazi makes an attempt to highlight his urbane credentials, he introduces himself as a Quaid Azam University (QAU) alumni and one who is interested in keeping in touch with all that is happening in academia. He starts the letter as a critique of the research methodology employed by academics associated with QAU who have appeared in media programmes related to the Lal Masjid, and particularly their views and prejudices regarding his socio-political movement, a prejudice he repeatedly points out as based on a shoddy inquiry. However, further down the page he shifts from his academic critique and resorts to the strong-arm techniques that the seminary was getting a reputation for. Making veiled threats of a tit-for-tat 'misinformation' campaign ('How would the VC feel if we were to spread rumours he drinks or is a RAW agent?'), Ghazi declares that his students are also capable of launching a mission against the person of the VC. He requests the Vice Chancellor to muzzle academics and students associated with the university. Ghazi is eager to present his institution as an academic body with a vibrant student population that is eager to host the university affiliates on fact finding and study trips:

> We feel that the system has failed and if it's working it is only to benefit a small privileged section when 99 per cent of the population does not have access to either justice or peace. We feel that this system has to change and be replaced by a just and peaceful Islamic system. As the elite do not find it acceptable therefore they are creating a ruckus...otherwise the people who have visited us have left with a good opinion. Through your good offices I want to invite the student population of QAU to visit us and our female and male student population and see the true picture (translation from the Urdu is mine).

The archives also include an 'open letter to multi-nationals operating in Pakistan'. The text is a scanned image of what appears as a newspaper report (the website does not give any details as to which publication) based on a media release/letter issued by Maulana Ghazi. The Maulana warns the companies to desist from using vulgar images of Pakistani women in their advertising campaigns; he directs most of his ire towards cellular companies.

The hyperlink to 'Coulumns' (sic) includes scanned images of letters to the public by concerned female students of the seminary. The letters are an attempt to convince their 'brothers' in the Pakistan armed forces to side with the students rather than taking up arms to defend an 'evil and morally corrupt regime'. The focal point of this section is a 'response to alleged grievances against the Red Mosque'. The creators of the website have included a Question-and-Answer-style document titled Aitrazat Jawabat (your grievances our response) which addresses the 'objections' anyone might have against the Red Mosque (I have included a translation of some of these queries as Box 6.1). The webmaster had very cleverly manipulated the platform of this 'town hall'-style debate, so that those associated with the Shariah movement emerge as valiant footsoldiers in a fight for Pakistan's soul.

**Box 6.1**

*Aitrazat jawabat (Queries/Answers)*

**Q:** *We have heard that a Jamia Farida student flung acid on a woman because she was without a veil?*
**A:** It's a blatant lie and we hold the government agencies responsible for spreading these rumours. In the history of Islamabad there has been no such incident of a seminary student involved in an acid attack. If he was, there should be an FIR in a police station, some mention in a newspaper, or any other media. These are all allegations to turn people against us.

**Q:** *Does Shariah allow Jamia Hafsa students to go with sticks to video shops? And does threatening video shop owners fall within the ambit of missionary activities?*
**A:** Our students have never gone to video shops, not even once. If anyone has proof of it, please come to us. These are all rumours and allegations spread by agencies and a biased media. Yes, once our students had gone to a video shop as part of missionary activities but they were not carrying sticks, they were not threatening the shopkeepers or warning them of any dire circumstances. Islamabad traders can vouch for the fact that our students counselled them gently, were affectionate in their approach and only asked of them to quit this terrible occupation. Our students explained to them how by running such establishments they were responsible for our youth being morally corrupt and immodest and putting our people's faith in peril. By the grace of God our students' missionary activities bore fruit and many traders decided to leave this way of life. In fact one trader put his shop holdings on fire; it was nearly fifteen lakh rupees of capital. From time to time we hear of other episodes where traders have sacrificed their worldly goods and revoked their previous heinous ways.

**Q:** *Have your students been threatening women drivers as well?*
**A:** This is wrong. Even the newspapers have reported that Maulana Abdur Rashid Ghazi's wife drives a car, and when need be, gets the groceries (but of course under Islamic dictates). When we haven't put any restriction on the women of our house, then why curtail the movement of those in the outside world?

**Q:** *Why are you bringing women to the forefront and using them as shields?*
**A:** We didn't bring them to the forefront. They rose to the occasion when the mosques were martyred and decided to occupy the children's library as retaliation. This was during the earlier days of the movement, now they have gone back to their books, yes they may participate in the movement from time to time. Both male and female students are active members of the movement but according to their roles defined by Shariah, it's just the mischievous media that overplays their coverage of the girls. Perhaps they do so because they find the students' behaviour unusual or it could be because they get more revenue out of publishing such stories.

**Q:** *Kidnapping Aunty Shamim was not Islamic.*
**A:** Aunty Shamim was a notorious madam and her neighbours were fed up of her. The police had raided her den a number of times, and had arrested her girls, but every time powerful figures would use their discretionary powers and pressurise the police into releasing her. People tried to use the courts of law but they could never get her name on the FIR as she had powerful contacts. They had no other choice but to contact Jamia Hafsa and Maulana Rashid. Our girls tried to counsel her, warn her about the afterlife, but she was not convinced. Our students returned again, hoping that they could lock up the brothel and ask her to leave. When we tried doing that, she created a ruckus. We wanted to avoid a public spectacle and decided to bring her to the seminary, hoping the positive environment in Jamia Hafsa would have a good influence on her. Everything is so peaceful and calm here, we hoped that she would give up her evil ways.

*Q: Aunty Shamim claims you used force against her and tortured her. In a TV interview she even showed the rope with which you had tied her up and had dragged her to the seminary.*
**A:** These people are involved in a way of life that encourages such lies and deceit; in fact people commend them for it. When she showed the rope on TV, she proved this. Are you to imagine that when the students bid her farewell they gifted her with the rope? That we used this to tie you up so take it away as a souvenir?

*Q: Why are the Ulema against you?*
**A:** Our question is—can only people who appear in the media be Ulema? The thousands of elders and Sheikh Hadees (those who have memorised the sayings of the Prophet) and who have offered us support, shouldn't they be counted? At the moment there are two groups of Ulema. They are those who are our elders, we respect them; they agree with our ideology in principle but are against our approach. They chide us because they love us. We respect them and beg their forgiveness. We wait for a day when they will come and guide us and lead our movement. If there are any shortcomings in the way we conducted affairs may they help us in rectifying our mistakes. If you remember their attitude towards the Taleban, they had chided them as well in the early days and claimed them as a creation of the agencies—but in later days they supported them and pledged their allegiance to the Taleban. There is another group and we can tell by their demeanour that they only oppose us out of jealousy. They want to hide their failures and benefit from the situation today. We can only pray for

their well being and that they find the righteous path. The Maulana brothers have often said that we will continue to suffer their arrows and barbs, they are after all our own and we will not cry out in hurt. We have never accused or have recriminated against anyone, and just want to concentrate on our good work.

*Q: Why don't you vacate the government land?*
**A:** We tried to buy the land adjacent to the seminary a number of times but the government never sold it to us even though we wanted to buy it for educational purposes and good work. On the other hand, we have witnessed up to 80 kanals being doled out each time when the rich and powerful would ask for farm houses. So according to the doctrine of necessity, we made extensions to the seminary. The other question is that even if we have occupied the land illegally, we have been doing so for the past ten to fifteen years. Why is the issue being raised now? The real reason is they oppose our movement to usher in Shariah, so at times they speak of illegal land occupation, at other times some extension of sewerage lines.

*Q: Occupying the children's library was illegal.*
**A:** But we were not planning to be there permanently, this was just a sit in. To create such a ruckus about such a small space! The library was not a sacred place, we didn't cause any damage. Have we uttered even a word against the destruction of the seven mosques? Why do people cry so much over a sit in at the library? The mosques were not occupied by the government like we occupied the library, they were destroyed! And they did this to a site that is affiliated with God, to reduce them to rubble, to dishonour the Quran.

*Q: So you don't want to call it occupation but rather a sit in. But why punish the poor students who visit the library?*
**A:** The library has been open to the public for a while, the students can come and visit it and use its facilities. You should read the statement of these young students in newspapers who claim they feel more secure now that their sisters from Jamia Hafsa are there and how happy they are.

*Q: You have created a state within a state. Is that right?*
**A:** The state is God's state after all, we attained this state in the name of God and the Kalima Tayyaba (specific verses dealing with the oneness of God and the finality of the Prophet). Our Pakistan constitution declares that the ruler is God, but have we not betrayed God's trust? For the past sixty years we have only thought of ourselves and our personal good, it is the Pakistani citizen who has created a state within a state by challenging God's Will at every step.

*Q: Isn't declaring Shariah Courts ushering in a parallel system of justice?*
**A:** It is strange why certain sections of society are so against the Shariah. Perhaps they know once Shariah is imposed, their personal whims, immoral activities and injustices against the weak will be a thing of the past. So they are making a big deal about the Shariah. You have to keep in mind that the present tussle is a clash between the rich and elite and the oppressed and the weak. The country has at the moment

jirga system, panchayat system and God knows how many others which pass rulings that are against our religion, traditions and constitution, even human rights through the concept of vani, bride price; but no one criticises these systems, or declares an operation against them, or calls them parallel systems? Why do people only object to Shariah courts? Is it because they have discovered that the poor can find speedy and quick justice from the mosques and that their system will fail? This can be the only fear according to us.

*Q: Why not use the constitutional and political road when it comes to bringing in Shariah?*
**A:** We did that for the past sixty years and the results are in front of you. Let us use the missionary and reformist path. There is a big class in Pakistan that speaks of a bloody revolution. No one has criticised them; we don't speak of bloodshed but of peace, well-being and reform. What's the harm in maintaining peace and speaking of reform?

*Q: You speak of peace and no bloodshed, then why does Maulana Abdul Aziz threaten Pakistanis with suicide attacks?*
**A:** You only report one per cent of the conversation; you don't pay any attention to the remaining 99 per cent. We had declared that if the government is threatening us with military operations then our only choice would be suicide missions. If the matters can be resolved peacefully, not even a firecracker will burst. Has anyone even lost a finger in the past three months? Yes, if they repeat the history of 19 July 2005, if they harass our female students and make it difficult for the Maulana and his followers to lead a good Muslim life, than everyone knows what will happen. When you trap a cat and she feels there is no escape she will attack you as a last resort. The Maulana in the end is a religious elder and teacher to thousands of people, the elderly, the young, men and women.

*Source*: Author.

Here, the spokesperson for the seminary has been very intelligent in framing the movement as a struggle between Pakistan's weak and exploited and the powerful establishment. There are references to a corrupt bureaucracy that has benefited from the lawless state of affairs, a political elite that does not welcome good governance, and a power structure that fears alternate sources of authority that can offer cheap and speedy justice to the people. The spokesperson builds on the average Pakistani's desire to have a system that works and if the Pakistani citizen views the solution coming from a space that is allegedly divine and sanctified by the Word of God, then why should they oppose it?

It is said that societies that privilege militaristic values are fond of creating or craving heroes. A common saying in Pakistan is that one needs another Mohammad bin Qasim or Jinnah to liberate the nation and take it towards progress—or how a politician is just another Jinnah or Qasim at best. They do so by attributing all the aspects of action and liberation to the hero in question. The Lal Masjid administration and their collegial networks exploited this desire by presenting their movement and high command as that particular hero, and their movement as the liberating force. In an opinion piece they present a convoluted version of reformist forces through history and draw parallels between their movement and vigilante forces in European history (translation from the Urdu mine):

> There have been heroes over the ages that have used their strength to steer society towards the righteous path. In Roman history, we had Nero. This king would organise a spring carnival very much like the Basant organised by Pakistani elite. There were orgies; beautiful women were procured from all over the world to participate in swimming galas and marathons. All this was done in the name of art, culture and heritage resulting in a macabre picture. Women had become commodities, but little were they to know that with the advent of Christianity this state-sponsored debauchery would become a tale of the past. The papacy took a strong stance against such filth.
>
> In 1469 Florence introduced carnivals and licentious behaviour, Venice was similar, decent family men were embarrassed by all the wantonness and shamelessness. This was when the Lutherans came in; university students too got involved, followed by the Muslims. The Muslim empire flourished and such depravity was confined to narrow quarters alone, no one had time for galas and carnivals. Elizabeth I's court was also notorious but Puritans came in to put a stop to that.
>
> History can bear witness that whenever the state forces lewd acts and debauchery on its people or uses the stick to bring in 'enlightenment' doing away with age old family values and traditions, there will be always be a group of righteous people that will oppose them. They will form a powerful force that will lash back at the state and champion the cause of conservative values.
>
> This revolution has been spearheaded by the valiant students of Waziristan and Jamia Hafsa, and people who get nervous by it, we just ask them to take a look at the past seven years. Have our people behaved in any way less than Nero? Basant, videos. We repeat history has borne witness to the fact that forcing depravity on people by force will always give rise to people who will resort to violence to stop this shamelessness. This is the only thing that can happen to such societies. These societies allow their dictators to ruin their social fabric, societal values. If they are willing to turn a blind eye, they should get ready to welcome anarchy. Their apathy will give birth to similar vigilante groups. They remained silent when society went to the dogs so now they should keep quiet and not pose any opposition to vigilante groups who have come to restore decent values.

The use of the terms Basant, marathon and enlightenment is strategic as the Musharraf government had employed these expressions and introduced these events to show Pakistan as a soft Islamic state. Organisations such as the Jamia Hafsa do enjoy support networks with prestigious, albeit, right-wing think-tanks in Pakistan, and therefore have the vocabulary and resources to analyse and criticise the research undertaken by others about their own institutions. Once renowned for their obsessive focus on Quranic studies, Pakistan's *madrassahs* today are increasingly tuned into international debates about a wide range of issues including north-south relations, the construction of knowledge, the hierarchy of global knowledge, the politics of aid and the 'real' agenda of western powers engaged in South Asia, Iraq and elsewhere. And therefore they have been very successful in casting Jamia Hafsa and Lal Masjid's struggle as a valiant fight between David and Goliath, and how Musharraf's evil regime was vehement in its intentions to drag Pakistan into a time of lawlessness, and moral corruption.

It is clear from Umme Hassan's eyewitness account of the events of July 2007[5] that the protagonists of the Shariah movement wanted to stick close to this script. The file-sharing website multiply.com that hosts a link for Jamia Hafsa scanned images of some of the publications of the Media Department of the Lal Masjid. (I include here one titled 'The Lal Masjid Tragedy: An Eyewitness Account' which narrates Umme Hassan's account of the siege). The day I accessed the document, there had been some 50,000 hits for that particular document, which can be seen as an indicator of the popularity of this material. In the long list of comments sent in as feedback, many of the readers have requested for the eyewitness account to be translated to English so it could be accessed by a wider audience. How ironic that it is I who get to do this in the following pages. The document starts with a preface penned by the Media and Information Department of the Students of Red Mosque. It eulogises the 'ornament that graces the fair head of Islamic history', referring here to Umme Hassan. The introduction goes on to praise her courage under fire, and the compassion, care and understanding she accorded to her wards in the seminary. The editors laud Umme Hassan and the noble family she belongs to for their willingness to sacrifice their lives in the cause of Islam. The publication refers to her as Mother of the Martyr Hassan (Umme Shuhda Mohtarma Umme Hassan). Umme Hassan's account of the siege reads at

---

[5] I accessed her account from http://jamiahafsa.multiply.com/photos/hi-res/upload/SMn74AoKCF0AACgdRiE1 on September 2009.

the time as popular Urdu pulp fiction, adopting as she does the tone of the protagonists of some of the prevalent Urdu digests. She speaks of demure young women who remain veiled as they dodge bullets and take food for the male students, of compassionate maidens who go hungry so the men can eat, of good Muslim women who go to their deaths defiant of a corrupt regime, and a little girl who laughs hysterically as she takes her last breath and finally realises how much God loves them. At times she refers to Islamic history mentioning how her students ate leaves and berries as food supplies dwindled during the siege, drawing parallels to incidents when the Prophet's companions did so in times of dire circumstances. In later pages she refers to Maulana Aziz sending out representatives and writing letters to the authorities that the seminary is not their enemy (a clear reference to traditions of the Prophet; the Prophet too had sent out emissaries to the various heads of state inviting them to embrace Islam or conduct peace treaties). Umme Hassan's testimony begins with a description of how she, the much pampered daughter of a prosperous family gets married into a family very different from hers. Her in-laws had given up all creature comforts and she is so motivated by their ideology that soon she too joined them in giving up worldly goods in the cause of Islam. In the coming years the family is set upon with trials and tribulations; her beloved father-in-law gets killed before her eyes and her husband Maulana Abdul Aziz is declared an offender, and false cases are filed against him. Their seminary is raided a number of times, its sanctity violated, and her students imprisoned and beaten up (Umme Hassan refers here to the 2005 incident). However, when the Lal Mosque siege unfolds she forgets all that had transpired in the past. She laments that no one realised that a city named the abode of Islam (Islamabad) would instead become a new-age Kufa (Umme Hassan refers here to the Prophet's grandson's trials and tribulations at the battlefield of Karbala, there are other parallels too in the document). She feels that there is a long list of incidents when they felt let down by the Pakistani government, that a number of distressing incidents led to the standoff; however, the straw that broke the proverbial camel's back was the 'martyrdom' of the mosque Masjid Hamza.

A country that was created to proclaim the Oneness of God had not been kind to Muslims. Muslims have been subjected to all kinds of torture in the state of Pakistan. Ataturk was declared as a model to emulate[6] and in the guise of moderation and enlightenment the powers that be tried to encourage

---

[6] She refers here to Musharraf's support of Kemal Ataturk's policies.

atheism and waywardness. Quranic verses and references to jihad were removed from the educational curriculum and textbooks in order to push the students into the quicksand of secularism but we didn't see anyone protesting. We could see pornographic literature and morally reprehensible material flooding our markets that was responsible for corrupting our future generations but no one paid attention. We saw justice becoming an economic commodity in Pakistan, being traded and compromised upon openly on the streets. Corruption became the right of the powerful and even then Pakistani people did not challenge the situation. The marathon race[7] was an excuse to bid farewell to dignity, the Women's Protection Bill was introduced to encourage vice. Seminaries were raided, and our Muslim intellectuals were martyred. Our citizens were sold off for a few dollars, the number of missing people increased with their heirs and children continuing to search for them. Dr Abdul Qadeer Khan who was Pakistan's well-wisher was shamed publicly and then jailed, the mujahideen were denied the plentiful expanses of the Land of God, the veil was declared an obsolete and archaic institution, and jihad was declared terrorism. This was followed by the process of destroying the word of God. Mosques are viewed as the 'daughters of God'; they are symbols of His grandeur—imagine the government is hell bent on martyring these icons of our faith. In a short span of time we heard of seven such 'daughters' being martyred, with each incident leaving us deeply wounded. Such incidents would be highlighted by the newspapers for a few days, relegated to the back pages soon after and then they disappeared completely from the pages. There would be some half-hearted consultations, a few processions would be taken out to protest the demolition, someone would conduct a seminar or two but over time people became involved in their lives of pleasure and ignored the call of God. We soon realised that we had to come up with some way to stem this flood of vice and evil. Earlier this year, our seminary started receiving a number of official notices. We also heard that a secret list of mosques was being prepared, which would lead to 80 mosques being martyred. Mosques were declared a security risk and became a victim of the stubbornness and ego of an evil dictator named Musharraf. I have never seen my husband as upset and concerned as he was when Masjid Hamza was martyred—not even at the murder of his own father. I had seen the bullet-ridden body of my father-in-law; you can understand being a woman and a daughter how I was mentally affected by the murder of such a humane and kind father. At the time I had drawn solace from the fact that our dear Abbaji had at least received the status of a martyr, but when I saw the broken bricks of the razed mosque I cried as I have never cried before. At such a dire stage

---

[7] In May 2005 human rights activists organised a symbolic mixed-gender marathon in Lahore to raise awareness about violence against women. The marathon was attacked by members of the clergy, intelligence agencies and the police.

in life our hearts could only wail for an Ibne Qasim[8] who would protect and give sanctity to the daughters of Kaba. We are still amazed at the fact that when the Babri Mosque fell in India there was condemnation from the entire Muslim world, but when the Masjid Ibne Abbas and other mosques in Islamabad lay in ruins, with the pages of the Quran scattered among the fallen bricks, there was a deafening silence on their part. I could not sleep the whole night. I would see Maulana Aziz distressed, and could only pity him. He spent the last hours of the night in hiccups as he cried and the tears rolled down his cheeks. It was Muharram 1, 21 January 2007—the start of the new Islamic year. When I got to the seminary in the morning some students came running to me and declared that students of Aliya (equivalent to Masters of Arts) and Aama (equivalent to a BA course) have taken over the children's library. When I confronted them, they became stubborn and said that they should not be pushed into returning to the seminary as their hearts bled at the state of Islamabad's mosques. I was amazed for these were students who had never even squeaked in front of me and today they were defying me, so steadfast were they in their belief. This was a time of challenge for me. I consulted with Maulana Aziz, he said he had spent the whole night in *istikhara* (reciting special prayers), asking God to make the right path obvious and easy for them but he could come up with no solution to the crisis. Perhaps what the students had done was the right option. He wanted to consult his brother Maulana Ghazi. In the meantime the news of the library sit-in spread, perhaps Maulana Ghazi had encouraged the media to publicise the sit-in as he wanted the administration to enter into talks and offer a resolution to the conflict.

In the coming days it seemed like a tornado had swept into town. Our students were very direct in their talk with the Ulema and the city administration. They wanted the demolished mosques to be rebuilt and to stop any further action against the mosques that were on the CDA's list of 80.

We decided to side with the students on this issue as these students were taking the 'prescribed' path, they had not gone out in the streets or spoken of their own interests, rather they remained in the private space of the '*chardevari*' and spoke of their constitutional and legal rights. Despite this, we witnessed them being subject to a war of propaganda and being threatened with violence.

In later pages Umme Hassan speaks of the then Minister for Religious Affairs Ejazul Haque (who also happens to be the son of the infamous

---

[8] Reference to Mohammad Bin Qasim; Pakistani textbooks credit him as introducing Islam to the subcontinent. They describe him as coming in to rescue a Muslim princess kidnapped by an evil Hindu king and setting up the Kingdom of Islam.

General Zia ul Haq) betraying their trust and threatening the girls by letting loose the special police force 111 Brigade on them. She accuses the
Minister of wickedness and of rushing to Karachi and turning the federation of the Ulema (whom they respected a lot) against them.

We held the council of Ulema in the highest esteem and humbly explained
our situation to our learned elders and implored them not to intervene. Over
time we had realised the futility of having talks with the government. A
pattern had emerged over the years, and we thought to ourselves that even
if we get the demolished mosques reconstructed in lieu of vacating the
Children's Library, what guarantee do we have for the security of the other
mosques? In the past the government introduced the insulting Women's
Protection Bill and we diligently registered our protest, when our Muslim
brothers were murdered we took out a procession, at times young women
are forced to run without head covering in the name of a marathon and we
lobbied against it. But all our efforts were to what account? We realised
we could only keep on protesting and this morally corrupt government will
continue unabated in its evil ways. So in the light of the Quran and Sunnah
the only choice was to work for the imposition of the Shariah. This was
the same demand raised by my husband and martyred father-in-law, and
has formed the crux of our struggle over the past six decades. However,
we were taken aback by the reaction, of friends and foes alike. There was
unrest in the corridors of power; the media which until now had only disseminated debauchery and vulgarity was forced to take us seriously and
give us coverage on their pages and TV channels. A caravan of young
people from all over Pakistan joined us *ammama* kerchiefs tied on their
heads, we witnessed women, students from seminaries, from schools and
colleges joining our movement. In a matter of days the Red Mosque and
the 'Shariah or Martyrdom' war cry became a rallying point for previously
disillusioned Pakistanis. We became a respected platform for giving out
justice to those who had been previously victimised by our system. The
agents of evil observed this challenge to their ways; they could witness
how we dispensed speedy justice. The wicked became busy in initiating a
propaganda war, we witnessed with dismay how even our 'own' bought
their lies and abandoned us.[9] We did not want to succumb to offers of 'give
and take' and compromises. Maulana Abdul Aziz remained concerned about
all those immoral spaces in Pakistan where young, innocent women are
exploited and young men tempted towards evil, these children are like our
own. We had no choice but to close down these 'springs of evil' and started
our campaign against computer discs and videos, God is our witness we did
not use force, we would counsel the shopkeepers gently. Yes some of them

---

[9] She refers here to Wafaq Madaris, the confederation of seminaries that 'expelled' them.

were so moved by our argument that that they would burn their inventory. Everyone knows about the gentleman who put to fire audio-visual material worth 15 lakh rupees in front of the Red mosque. One man in Bara Kahu put a match to all that was in his shops and the police arrested him along with some of our students who were passing by. We should have been rewarded for ridding society of evil, of removing Pakistan's youth from the path of temptation and corruption. But we found instead our teachers and students arrested and tortured.

During this process the residents of G-6 contacted us to complain about a den of vice in their neighbourhood. This was the infamous madam Shamim and her brothel. She had powerful contacts within the city administration and no one could stop her nefarious activities. We counselled her from time to time and finally brought her to the Red Mosque hoping that perhaps the good Islamic environment in our institution would show her the evil of her ways. She sought repentance and spoke in front of the media of learning the evil of her ways. This was but one tactic to clean society and the city administration paid heed and closed a number of dens and brothels after our operation. We continued with our educational activities, our students continued to be harassed, and we watched in dismay as some of our teachers, and female students were arrested. In retaliation some police officers were taken in by our students but we never mistreated them.

Following this incident the *Tehreek* (Movement) of Students continued peacefully. From time to time we would point out to the government certain businesses that we knew were spreading vice but the government would make excuses and claim they were helpless. They would shy away when any of these businesses involved foreign nationals. We screamed hoarse that the government is refusing visas to young students from foreign lands who want to enrol in our seminaries to get a religious education, but has no qualms allowing dubious foreign nationals who come to our country for no purpose but to spread corruption and evil ways. In the coming days we were approached by young women who belonged to Islamabad's elite, also other concerned citizens of the city who were not affiliated with the seminary. They were all getting worried about the wayward ways of Pakistani youth; they had seen disturbing things transpiring at farm houses, motels and hotels. Students from Bahria (Naval) College in Islamabad wrote to us about what was happening in massage centres. We could have ignored these massage centres if their clientele included foreigners only. But here we were listening to stories of our bureaucrats frequenting them, names of our honourable ministers and members of parliaments featured on their lists of 'favourite customers'. We had no intention of bringing the Chinese masseurs to the seminary, in fact what we would have preferred was if the city administration that was hell bent on conducting crackdowns on seminaries could have directed some of their ire towards these places as well. However, we observed that they would develop cold feet any time they would hear the name of a foreigner. In the end though this was not a desirable step to take we had no choice but to do what we did. We never harmed the Chinese masseurs; to tell you the truth, keeping in mind the close ties between Pakistan and China and not wanting to ruin this friendship we handed them over to the Chinese Ambassador. The ambassador was appreciative of our actions and praised our taking such good care of their nationals. However the particular section of society that has been against us from the beginning created such a furore. These are the people who have always wanted to ruin the peaceful environment in Pakistan and bring about anarchy and civil war. For this purpose they set up trenches in surrounding buildings. Even as they prepared for war they would feed us lies and pacify us by declaring that they had no intentions of conducting an operation. We now have the bitter experience of discovering that there are some in the government who are paid a salary only to lie to and betray Pakistani citizens. At times someone would come to conduct talks and when the talks would inch towards fruition they would shrug their shoulders and say they were powerless. Later someone else would come to start talks and the same process would begin. We had great faith in Chaudhry Shujaat, we sincerely believe that he could have worked out an arrangement but all his efforts were foiled. He has gone on record to state that the resource persons at Lal Masjid 'are cooperating with me and it's only CDA and some anonymous personalities who are sabotaging the talks'.

In her account Umme Hassan repeatedly declares that her institute and affiliates never wanted trouble. She goes on to narrate how:

> ...our six-month peaceful struggle is testimony to the fact that our intentions were non-violent. Not a finger cut or a drop of blood spilled. It makes for an interesting anecdote that the night of 3 July when the security forces were ready to storm the seminary, Maulana Aziz was busy writing letters to the authorities that we are not your enemies and we are only struggling to change the system.[10] He implored the security forces asking if they were ready to fire bullets on the Quran, unarmed students and innocent girls on the behest of others? But clearly they were not ones to heed the words of the righteous and stay away from their evil mission.

> They first fired shells of tear gas at us and then came a hail of bullets. I can still remember that there was a little girl standing next to me who said I cannot believe that these are our soldiers, our brothers who are firing at

---

[10] A clear reference to the time the Prophet sent out emissaries to the various heads of state inviting them to embrace Islam or conduct peace treaties.

us, God works in mysterious way. As she was crying her lament a bullet came and injured her, she hovered between life and death for long and kept on repeating in disbelief, 'I cannot believe these are our brothers, this is Pakistan's army.'

Umme Hassan is guarded when she talks about the infamous arrest of Maulana Aziz and the circumstances under which he was arrested.[11] She begins with reiterating their loss of faith in the Pakistani security forces:

What happened between 3 and 10 July is beyond description; the same soldiers that we have always considered our protectors and guardians, we never expected them to go to such limits—our defenceless students being martyred, their exposed bodies lying in the courtyard. Maulana Aziz would pass his hands over the bodies of the dying with such an anguished expression. Maulana was soft hearted and he did not want bloodshed and the lives of the innocent to be wasted, he decided to go out and enter into discussions. I was not supportive of this decision. From day one I had braced myself for news of his martyrdom or arrest. Now under what circumstances he was captured and what happened to him after that event I do not want to get into the details, I will only repeat the Quranic verses of leaving some matters to the Almighty.

In brief he was captured in a very dishonourable way and was later subjected to humiliation. All of this was a trick, just to demoralise us. People were given the impression that he had left the seminary to save his life, but if he wanted to save his life why would he leave his mother inside. Would he have left his young son Hassan behind? If nothing else he would have taken his beloved daughter Isma. We were under the impression that once the Maulana was arrested and their nefarious purposes achieved the operation would stop. But we were dealing with such bloodthirsty souls, they continued with their nefarious purposes. Of putting our seminary on fire, of using all their ammunition and bullets to silence us. We realised at that moment that their aim was not just to arrest Maulana Ghazi and Aziz but to prolong the reign of their evil rulers, to give a good impression to the US. They were ready to slaughter their innocent children in order satiate their hunger for dollars and F-16s.

She narrates how she will never forget the events of the terrible seven days of siege, of her students dying of hunger and thirst, and their wounds. She describes the Lal Masjid and the seminaries as sites where hundreds

---

[11] The Maulana was disguised in a woman's *burqa* and was apprehended when a vigilant policewoman became suspicious of the 'aunty' being taken out by students for medical aid.

would be fed every day but they were left with not even a single piece of bread, as their cruel adversary had first attacked their kitchens and put to fire their stocks of food.

One might have seen the sick dying of their illness but not the ruthless plunder of a garden of flowers, of young flowers being trampled under gumboots.... We were only left with stocks for two days; we discovered some biscuits and sweets in the canteen. But how could the hungry be satiated with candy? We resorted to eating leaves. This was a time when all of Pakistan was eating the best of God's bounty while my girls were starving. My heart would sadden when I would see the little girls eating leaves but I would draw solace from incidents in Muslim history when the Companions of the Prophet would eat leaves and tie bandages on their feet.

We had always wanted the students to leave the seminary and avoid the bloodshed. We would make efforts to cajole and convince the innocent girls to leave but they would fall at our feet and beg us to let them stay. One day a father came to take away his daughter, she burst into tears and sat at his feet pointing to the dead bodies in the courtyard, imploring her father that she too be allowed to join her colleagues and embrace martyrdom. What were we to say after that? And the father, how could he deny her such an honour?

I tried convincing my students to leave as our rations were depleting. But they replied 'Aapi Jan! Those who dishonoured our beloved teacher and tried to blacken his name, they who tricked our brothers into giving themselves up and then threw them in jails and torture chambers, took off their shirts and tied their hands behind their backs, you want to throw us in front of those hungry animals?' I was without words. Till the end none of them even hinted to me that they were having second thoughts, that they regretted their decision of staying behind in the seminary. They were always steadfast in their intentions to live a life of dignity while alive and to die a martyr's death.

Towards the end of the operation we had two groups of female students staying back. There was the group that had beseeched their parents in the name of God and the Prophet into not making them leave the seminary, and the second group of girls who had no families outside the seminary. After the 2005 earthquake the Maulana had asked the Al Qasim Foundation and their volunteers to bring any children who had no guardians to the seminary and when these destitute children arrived, he reminded me of the time when the Prophet had brought an orphan home for Eid and told the child that from this day on, I'm your father and Hazrat Ayesha your mother.

We realised after the earthquake that now we too had the opportunity to emulate that particular episode of our beloved Holy Prophet. We arranged for the orphans to have a secure place to stay, a full stomach's food, a place to sleep, toys to play with. Now the only life they knew was that of Jamia Hafsa. They had witnessed a life of destitution and exile after the earthquake, and under no circumstance wanted to go back to that tough life again. They were very forthright and told me in clear words that why should they want to leave the seminary. Who was there to take care of them? Who would love them like I had? I was so helpless in the face of their love for me and their attachment to the Jamia Hafsa. And in the following days I administered the last rites to so many of the innocent who had died loving their alma mater. I remember once we had found some potatoes lying behind a door. One of the students asked me whether she should take them for the male students who might be hungry after such a long siege? I told her to go and offer them to any male student who might be sitting outside hungry for food. I told her to go out reciting the Kalima, but within 15 minutes a young male student was outside our door calling out for me. We were all in our *burqas*, I came out and saw him holding her bleeding body in his arms; the boy told me that when he leaned forward to recite the *Kalima* for her, the girl told him that Aapi Jan had already told her to recite that prayer before stepping into the compound. She died soon after. Such are the ways of God; we didn't need to recite the last rites for her, as she had already declared them for herself.

I had been praying to God all those days, and I would keep on explaining to my students how God tests those whom He loves. A little girl who was a student in grade one told me that she could not believe that God loved them and was putting them through this trial. It happened so that it had been raining the past days and we had collected rainwater in buckets. When it came to the *Maghreb* prayers I told the girls to continue with their dry ablutions and to not use that water. But this particular little girl was in a strange trance and proceeded to use the water in the buckets and in the same heady state of mind went about to offer her prayers. A bullet came from the skies and pierced her jugular vein. As the blood poured forth she looked at me and laughed hysterically. Laughing, that she knew now how much God loved them, she turned towards the heavens and gave up her fight for life.

In the same week we discovered some rice. There were some shattered window panes and doors, we decided to burn them and boil the rice. I told my students to drink the water and give the boiled rice to the injured male students. My students died delivering that rice.

While we were under siege my daily routine was to visit the different rooms hosting the students. I would console the students as they went about their prayers and tended to the sick. Some would be crying as they prayed to

God. Even after putting us through so much stress and pain, the cruel were not satisfied. They started lobbing fire bombs at the building, set on fire our libraries with valuable copies of the Quran and holy texts. We would try to use our *burqas*, our *chadors* to put out that fire. Some of my valiant students were burnt alive trying to save the holy texts.

I saw God from so close during those seven days and I can now say that he is kinder than 70 mothers. I think it was a Friday night when I sent a message to Maulana Inamullah that God listens to your prayers, please ask Him who has promised to send manna from the heavens to his people, to do something for my students. They are hungry. I begged him to beseech God on our behalf to keep my students safe from the tear gas. My students could bear all fortitudes with grace but they would cry to me to save them from the blight of the tear gas shells.

And a kind God sent us rain which we could collect in buckets, he arranged for thunder storms that rendered useless the tear gas. The same night we discovered two gallons of honey behind the minarets of the mosque. The fragrance of that honey was unrivalled; to this day it remains a mystery where the honey had come from. But has not God promised His beloved people that He will provide them with sustenance from sources they never imagined. If Bibi Mariam was given fruit 'out of season'[12] so why could he not provide honey for the numerous other Mariams in the seminary?

But this was not the only miracle of God that we witnessed. How can I forget the fragrance that emanated from the body of martyrs? It was a sweet smell that still lingers with me. And how thunder clouds would gather on the horizon the day they would be ready to launch their most poisonous tear gas shells. We had between us only 14 Kalashnikovs and a negligible number of bullets. We had recieved strict instructions from Maulana that we should only fire in a sporadic fashion so the security forces outside should not suspect that we were unarmed.

But the unending miracles of God. The wretched soldiers would die in their own crossfire. They had surrounded us from all sides and what happened was that their bullets crossed over our building and hit their comrades on the other side, and here they were thinking that we too had weapons and it was our bullets that were taking them out.

Every day brought one heartrending sight after the other. My heart mourned at the death of the students but more than that would grieve at the sight of the Quran and Hadith books being disgraced. I would see them burning in the fire, the bullets tearing the pages. We would try to put the fire out with

---

[12] The miracle of the birth of Jesus Christ.

our *burqas* and *chadors*, but how much was I to do? I would rush about trying to console the students, would recite my prayers and the specific Quranic verses for protection. I was trying to give hope and courage to those whom I knew were losing hope. I would tend to the injured as they lay on the grounds. To date my number one regret was that we couldn't save the Quran from burning. We were also depressed by the attitude of our respected Ulema. I still remember how they would refuse to take Maulana Ghazi's calls, and would promptly switch off mobiles when they saw his number displayed on the screen. At times they would shut him off in the middle of the conversation if he referred to the events transpiring at Lal Masjid.

During that time I was amazed at Ghazi Sahib's courage and patience. I would implore him to write a will for his children and he would only reply in a confident manner that I trust God with my wife and children. I am sacrificing my life for Him, I am sure He will look after them. My mother-in-law's attitude was also impressive, she said I had told everyone I would be martyred in this bed, and see it is coming true. What is there to do in this corrupt world, it is a filthy place. I will soon be in heaven with my Maker; it will be a place free from the evil, the cruel, and the dictators. Anyone who had met her in those days had their faith renewed. My son Hassan would also talk in a strange manner. He would tell me that this year I will break my fast with my grandfather, and see he was right. He was martyred at such a young age and was blessed to join his martyred grandfather in heaven.

After the arrest of Maulana Aziz, my brother-in-law Maulana Ghazi and my son would convince me every day to leave the seminary, but I would refuse their request. On 8 July they ordered me in their capacity as Amir and I could not refuse our Amir's orders. They warned me that the troops would make me disappear if they ever captured me alive. And now it is very clear after how they caused my deceased mother-in-law's body to vanish in thin air, what they could have done with me.

When I left, I had to leave my injured daughters behind in the seminary. My heart was crying for all the dead I had left behind. I had left behind my books, my whole life there. Only a mother can understand what went through my heart as I kissed my young son for the last time. But I told him we have raised you for this day, not to lose hope, to stay steadfast in the cause. I told him I am leaving you to protect the sanctity of the mosque, to protect your innocent brothers and sisters, the dignity of the Quran. If God accepts your sacrifice in lieu of the noble task you are performing we will be honoured. Please do not embarrass us. I beg you to take a bullet in your chest, and to not humiliate us in front of our Holy Prophet.

I declare today that I do not have the courage of the Prophets to bear these matters with fortitude. I am after all human and a woman at that. And the

Prophet too had cried when his son Ibrahim lay dying in his lap. These days I frequently think of some lines that are attributed to Hazrat Fatima.[13] She had cried out one day that so many burdens have been cast upon us, that if these were to be shed on the morn, the daylight would turn into night.

Towards the end of her testimony Umme Hassan praises the souls of the martyrs, and the courage of their families. She reiterates how she will never forget the events of the dark days and how today, much like the earthquake survivors she had sheltered, she cowers at every distant rumble. Every loud noise seems like a volley of bullets to her, and the thunder in the sky a hail of gunfire.

Has there been any good outcomes of the sorry events of July 2007, she asks of her readers. And then answers her question herself in the next breath. She writes that she now believes that the events had some positive results. For one the Pakistani public finally started contemplating the state of affairs in their country. People have since then started writing about the merits of an Islamic system, openly discussing the perils of the current political system in the public and coming to the conclusion that perhaps welcoming the Shariah is the only solution. She begs of the Pakistani nation and her comrades to overlook the shortcomings of those who had betrayed them in the past and to forget and forgive the ambivalent allies of that particular chapter in the mosque's history. Rather than wasting energy accusing certain figures who didn't act when they should have, she would rather that each and every one of her readers look within and ask of themselves, 'What did we do?' 'Didn't we behave like nothing more than passive spectators?' Rather than pointing fingers at others it is time that you, the reader decide to be more proactive in the future.

(In the final pages of her testimony she concludes that) though in the past there was a great deal of confusion regarding the motives of the Lal Masjid administration, people doubted whether they were nothing more than the government stooges out to broker a better deal for themselves. But hopefully matters are much clearer today and there are no doubts regarding their sincerity.

The confusion of the past should have disappeared after the Lal Masjid tragedy. Our message is now clear. I implore of you, consider the blood of the martyrs, those who had set forth to memorise the Quran as my emissary. Spread the word of God and use all your energies towards that cause.

---

[13] The youngest daughter of the Prophet.

Our mission does not cease if one mosque was destroyed, or if the seminary is no longer there. Tomorrow we can study under trees. I want you to set up seminaries in every village, to have a presence in every corner. Today I see our cause spreading to spaces which never imagined our student movement flourishing. Countless people take oath every day. I see them joining the thousands of martyrs and their noble cause of introducing Shariah to Pakistan. They are shoulder to shoulder with the 65,000 martyrs who gave up their lives in the cause of Pakistan. I implore you to join hands and march with them today.

What stays with us after perusing this document? It is a litany of lament which extends beyond their grief at the alleged desecration of the Abbas mosque and other mosques; and by her own admission she makes it clear that their struggle would not have stopped with the rebuilding of the mosques bulldozed as part of the CDA project. Umme Hassan and her colleagues list a host of issues, the Women's Protection Bill, the shift towards Islam as Secular, the change in the visa regime towards foreign students at Pakistani seminaries—a whole gambit of issues that form the focus of Pakistan's post-2001 foreign and domestic policy. Were they now willing to cut off their alleged umbilical cord with certain sections of the Pakistani military and secret service agencies? It is not evident from the statements issued by the administration and affiliates of the seminary. During the *Shariah or Jihad* conference, the speakers laud the Pakistani security forces and refer to them as their 'dear brothers'. They remind them of their duty to defend Pakistan's borders and not to train their guns towards their well-wishers within. They beseech God that they are aware that the soldiers too have families and to protect them, that the Almighty soften the hearts of the soldiers, and to give them guidance. And if the soldiers don't have the *naseeb* (good fortune) to get guidance, to take them in His hold.[14]

Why is it that the discourse of the Lal Masjid found so many consumers? Particularly since there were many at the time of the Operation Silence who had questioned how a campus in the vicinity of Pakistan's military intelligence offices could stockpile weapons and provide sanctuary to hardened terrorists as was claimed by General Musharraf and the commanders of the operation. There was no explanation on the part of the establishment when people questioned them how their 'friends of yesterday have become the enemies of today'. The citizens also bemoaned the 'understanding' between the media houses and the commanders of the operation since the

---

[14] http://www.youtube.com/watch?v=Fex56lP5E5c&NR=1

electronic media refrained from giving the exact figures of the dead, neither did they release any images of the dead or reactions of their relatives. In fact the media coverage only concentrated on showing what the security forces were doing in the area. The Pakistani nation was left looking for answers and they turned to the only organisation that had something to say—the Lal Masjid sympathisers. They did not question the authenticity of the information, at least someone was ready to tell them what had transpired during the days—whether it was the truth or not. In addition, many had been disturbed by the behaviour of certain TV news anchors who conducted interviews with Maulana Aziz, making him put on the *burqa*. They also did not approve of how students who sought amnesty were ridiculed by the Pakistani security forces and in the electronic media. 'The US treated the prisoners in Guantanamo better', remarked some.

In later years, the discourse (of the Jamia Hafsa website[15]) shifted to Dr Afia, the Pakistani-American physicist who was arrested by US forces for allegedly plotting to kill US servicemen in Afghanistan. There are interviews with Dr Afia's mother and newspaper op-eds sympathetic to her case.

A recent edition is a pamphlet in English titled 'The Role of the Women in Fighting the Enemies'. It is published by Al-Tibyan publications. The cover page has an image of a woman in a *burqa* in profile holding a Kalashnikov, superimposed upon a background of lurid purple and a huge pink rose. The author of the pamphlet is Yusuf al-Uyairi, who has been described by political scientists as 'one of the most interesting examples of the transnational experience of the Salafi Jihadi movement in Saudi Arabia (Meijer, 2007)'.[16] In more than 2,000 pages of articles, books, and pamphlets, this particular Al Qaeda actor has spread the radical revolutionary ideas of Jihadi Salafism. Even after his death he left an important legacy of this movement in the form of e-magazines as Sawt al-Jihad and al-Battar. This particular pamphlet has been published as a letter to young Muslim women warning them of becoming one more hindrance in the path of jihad.

> By mentioning one hindrance that we see the *Ummah* is in need of removing quickly and before anything else. And that obstacle is the woman who is manifested as the mother, or the wife, or the daughter or the sister. They all

---

[15] http://www.jamiah-hafsa.com/index.php
[16] Roel Meijer, 'Yusuf al-Uyairi and the Transnational Expansion of Salafi Jihadism Expansion'. Conference abstract Kingdom without Borders Saudi Expansion in the World Conference programme and abstracts, September 2007 http://www.kcl.ac.uk/artshums/depts/trs/research/certap/archive/kingdom.pdf (Accessed 2 June 2011).

fall under the Verse detailing the obstacles to jihad. And our research into the obstacle of the woman will not be new to her, but we will nevertheless address her in these papers and we will inform her that she is one of the biggest impediments before the Victory and Honour of Islam. And when we say that the woman is one of the greatest obstacles to the Victory of Islam, we must also mention the opposite notion, and it is that the woman is one of the primary and most influential factors in the Victory of Islam, with the condition that she fulfils her role with complete courage and sacrifice. And here we will transmit for her biographies that she must take as her example in order for Islam to be victorious.

But the women of our era... they are unaware—and what kind of unawareness is it? It is the unawareness of (everything except) following the latest trends and fads, the adornment and pomp. Rather, some of them are, if you wish, drowning in the prohibited things. They've become relied on for destruction. The enemies of the Religion use them against the *Ummah* in its own lands. After we had expected them to contribute to the building of the tower of the *ummah,* we find ourselves instead working to stop them from destroying Islam. And the enemy's focus on 'freeing' women was only after they realised that the woman is the custodian of the *Ummah.* If she is corrupted, her creation will be corrupted, as well as those around her. So they (the enemies) used her in the worst way, while she is delusional and drowning, and believes all of these false calls, and there is no Might or Power except with Allah.

The rest of the pamphlet gives brief sketches for Muslim women in the past who supported the cause of holy war by either inciting young men to participate in war, or by participating directly. There is Umm Umairah who fights alongside the Holy Prophet and avenges her son, Umm Hakim who gets up from her marriage bed and uses the pole of the tent to kill seven Romans, of Saffiyah Bint Abdil-Muttalib who not only fought but used the power of words:

As for her incitement of the men to fight, then she never fell short in inciting them with her tongue. And she did not (just) incite those who remained behind; rather, she incited the fighters who were not victorious over their enemies. And this incitement was with her limbs also.

Umme Hassan and her colleagues have been conscious of employing linguistic traditions and a discourse similar to oratory performances of the *kissa khwan* storytellers, and narrators of *marsia* dirges of the old. Pakistani audiences are familiar with and are moved by the standard format of motivational slogans, use of powerful poetry and a reading of particular

Arabic verses. One can observe their public performances in the dozens of media files and file-sharing forums. In one such recording at the time of their Shariah or Jihad conference, the camera pans over a sea of black *burqa*, the monotony broken only by some young Pathan girls, not more than eight years in age, sitting on their haunches in the back row in their unique shawls of pink and turquoise. The camera pauses on a little boy held aloft in the front lines. He sports a headband declaring him a martyr in the cause of the Lal Masjid. The speakers (including Umme Hassan) take to the mic and refer to their army of young *ababeels,* the birds mentioned in the Quran that took on an army of infidels. This time they assure us that the *ababeels* of the Jamia Hafsa will take on the Pakistani army. The speakers make one last plea to the Pakistani security forces and ask whether among the 12 lakh soldiers, there is any Mohammad bin Qasim, or a contemporary Khalid bin Walid. This is an intelligent choice of historical figures, as Pakistani textbooks and the media are replete with the image of the young Mohammad Bin Qasim who came to South Asia to 'free' Muslim women taken hostage by an evil ruler.

As Jamia Hafsa alumni made media appearances in later weeks, one was distracted from the melancholy of the moment by the irony of their words—'Look at our hands, look at us,' exclaimed the gloved, veiled voices behind the intimidating *burqa.* There were references to the bloodstained hands (theirs) and their sisters in Kashmir who they declared had decided to decorate their hands with blood rather than henna. They repeated what had been said by Umme Hassan and the Maulana brothers earlier. That they as citizens of Pakistan had the right to protest and they had staged a sit-in and not occupied the Children's Library, that they had not 'wasted' any of the library collections. 'There were VCDs there, videos, we considered them our nation's *amanat,* a trust, and did not waste anything.' They believed that their protest had given a second life to 80 mosques in Islamabad, preventing them from being demolished. They maintain that Aunty Shamim had been brought to Lal Masjid with the full knowledge of the Islamabad DSP and SSP. Their hands were tied because of Shamim's connections, so they had nudged the Maulana into bringing her in. The police, like them, did not trust the government.

The Lal Masjid cadre and their struggle, Pakistani women and their involvement in project militarism reminds me of what Mary Hegland had written elsewhere regarding how women gain skills, experience, and awareness of their own capabilities by serving in a revolution, a particular organised group, or a movement (Hegland: 2002). Hegland had explored the paradoxical demands on women of the Shia movement:

that they should be capable political workers as well as obedient, pure, self-abnegating, covered, and secluded symbols of the strength and rectitude of the Shia religion and movement—providing a gender situation with some fluidity and dynamic potential. Their experiences with diverse people and situations; and their growing awareness of their capabilities presented them with opportunities to think differently about themselves, women in general, and women's place in society. It is ironic that the meeting these women participated in brought women *fundamentalism and* freedom as well as a female community *both* coercive *and* enabling. However, they were to place all they were gaining at the disposal of the revolutionary movement or, more precisely, its male leaders. Then, when the struggle is over and they are no longer needed, much like the female Algerian and Palestinian freedom fighters, the French and Iranian revolutionaries, and the American 'Rosie the riveters' they are all supposed to go home and revert to earlier, narrower gender roles, as if all of their experiences had not happened and nothing had changed (Hegland, 2002: 95–97).

Were Lal Masjid's semantics feminist? Would one view their struggle as fundamentalist with feminist sympathies? Would feminists who appeal to fundamentalism (mother/nature, the feminine in divine) find solidarity with the movement? No, for they continued to disseminate the idea of the feminine as passive, as the ideal. For all the furore of the new face of political Islam, it goes without saying that what one witnessed was a reinforcement of traditional, static and unchanging articulations of Muslim women.

# Conclusion

This project began by deliberating the legacy of one death—Benazir Bhutto's. It is now ending with the death of another protagonist of the previous pages, Junaid Jamshed. The furore over him being remembered for his musical legacy rather than being an Islamic scholar highlights all the schisms in Pakistani society.

*Where Are They Now?* In the period since I last wrote about Pakistan's particular nexus of gender, militarism and religious revivalism, some of the actors mentioned in these pages have been living (as some may have wished upon them) in quite interesting times.

Junaid Jamshed, the singer-turned-Islamic motivational speaker had struggled with a blasphemy case (in 2014) and a strong social media campaign against him for using insensitive comments with regard to women and the women of the Holy Prophet's family. His mentors then derided his evangelist avatar declaring him '*ignorant and uneducated as a scholar*' (Maulana Tareeq Jamil as quoted in *The Tribune*).[1]

Jamshed on his part apologised for his comments saying:

*This is my mistake and it happened because of my ignorance and lack of knowledge and I seek forgiveness from the Muslim world. I request my brothers to forgive me and I am thankful to them for pointing out my mistake, it happened unintentionally and I seek forgiveness from Allah.*[2]

In 2015, Jamshed was in the news again when he inferred that God dislikes that any woman should be named [in the Quran]. In February 2016, he was beaten up by a group of irate clerics who still held him guilty for his earlier alleged blasphemy about the Prophet's wife. After his death, the same people obliterated his musical legacy.

---

[1] http://blogs.tribune.com.pk/story/33769/the-b-side-junaid-jamshed-and-untold-stories-behind-the-controversies/ (Accessed 19 January 2016).

[2] http://www.pakistantribune.com.pk/blasphemy-case-registered-junaid-jamshed.html (Accessed 19 January 2016).

**What we learnt**—that for all their talk of how it is possible to meld the secular and the spiritual aspects of institutions and their formulaic promises of offering the best of both the worlds, the religious right will never welcome hybrid spaces, and/or personalities that are not from more familiar and traditional backgrounds.

Apa Naseem retreated to the outer margins of social media and the last bastion of having a political voice, her own Facebook page. For it is her brother-in-law Maulana Abdul Aziz who remains the face of the Red Mosque. Apa Naseem will pop up in the odd interview where she will chide a Malala for being extremely misguided,[3] or her students will raise the political temperature by inviting the ISIS to Pakistan (or naming their library after Bin Laden), or there might be an update on her Facebook page where she laments the operation to take down her school when other favourites like Imran Khan or Tahir-ul- Qadri were allowed to camp out in front of the Parliament and conduct a siege for four months with nary the state violence that the Jamia Hafsa faced. But for all purposes, it is back to business for Maulana Aziz (despite the extreme censure post-December 2014, when a group of Pakistani citizens attempted to register an FIR against Maulana Aziz for not condemning and justifying the Peshawar school attacks, and therefore abetting crime).

**What we learnt**—that even during social revolutions, the empire and the patriarchal face of the revolution will strike back.

Dr Hashmi and the Al Huda apparatus moved to Canada, proving as I had predicted earlier that even if the organisation were to lose favour in urban Pakistan, since a significant section of Hashmi's support came from the diaspora, Pakistani's overseas community would be eager to support them. So other than the odd news item that Canadian authorities were looking into the working of Al Huda and Dr Hashmi's background, the organisation had gone quiet. Leading to some declaring that like many other Islamabad institutions that lose patronage and profile with a change in regime and political weather, the organisation too had to contend with a new generation of more powerful and eloquent evangelists moving in on its turf. However, with Tashfeen Malik (a former Al Huda alumni) and her involvement with the San Bernadino killings, Al Huda was back in the news. Unfortunately for me, a group of interviewees I was in contact with for a profile of how their lives and politics had evolved in the past decade, suddenly withdrew and requested that they would rather I destroyed records of my conversations with them.

---

[3] http://abcnews.go.com/2020/battle-young-souls-veil/story?id=20521784 (Accessed 19 January 2016).

**What we learnt**—that the next decade will be interesting to watch as we see a more firebrand generation of young women. These women will not just be content with consuming Hashmi's commentaries. We have already seen new actors and voices emerging, not all of them are as malleable and discernible as the first generation of the living room seminaries were. The alarm bells for some start going off when some (of what the Americans quaintly quote as 'lone wolves'—the Tashfeen Maliks) who may have frequented the campus and the discussion groups in their need for a support system and to remedy their exclusion from certain networks of their host city, drift in and out of the Al Huda system with a very problematic reading of millennial Islam.

Working with Pakistani women in the diaspora, it was more than clear that these women found themselves in a host of conflicts and contradictions on the issue of Islamic law as interpreted from the Quran and/ or resulting from what their extended Pakistani family understood of them. The Pakistani state law did not directly influence them wherever they were now, but a significant group among them belonged to or were being raised by a generation which had grown up under these laws. It also affected them every time they visited the Pakistani diplomatic missions. We are constantly reminded that culture is transmitted and internalised as a socialisation process and is frequently a more important control mechanism than formal law. Members of the Pakistani diaspora regulate personal affairs by reference to what they see as 'good Pakistani norms'. Community elders unhappy with any challenge to their status as sole mediators and adjudicators in their community may deliberately perpetuate the disjuncture between the legal provisions and institutions of the Australian state and the lives of the Pakistani community. These 'good Pakistani norms function as informal laws which are either internalised and operate through a system of self-censure, or are imposed and enforced through the use or threat of violence, and usually through a combination of these two. Of course women's multiple layers of identity would come into direct conflict with each other during interviews. They found that they were women, of Pakistani origin, Muslim/ non-Muslim, Punjabi/Pashtun/Sindhi/Mohajir, South Asian, mothers, daughters, professionals, in short that they were located within several contradictory and competing discourses simultaneously. Some women found that they could not reconcile their identity as women with their identity as Muslims. Others felt that their loyalty to Pakistan as a country conflicted with their struggle against the oppression of women. This is particularly important to keep in mind when we struggle to understand Pakistani (men and women) disdain for particular narrations—such as Malala Yousafzai (Pakistan's young Nobel laureate) or Sharmeen Chinoy (whose well-lauded documentaries feature courageous Pakistani women taking on social evils); why certain members of the Pakistani community constantly complain that such episodes 'shame' Pakistan and a 'good' citizen would have kept quiet and carried on rather than shame the nation by such a declaration of facts.

Let me share a particular incident disclosed by one of my interviewees Maria to elaborate how the Pakistani community in the diaspora reminded women of the content of the roles appropriate to them. It will explain the mechanisms behind an off-hand remark ('casual comment' as other interviewees excused it) through which women of the Pakistani community acquire the cultural ideas and values that shape their image of themselves and which in turn inform the visions they have of their political future in the diaspora.

The incident took place at a meeting organised to discuss the future of the community organisation, the Pakistan Host Country Friendship Association. Spaces like this organisation had become an interesting site of an ongoing battle between the women and the male elders, who saw this, the women's struggle for recognition, as a challenge to their monopoly, and a subtle allusion to women's 'lesser capabilities' in the group meetings proved a useful tactic. For while women's roles after moving abroad might have enlarged to include both domestic manager and economic worker, by comparison men's role might not have changed as favorably. Maria, a university student, narrated what was an embarrassing incident for her; she had stood up to argue changes in the Friendship Association's charter and had heard someone from the 'back of the room loudly saying *ek tau adhee guwahee aur itna bolna* (she has half a testimony and still has to talk so much)'. The comment referred obliquely to legislation in Pakistan that denies equality to women, limits their choices and reinforces their subordination.

Why did Maria's participation in a public debate make the male elders in the community nervous? Did her age place her as representative of a younger generation challenging the elders' authority? Or did her gender make her appear to be encroaching upon what had been till now a male preserve? In either case we are reminded of Werbner's queries on the question of ownership of the public sphere where the Pakistani diaspora is concerned:

Who controls the discourses allowed to be made 'public'? Who dictates what is 'official', that is, legitimate, as representative of the group or its 'culture', or 'unofficial', illegitimate, and hence denied public voice? Control of the public sphere as a contested arena is constitutive of authority, just as authority constitutes the public sphere (Werbner, 2002: 191).

What I want to narrate through Maria's story is how the deduction that men were more reliable in the outside world, based on legislation confirming their superior intelligence (making them the only ones who could legitimately represent and speak for the community), influenced Pakistani women's life-choices and their very image of their self-worth even in the diaspora. Though the executive committee of the Anglo-Pak Friendship Association was eager to emphasise that the Pakistani diaspora was growing more inclusive, Pakistani women in the city were still oppressed by interpretations of religion, kinship, ethnicity and access to public spaces. Though none of these factors were static and they have been constantly changing since the move abroad, they still play a repressive role for women. For instance, even if Pakistani families in the diaspora may no longer feel that their daughters should marry within their own immediate kinship group, and may become engaged to somebody in another group; even so, the decision is still made by the family. I have to acknowledge that the women take none of these intrusions lightly, and they have responded with vigour and initiative. However, any analysis of which of the many ethnic, sectarian, gender and age groups in the diaspora rise to challenge the community elders immediately raises the question of class and gender and the linkages between them. At one level economic and class relations among Pakistanis are dominant, but this remains just one of the many levels.

For there is a range of processes at work in the Pakistani communities that have kept women's political participation marginal, and not all of them reveal the hand of the community elders directly. As Helie-Lucas explains:

> At independence of Pakistan, in 1947, women found themselves with NO right to inheritance, at all. When they challenged this with the political leadership, they were told, this was Islam. Knowing too well that women may have an unequal share to inheritance, but still have something, according to the most common interpretations of Muslim laws, the women then went through the debates of the Parliament, and discovered that the new independent Pakistani Parliament had used the old British Victorian law (not even in use in Britain anymore) to deprive them of all rights. Like the Algerian government, they did not mind cynically using a colonial law and labelling it Islamic if it suited them (Helie-Lucas, 2004).

This along with other interventions increased women's economic dependence and reinforced the popular image of women being biologically unsuited for participation in the public sphere. In the end it is the integration of social, cultural and religious relations that oppresses women no matter which background they come from. What Pakistani women in the diaspora and home are constantly challenging is who has the authority to determine what is an essential Pakistani Islam? This question directs attention to similar power struggles in Muslim communities all over the world—that is, who has the power to define and enforce particular ways of being 'complete' rather than 'half' citizens (Maria's protest) and being a good Muslim (as Maria insisted she was). It may have perplexed community elders like a host country—Pakistani diaspora community forum president and administrators—that their endeavours to make the organisation appear more inclusive and 'forward-looking' to meet the concerns of the changed political climate did not find overseas Pakistani women stepping forward to participate in the task of improving the particular image of the Pakistani overseas community.

To understand this it is essential to examine all the mechanisms that had rendered these women powerless till then; and an overnight decision to 'include more women' in community forums, or the military, or the clergy, or political parties could not reverse the previous process of sidelining them and their voices.

# Bibliography

Abu-Lughod, Lila (1990), 'The Romance of Resistance: Tracing Transformations of Power through Bedouin Women', *American Ethnologist* 17 (1), pp. 41–55.

——— (2002), 'Do Muslim Women Really Need Saving? Anthropological Reflections on Cultural Relativism and Its Others', *American Anthropologist* 104 (3), pp. 783–90.

Ahmed, Akbar S. (1986), 'Death in Islam: The Hawkes Bay Case', *Man*, New Series, 21, No. 1.

Ahmed, Durre S. (2002), 'Introduction: The Last Frontier', in D. Anwar (ed.), *Gendering the Spirit: Women, Religion and the Post-colonial Response*, Zed Books, London and New York.

Ali, Mubarak (1998), 'History and War', *In the Shadow of History*, Fiction House, Lahore, pp. 32–34.

Ali, Saleem (2005), 'Islamic Education and Conflict: Understanding the Madrassahs of Pakistan', Washington Draft Report Submitted to the U.S. Institute of Peace Report, 2005.

Anderson, Jon W. (1999), 'The Internet and Islam's New Interpreters' in Dale F. Eickelman and Jon W. Anderson (eds) *New Media in the Muslim World: The Emerging Public Sphere,* Indiana University Press, Indiana, pp. 41–56.

Armstrong, John (1982), *Nations before Nationalism,* University of North Carolina Press, Chapel Hill.

Babar, Aneela Z. (2001), *Texts of War: The Religio-military nexus in Pakistan and India*, Bangkok, Asian Institute of Technology.

Bahri and Vasudeva (ed.) (1996), *Between The Lines—South Asians and Postcoloniality,* Temple University Press, Philadelphia.

Bhabha, Homi K. (1994), *The Location of Culture*, Routledge, New York.

Bhattacharjee, Annanya (1997), 'The Public/Private Mirage: Mapping Homes and Undomesticating Violence Work in the South Asian Immigrant Community', in M. Alexander and C. Mohanty (eds), *Feminist Genealogies, Colonial Legacies, Democratic Futures*, New York, Routledge, pp. 308–29.

Bouhdiba, Abdul W. (1985), *Sexuality in Islam*, Routledge, Kegan and Paul, London.

Chatterjee, Partha (1993), *The Nation And Its Fragments: Colonial And Postcolonial Histories,* Oxford University Press, Delhi.

Chaudhry, Muhammad S. (1991), *Women's Rights in Islam,* Adam Publishers, New Delhi.

Cobin, Henry (1987), *Creative Imagination in the Sufism of Ibn 'Arabi,* Princeton University Press, Bollingen Series, Princeton.

Cohen, Phil (1988), 'The Pervasions of Inheritance: Studies in the Making of Multi-Racist Britain' in P. Cohen, and H. S. Bains (eds), *Multiracist Britain,* MacMillan, London, pp. 9–118.

Cohen, S. (1990), *The Pakistan Army*, Himalayan Books, New Delhi.

Dalrymple, William (1999), *The Age of Kali: Indian Travels and Encounters*, Flamingo, London.

Dietrich, Gabriela (1997), 'Women and Religious Identities in India After Ayodhya' in K. Bhasin, R. Menon and N. Khan (eds), *Against all Odds: Essays on Women, Religion and Development from India and Pakistan*, Kali for Women, New Delhi.

Doxiadis Associates (1960), *Programme and Plan, Vols 1 and 2*, Capital Development Authority, Rawalpindi.

Ellis, Carolyn and Arthur P. Bochner (2000), 'Autoethnography, Personal Narrative, Reflexivity: Researcher as Subject', in N. Denzin and Y. Lincoln (eds), *Handbook of Qualitative Research*, SAGE, California, pp. 733–768.

El Saadawi, Niwal (1997), *The Nawal El Saadawi Reader*, Zed Books, London.

Esposito, Richard (2009), 'Mumbai Terrorist Wanted to "Kill and Die" and Become Famous', retrieved from http://abcnews.go.com/Blotter/Story?id=6385015&page=1

Fremson, Ruth (2001), 'Allure must be Covered: Individuality Peeks Through', in *New York Times*, 4 November, pp. 4–14.

Gardezi, Fauzia (1997), 'Nationalism and State Formation: Women's Struggles and Islamisation in Pakistan' in N. Hussain, S. Mumtaz and R. Saigol (eds), *Engendering the Nation State*, Vol. 1, Simorgh Publications, Lahore, 1997, pp. 79–110.

Göle, Nilüfer (2002), 'Islam in Public: New Visibilities and New Imaginaries' in *Public Culture*, 14 (1), Duke University Press, pp.173–90.

Guindi, Fadwa (1999), *Veil: Modesty, Privacy and Resistance*, Berg, Oxford.

Haroon, Anis (2001), '"They Use us and Others Abuse us": Women and MQM Conflict', in Rita Manchanda (ed.), Wome, War and Peace in South Asia: Beyond Victimhood to Agency, SAGE Publications, New Delhi, pp. 177–213.

Hassan, Riffat (2002), 'Islam and Human Rights in Pakistan: A Critical Analysis of the Positions of Three Contemporary Women', *Dawn Review Magazine*, Karachi, 7–14 November.

Hegland, Mary Elaine (2002), 'The Power Paradox in Muslim Women's Majales: North-West Pakistani Mourning Rituals as Sites of Contestation over Religious Politics, Ethnicity, and Gender', in C. Allen, T. Saliba and J. Howard, (eds) *Gender, Politics and Islam*, The University of Chicago Press, Chicago, pp. 95–132.

Helie-Lucas, Marieme (2004), 'The Construction of "Muslim Women's" Sexuality and the Political use of Tradition and Religion', presentation at the workshop on *Muslim Women and Sexuality* at the 2004 World Social Forum, retrieved from http://www.wluml.org/english/newsfulltxt.shtml?cmd%5B15%7/%5D–x-157-41086 (Accessed on 30 November 2005).

Hull, Matthew (2003), *Paper Travails: Governance, Graphic Artifacts, and the Built Environment in the Islamabad Metropolitan Area (1959–1998)*, PhD dissertation, Department of Anthropology, University of Chicago.

Hussain, Akmal (1993), 'The Dynamics of Power: Military, Bureaucracy, and the People', in A. Hussain and M. Hussain, *Pakistan, Problems of Governance*, Konark Publishers, Delhi.

Hussain, Neelam (1996), 'Women in Pakistani Context: An Overview' in M. Malik and N. Hussain (eds), *Reinventing Women*, Simorgh Publications, Lahore, pp. 11–21.

Hutnyk, John, Scoot McQuire and Nikos Papastergiadis (1990) (in conversation with G. Spivak), 'Strategy, Identity, Writing' in S. Harasym (ed.) *The Post-Colonial Critic: Interviews, Strategies, Dialogues*, Routledge, New York.

Imam, Ayesha M. (1997), 'The Muslim Religious Right ('Fundamentalists') and Sexuality', *Women Living under Muslim Laws*, Dossier 17, WLUML Publications, pp. 7–25.

International Crisis Group Report (March, 2006) Pakistan: Political Impact of the Earthquake, ICG Asia Briefing No: 46, Islamabad/Brussels.

Jalal, Ayesha (1992), 'The Convenience of Subservience' in Kandiyoti, D (ed.), *Women, Islam and the State,* Temple University Press, Philadelphia.

———— (2002), *Self and Sovereignty,* Sang-e-Meel Publications, Lahore.

Javed, Tazeen (2009), *A Reluctant Mind,* http://tazeen.net/2009/09/16/gift-of-gall-or-permanent-lapse-of-reason/ (Accessed on 1 October 2009).

Kandiyoti, Deniz (1992), *Women, Islam and the State,* Temple University Press, Philadelphia.

Kazmi, Fareed (1994), 'Muslim Socials and the Female Protagonist: Seeing a Dominant Discourse at Work' in Z. Hasan (ed.), *Forging Identities: Gender Communities and the State,* Kali for Women, New Delhi, pp. 226–43.

Khattak, Saba (1994), 'A Reinterpretation of the State and State Discourse in Pakistan (1977–88)' in N. Khan, R. Saigol and A. Zia (eds), *Locating the Self: Perspectives on Women and Multiple Identities,* ASR Publications, Lahore, pp. 22–40.

———— (2010), 'Inconvenient Facts: Women and Political Representation under Military Regimes', *Democracy Asia,* http://www.democracy-asia.org/casestudies_studies_saba_gul_khattak_p2.htm.

———— (1997), 'Gendered and Violent: Inscribing the Military on the Nation- State' in N. Hussain, S. Mumtaz and R. Saigol (eds), *Engendering the Nation State,* Vol. 1, Simorgh Publications, Lahore, pp. 38–52.

Knott, Kim and Sadja Khokher (1993), 'Religious and Ethnic Identity among Young Muslim Women in Bradford', *New Community,* Vol. 19, pp. 593–610.

Lalarukh (1997),'Image Nation: A Visual Text' in N. Hussain, S. Mumtaz, and R. Saigol (eds), *Engendering the Nation State,* Vol. 2, Simorgh Publications, Lahore.

Leblanc, Robin (1999), *Bicycle Citizens: The Political World of the Japanese Housewife,* University of California Press, Berkeley.

Macleod, Arlene E. (1991), *Accommodating Protest: Working Women, the New Veiling, and Change in Cairo',* Columbia University Press, New York.

Majid, Anouar (2002), 'The Politics of Feminism in Islam', in T. Saliba, C. Allen and J. Howard (eds), *Gender, Politics and Islam,* The University of Chicago Press, Chicago, pp. 53–94.

Manchanda, Rita (2001), *Women, War and Peace in South Asia: Beyond Victimhood to Agency,* SAGE Publications, New Delhi.

Maududi, Syed A. (1930), *Aljihad Fil Islam, Islamic* Publications, Lahore.

Meijer, Roel (2007), 'Yusuf al-Uyairi and the Transnational Expansion of Salafi Jihadism Expansion'. Conference abstract, Kingdom without Borders: Saudi Expansion in the World, Conference programme and abstracts, September, http://www.kcl.ac.uk/artshums/depts/trs/research/certap/archive/kingdom.pdf (Accessed 2 June 2011).

Mernissi, Fatima (1991) (translated by M. J. Lakeland), *Women and Islam,* Basil Blackwell Ltd., Oxford.

Metcalf, Barbara D. (1994), 'Reading and Writing about Muslim Women In British India', in Z. Hasan (ed.) *Forging Identities: Gender, Communities and the State,* Kali for Women, New Delhi, pp. 1–21.

———— (1996), 'Introduction: Sacred Words, Sanctioned Practice, New Communities' in B. Metcalf (ed.), *Making Muslim Space in North America and Europe,* University of California Press, Berkeley, pp. 1–27.

Minault, Gail (1986), *Voices of Silence: English Translation of Hali's Majalis un nissa* and *Chup Ki Dad,* Chanakya Publications, Delhi.

Moallem, Minoo (1999), 'Transnationalism, Feminism, and Fundamentalism' in C. Kaplan, A. Alarcon and M. Moallem (eds), *Between Woman and Nation: Nationalisms, Transnational Feminisms, and the State*, Duke University Press, Durham and London.

Moghadam, Valentine M. (1992), 'Patriarchy and the Politics of Gender in Modernising Societies: Iran, Pakistan and Afghanistan', *International Sociology*, 7(1), pp. 35–53.

Moghissi, Haideh (1999), *Feminism and Islamic Fundamentalism: The Limits of Post-modern Analysis*, Oxford University Press, Karachi.

Mumtaz, Khawar and Farida Shaheed (1987), *Women of Pakistan: Two Steps Forward, One Step Back*, Zed Books, London.

Mumtaz, Khawar (1994), 'Identity Politics and Women: 'Fundamentalism' & Women in Pakistan', in V. Moghadam (ed.), *Identity Politics and Women: Cultural Reassertions and Feminisms in International Perspective*, Westview Press, Boulder, pp. 228–42.

Naipaul, Vidya S. (1998), *Beyond Belief: Islamic Excursions among the Converted Peoples*, Viking, New Delhi.

Naqvi, Muneeza (2000), *On Air*, Oxford University Press, Karachi.

*Newsline* (2001), February and April issues, Fazlee Sons, Karachi.

Papanek, Hanna (1982), 'Purdah in Pakistan: Seclusion and Modern Occupations for Women' in H. Papanek and G. Minault (eds), *Separate Worlds*, South Asia Books, Delhi, pp. 190–216.

The Pearls of Wisdom (2004), Al Huda Publications.

Rahman, Fazlur (1984), *Islam and Modernity: Transformation of an Intellectual Tradition*, University of Chicago Press, Chicago.

Rahman, Tariq (1998), *Language and Politics in Pakistan*, Oxford University Press, Karachi.

Rouse, Shahnaz J. (1997), 'Gender(ed) Struggles: The State, Religion and Civil Society', in K. Bhasin, R. Menon, and N. Khan (eds), *Against All Odds: Essays on Women, Religion and Development from India and Pakistan*, Kali for Women, India, pp. 16–34.

Rushdie, Salman (1984), *Shame*, Picador, London.

——— (1991), *Imaginary Homelands: Essays and Criticism 1981–1991*, Granta Books, London.

Saigol, Rubina (1995), *Knowledge and Identity: Articulation of Gender in Educational Discourse in Pakistan*, ASR Publications, Lahore.

——— (1997), 'Introduction', in N. Hussain, S. Mumtaz, and R. Saigol (eds), *Engendering the Nation State*, Vol. 1, Simorgh Publications, Lahore, pp. 1–28.

——— (1997a), 'The Gendering of Modernity: Nineteenth Century Educational Discourse', in N. Hussain, S. Mumtaz and R. Saigol (eds), *Engendering the Nation State*, Vol. 1, Simorgh Publications, Lahore, pp. 155–86.

Saktanber, Ayse (2002), *Living Islam: Women, Religion & the Politicization of Culture in Turkey*, I. B. Tauris, London.

Sardar Ali, Shaheen (2001), 'Misogynistic Trends in Islamic Jurisprudence—A Feminist Perspective', in K. Naheed (ed.), *Women: Myth and Realities*, Hawa Associates, Lahore, pp. 142–158.

Shamsie, Kamila (2002), *Kartography*, Oxford University Press, Karachi.

Shamsi, Amber Rahim (2002), 'Unveiling Pakistan', *Herald*, Issue (1) Dawn Publications, Karachi, pp. 140–43.

Siddiqa, Ayesha (2007), 'June 07: The Pakistan Military Economy', http://www.individual-land.com/index.php?option=com_content&view=article&id=52:june-07-the-pakistan-military-economy&catid=7:2007&Itemid=98

Siddiqui, Maleeha Hamid and Zahir Shah Sherazi (2009), 'The Caste of Faith', Herald, Dawn Publications, Karachi, January, pp. 84–87.

Suleri, Sara (1992), *The Rhetoric of English India*, University of Chicago Press, Chicago.

*Taleem-ul-Quran Diploma Brochure*, (2002) (Brochure for Enrolling in Al Huda Diploma Classes) Al Huda Publications, Islamabad.

*Taleem-ul-Quran Parah 4*, (2002a) (Audio-cassette of Hashmi's commentary of the Quranic Surah 4 *Al-Nisa*), Suniyay Aur Sunwaiyay Products, Al Huda Publications, Islamabad.

Thanvi, Ashraf (2002), *Behishti Zewar* (translated by Darul Ishat), Matba'al Rasheed, Karachi.

Toor, Saadia (1997), 'The State, Fundamentalism and Civil Society', in N. Hussain, S. Mumtaz and R. Saigol (eds), *Engendering the Nation State*, Vol. 1, Simorgh Publications, Lahore, pp. 111–46.

Vertovec, Steven (2000), 'Religion and Diaspora', Paper presented at the conference on *'New Landscapes of Religion in the West'*, School of Geography and the Environment, University of Oxford.

Werbner, Pnina (1990), *The Migration Process: Capital, Gifts and Offerings among British Pakistanis*, Berg Publishers, Oxford.

——— (1996), 'Stamping the Earth in the name of Allah: Zikr and the Sacralizing of Space among British Muslims'. *Cultural Anthropology* 11(3), University of California Press, pp. 309–38.

——— (2002), *Imagined Diasporas among Manchester Muslims*, School of American Research Press, Santa Fe.

Yuval-Davis, Nira (1997), 'Ethnicity, Gender Relations and Multiculturalism' in P. Werbner and T. Modood (eds), *Debating Cultural Hybridity*, Zed Books, London, pp.193–208.

# Index

# About the Author

**Aneela Zeb Babar** is a researcher and consultant working on Islam, gender, migration and popular culture. Over the past eighteen years she has been pursuing a career within the academic, research and development sector being employed with universities and non-governmental and international developmental agencies in South and South-East Asia and Australia. She has a strong track record in advocacy of development, governance, gender and cultural issues.